FOREIGN VOCABULARY IN SIGN LANGUAGES

A Cross-Linguistic Investigation of Word Formation

Edited by
DIANE BRENTARI
Purdue University

2001

LAWRENCE ERLBAUM ASSOCIATES, PUBLISHERS
Mahwah, New Jersey   London

Lawrence Erlbaum Associates, Inc., Publishers
10 Industrial Avenue
Mahwah, New Jersey 07430

Cover design by Kathryn Houghtaling Lacey

Library of Congress Cataloging-in-Publication Data

Foreign vocabulary in sign languages : cross- linguistic investigation of word formation /
Edited by Diane Brentari
    p. cm.
    Includes bibliographical references and index.
    ISBN 0-8058-3208-4 (cloth : alk paper)
    1.   Sign language. 2. Language and languages—Foreign words and phrases. 3. Language and culture. I. Brentari, Diane

HV2474 .F67 2000
419—dc21
                                                                        99-089780

Books published by Lawrence Erlbaum Associates are printed on acid-free paper, and their bindings are chosen for strength and durability.

Printed in the United States of America
10   9   8   7   6   5   4   3   2   1

Contents

List of Contributors

Penny Boyes Braem is Director of the Center for Sign Language Research in Basel, Switzerland. She has published in German a widely used overview of research on signed languages in *Einführung in die Gebärdensprache und ihre Erforschung* (Hamburg: Signum, 3rd ed., 1995). Her recent research has focused on a comparison of the signing of deaf early and late learners of Swiss German Sign Language (DSGS) with respect to their prosodic characteristics, published in the journal *Language and Speech* (1999, Vol. 42). Boyes Braem is currently directing a multimedia databank project for the lexicon of Swiss German Sign Language which should serve as a basis for learning and teaching materials as well as research on this language.

Mary Brennan has been involved in sign language research since the 1970s. Her work has primarily focused on metaphor in signed language and the productive lexicon in British Sign Language (BSL). She has a particular interest in the application of signed linguistics to the fields of Deaf Education and interpreting. She is currently Senior Lecturer in Deaf Studies at the University of Edinburgh, Scotland.

Diane Brentari is an associate professor of linguistics and Director of the ASL Program at Purdue University. Her work has focused on studying the phonological and morphological structure of sign languages and on the biological bases of language. She has recently published *A Prosodic Model of Sign Language Phonology* (MIT Press, 1998) and *Morphology and Its Relation to Syntax and Phonology* (SCLI, 1998). She is currently working on a project investigating the argument structure of classifier predicates.

Nini Hoiting is a psycholinguist at the Royal Institute for the Deaf "H. D. Guyot" in Haren, The Netherlands. She specializes in early acquisitions of Sign Language of the Netherlands (SLN), including training and guidance of hearing parents with deaf children. She has been active in developing programs of bilingual education for the Deaf in the Netherlands.

Christopher Miller is an associate professor of linguistics at Université du Québec à Montréal. His work has focused on the phonology of Quebec Sign Language (LSQ) and multichannel structure in sign syntax. He is currently working on the interface between rhythmic phonology and syntactic and discourse structure in LSQ.

Carol A. Padden is a professor in the Communication Department at the University of California, San Diego. Her work has recently focused on sign language structure, representational systems in sign languages for representing cross-modal borrowings, and she has published (with Clair Ramsey) several book chapters and articles on fingerspelling and English reading abilities in young deaf children. She is also the coauthor (with Tom Humphries) of *Deaf in America: Voices from a Culture* (Harvard University Press, 1989). She is currently working on a book exploring cultural changes in the signing deaf community.

Dan I Slobin is a professor of psychology at the University of California, Berkeley. His work has focused on child language acquisition and cognitive/functional linguistics. He has edited a five-volume collection, *The Crosslinguistic Study of Child Language Acquisition* (Lawrence Erlbaum Associates, Vols. 1-2, 1985; Vol. 3, 1992; Vols. 4-5, 1997). He is currently working in collaboration with Nini Hoiting and a group of American and Dutch researchers on the early acquisition of sign language (SLN, ASL) by deaf children of hearing parents.

Notational Conventions

BALL	Words in upper case, plain type are glosses for lexical signs. These glosses are not intended to be American Sign Language glosses alone, but rather generic semantic glosses.
BALL	Words in upper case italics are specialized glosses in the language of the surrounding spoken language community. These appear in the DSGS and the LSQ chapters since the material discussed warrants that the relation between the written or spoken form and the sign form used be made apparent.
THAT-WAY	Upper case words separated by hyphens are single signs which are glossed as more than one English word.
#JOB	Upper case words preceded by a '#' symbol are loan signs which have undergone some restructuring.
B-A-L-L	Upper case letters with intervening dashes are fingerspelled words in which every letter is expressed.
-8-	A letter or number in single quotes refers to a single letter of the manual alphabet.
<u>M</u>ATH	Initialized/abbreviated signs are represented by an underline below the letter(s) corresponding to its fingerspelled handshape in the form.
[CH]-I-L-D	Strings of upper case letters in square brackets within a fingerspelled word indicate handshapes that have undergone an operation of handshape merger.
FAITH	Capitalized words in small capitals are labels for phonological constraints within Optimality Theory.
biscuit	Italicized lower case words are either: 1. non-English words, or 2. forms whose source is a mouth pattern of a word in a spoken language.

'biscuit'	Words in single quotes refer to an English translation.
"loan"	Words in double quotes are used to indicate words with a specific or technical definition in the text.
[ri]	Strings of lower case letters or symbols in square brackets indicate either: 1. phonetic forms rendered in the International Phonetic Alphabet, or 2. distinctive feature specifications.
*FREE	An asterisk indicates a form that is ungrammatical in the specific context discussed.
$INDEX_a$	A gloss with a letter subscript indicates a spatial referent.
$_3GIVE_1$	A gloss with a number subscript indicates person agreement.

INTRODUCTION

Borrowed Elements in Sign Languages: A Window on Word Formation

Diane Brentari

LEXICAL INNOVATION AND LANGUAGE CONTACT

Sign languages change and stabilize themselves within their own language grammars. Each sign language community has its own cultural history embodied by values and practices that influence language change and innovation, but each language is also used by a minority linguistic community that is integrated within a neighboring spoken language community. New words in sign languages (lexical innovations) are created by: language-internal means, such as lexicalization of productive classifier forms (e.g., AIRPLANE, ROCKET, HELICOPTER); language contact with other sign languages (e.g., the names of countries and cities); and language contact with the surrounding spoken language community.

The focus of this volume is language contact with the surrounding spoken language community, although examples of language contact with other sign languages are also included in the discussion of the case of

Langue des signes québécoise (LSQ). Within every Deaf[1] community there is a contingent of bilinguals who facilitate this process.[2] Bilingual communities are well studied, and there are four major types of language contact that have been identified (Berruto, 1995; Grosjean, 1982, 1992, 1999; Hasselmo 1970, Haugen, 1950). First, there are "contact varieties" in which a single system is created by combining components of two or more languages. Pidgin and Creole varieties of spoken languages, such as Tok Pisin and Guyanese Creole, and sign varieties, such as contact signing, are examples of this (see Romaine, 1992, and references therein; Rickford, 1987; Lucas & Valli, 1992). For example, in contact signing the lexicon of American Sign Language (ASL) is combined with the word order of English to create this language variety. Second, "codeswitching" is the use of two different languages (a source language "x" and a recipient language "y") in a discourse, where language "x" is used to express a specific cultural identity within a language "y" context. An example of codeswitching might occur between Spanish and English when two people in a Hispanic section of Chicago, who are business associates, use English when discussing shipping details for their products, but switch to Spanish when talking about an upcoming neighborhood festival. Third, "codemixing" is the use of languages "x" and "y" in a single sentence, without changing the meaning, phonology, morphology, or syntax of the word or expression of language "x" when used in language "y." An example of codemixing is the use of the German word *mitarbeiter* in American English without applying the flapping rule to the two "t's" and which retains the German meaning. Fourth, "borrowing" is the use of single words from one language "x" in language "y"; crucially, the phonological structure of the word has been altered to assimilate to the grammar of language "y," and the meaning may also be different in language "y" than it is in language "x." In borrowings, single words or expressions from a source language "x" are filtered through the target language "y" (Poplack & Meechan, 1998).

The seminal work in this area for sign languages is Battison (1978); this volume expands on his findings by investigating this question cross-linguistically. We have case studies of borrowing in five sign languages among the contributions in this book—American Sign Language (ASL),

---

[1]Throughout this book "Deaf" refers to the cultural and linguistic identity of this group of people, and not to the hearing loss (Padden, 1988; Lane, Hoffmeister, and Bahan, 1996).

[2]What counts as "bilingual" within a Deaf community varies according to one's definition of bilingualism. If the term is defined as someone with equal fluency in both languages, the number of bilinguals is quite small, but if the definition is "someone who uses two languages in their daily lives" (Grosjean, 1992), almost every Deaf person is considered bilingual.

British Sign Language (BSL), Swiss German Sign Language (DSGS), Quebec Sign Language (LSQ), and Sign Language of the Netherlands (SLN). Although not all of the forms in all of the languages included here can be called "loan words," they are definitively part of the non-native lexicon. Using the labels loan words or codeswitches would depend on how well the two categories can be discriminated from each other, and for our purposes, I am using the term borrowing somewhat loosely to include all non-native vocabulary. The non-native words in the sign language cases that are of interest are primarily of two structural types. One type consists of words that contain "mouth patterns" borrowed from the surrounding spoken language that become a part of the sign. The German term *mundbilder* (Eng.: 'mouth pictures') is commonly used for this phenomenon. The other type of non-native vocabulary consists of words that contain letters of the manual alphabet in some form.

What is of particular theoretical interest in the sign language case studies contained in this volume is the degree to which an item has been assimilated into the core grammar of the sign language in question and the range of modification that is possible. We can learn a great deal about the word formational operations of individual grammars by studying foreign elements in them. There are few unitary analyses of lexicons that come from a variety of sources and historical periods. Itô and Mester (1995a, 1995b) have proposed such a model of the Japanese lexicon that is useful in the sign language context, because it allows for different types of non-native vocabulary to be systematically stratified according to how such items behave with respect to the native or core grammar of the language. In addition to Japanese, the Itô and Mester model has been used to analyze French loan words in Fula, a language spoken in the West Indies (Paradis & Lacharité, 1997) as well as foreign vocabulary in ASL (Brentari & Padden, this volume, chap. 3). The analysis of ASL foreign vocabulary shows that, although some foreign words do eventually conform to all of the phonological and morphological rules of ASL, many do not, and some of them are stable items in a peripheral stratum of the lexicon. In each successive stratum, the forms conform to fewer and fewer constraints in a predictable way. One reason why some non-native items can remain stable in a peripheral stratum might be that they are not very common, or that they maintain a necessary semantic or grammatical category distinction between the native and the non-native form. In the case of some sign+fingerspelled compounds, where the use of an English term is unrelated to the meaning of the ASL sign, a fingerspelled form can be used—e.g., SUGAR+F-R-E-E (not SUGAR+*FREE), since the ASL sign for FREE only means 'liberated,' not 'without'; LOVE (verb), but L-O-V-E (not *LOVE) (noun), since LOVE is a form which diachronically includes a body classifier, a type of classifier that appears to be rarely used in nominalized forms.

A complete explanation of the borrowing phenomena analyzed here cannot be found solely by using formal means; rather, it is a combination of the grammatical operations performed on structures and factors dependent on use. Grosjean (1999) has identified four factors in the language context or "mode" that are important in any bilingual situation: factors related to the interlocutors—e.g., language proficiency, kinship relations, attitudes toward language mixing, socioeconomic status, usual language of interaction; factors related to the situation—e.g., degree of intimacy, presence of monolinguals, location; content—e.g., discourse topic; and factors related to the communicative function that create social distance or intimacy. Following work on English loan words used in the Japanese-American community (Lovins, 1974), and on Spanish loan words in the bilingual, bicultural Tewa community in the border region of Mexico (Dozier, 1956), Battison (1978) argued that—contrary to what one might expect—loan words are less likely to be used in heterogeneous contexts, where interlocutors do not share the same language, and they are more likely to be used in homogenous groups of speakers using the recipient language.

The study of foreign items in sign languages is not solely one of theoretical interest. Because cultural identity and empowerment in Deaf communities are primarily expressed through the language, the status of foreign material in sign language becomes very important. During the 1960s and 1970s, linguists argued and proved that sign languages are independent languages from that of their surrounding spoken language communities by focusing on those grammatical aspects of the language necessary to show the large differences between the two. Now the discourse has taken a slightly different turn. This issue is most directly discussed in Boyes Braem (this volume, chapter 1) because a debate about the role of mundbilder in German Sign Language DGS has recently received a great deal of attention. A synopsis of the two positions in this debate is the following. One view appears in Schermer SLN (1990) and in for DGS an interview with Helen Leuninger (Wempe, 1997). This view considers mundbilder an unwanted intrusion in DGS and expects these phenomena to die out of DGS as new, indigenous forms take their place. This view argues that mundbilder are unsystematic, are not handled by the phonological grammar and are, therefore, not a part of the language in question. The other view (Ebbinghaus, 1998) is that mundbilder must be a part of DGS, because they can be used to establish contrast between core

TABLE I.1. *Comparison of borrowed elements in signed and spoken languages*

French	3.3% English words (Poplack et al., 1988)
BSL	<10% fingerspelled elements (Brennan, this volume, chap. 2)
ASL	10% fingerspelled elements in ASL (Padden, 1991)
DSGS	79% Swiss German mundbilder (Boyes Braem, this volume, chap. 1)
DGS	86% German mundbilder (Ebbinghaus & Hessman, 1996)
SLN	16% Dutch mundbilder (Schermer, 1990)

lexical items, such as kinship terms, because they are in widespread use, and because Deaf people cannot imagine their language without them. Under the latter view, a sign language is seen as a flexible multichannel system rather than a system that behaves according to a fixed set of grammatical rules. Without a doubt, there is an ideological anxiety about the presence of mundbilder or fingerspelling in a natural sign language, especially because of the high percentage of mundbilder reported in SLN, in DGS, and in DSGS as compared with words containing fingerspelled letters in ASL and BSL, or English forms in Canadian French (Poplack, Sankoff, & Miller, 1988; Table I-1).

After reading the chapters of this volume, I believe the reader will conclude that at least some *mundbilder* and signs containing fingerspelled letters—although not necessarily part of the native vocabulary—can be handled by the grammar of the sign language in question because they are subject to at least some of the constraints that govern the native vocabulary in systematic ways. One example is seen in the way that the shape of the *mundbilder* or the fingerspelled forms may undergo some or all of the deletion and restructuring operations to which native words are subject (Brentari & Padden, this volume, chap. 3; Miller, this volume, chap. 5). Another example is the analysis proposed in Boyes Braem (this volume, chap. 1), in which DSGS *mundbilder* play a role in marking prosodic boundaries of the phonological phrase. The use of nonmanual markers to mark constituent boundaries is seen in native sign language grammars (Nespor & Sandler, 1999; Wilbur, 1994). These examples can be seen as non-native material stratified in layers of the periphery of the given sign language lexicon.

RANGE OF ALTERATION
OF NON-NATIVE FORMS

The operations that modify a non-native form in order for it to conform to the sign language grammar are quite varied. Forms can add a prosodic function in the process of borrowing, as we see in Boyes Braem's contribution (this volume, chap. 1). In the Hoiting and Slobin contribution, we see the morphosyntactic properties of a form modified to fit SLN grammar (this volume, chap. 4). Phonological adaptation of similar sorts occurs in three sign languages discussed in this volume, with different results achieved in each. In Brennan's, Brentari and Padden's, and Miller's contributions, we see the range of altered phonological form and meaning that can occur when a form is borrowed via fingerspelling into BSL, ASL, and LSQ (chap. 2, 3, & 5, respectively). Short descriptions of the findings in each of the chapters are given in the following sections.

Syntactic Alteration of Dutch Forms in SLN

In this case, two words from Dutch that are separable verbal particles are used as signs in SLN (i.e., *door* and *op*). These words have undergone a grammatical shift in category from verbal particles to that of auxiliary verbs in the borrowing process (Hoiting and Slobin, this volume, chap. 4). The evidence for this shift in grammatical category is that typical verbal morphology appears on these forms—grammatical aspect in the case of *door;* agreement morphology in the case of *op*. We discuss only *op* here (1)-(2), glossed as ACT-ON. Additional differences between *op* and ACT-ON are: In Dutch, *op* can appear only on verbs that require prepositional phrase (PP) complements; direct object noun phrase (NP) complements are not allowed. In SLN, ACT-ON can appear with PP and NP complements; also, ACT-ON in SLN can occur with a wider semantic range of verbs than in Dutch—SLN verbs which denote processes that cause various emotional states allow ACT-ON, while in Dutch *op* occurs only with emotional state verbs. Forms that co-occur with ACT-ON also have structural conditions in SLN that are unrelated to Dutch; namely, in order to co-occur with ACT-ON, the verb must have a stem movement shape or direction that cannot otherwise be inflected, or it must touch the body.

> *(1)* op *in Dutch*
> *Hij is verliefd op mij* ('in love with') (PP complement)
> i.   *boos op* ('angry at')
> ii. *trots op* ('proud of')
> iii. *jaloers op* ('jealous of')
> iv. **lieft* ('loves')

> *(2)* ACT-ON *in SLN*
> i. $INDEX_{3a}$ $INDEX_{3b}$ TEASE $_{3a}ACT-ON_{3b}$
> ii. $INDEX_{3a}$ $INDEX_{3b}$ ACCUSE $_{3a}ACT-ON_{3b}$

Semantic Mismatches: English and French Forms in ASL and in LSQ

The distribution of meaning-to-meaning pairings across languages is not a perfect match in the borrowings in ASL and LSQ. The ASL signs for words in English that have more than one meaning may correspond to just one of these in ASL. Where gaps exist, fingerspelled forms are sometimes used to show the relatedness to an English word or expression when the English-to-sign pairing would result in a semantic mismatch (3).

> *(3) Semantic Reduction in ASL ; English source (Padden, 1998)*
> a. FREE 'liberated' versus F-R-E-E 'without'
> b. PICK (i.e., PICK U-P an object or child) versus P-I-C-K-U-P (i.e., a kind of truck)
> c. OUT 'external' or 'outside of' versus O-U-T (i.e., WORK O-U-T)

> *(4) Semantic Expansion in LSQ; French source*
> a. [biwi]+BISCUIT means both *biscuit* and *Buick*
> b. [ri]+RIRE means both *rire* and *riz* ('laugh' and 'rice')
> c. [rum]+RHUME means both *rhume* and *rum* (Eng: 'head cold' and 'rum')
> d. [avocat]+*AVOCAT* means both *avocat* and *avocado* (Eng: 'lawyer' and 'avocado')
> e. [ku]+*COU* means both *cou* and *couscous* (Eng: 'neck' and 'couscous')

In LSQ, the shape of the mouth pattern can, in certain instances, take precedence over the semantic value of the sign, and the combination of sign+mouth pattern takes on a new meaning of the spoken French word, thereby expanding the field of meanings a manual sign is used for. Miller (this volume, chap. 5) calls this phenomenon "visual homonymy" (4).

Prosodic Modification of Swiss German Forms in DSGS

The use of *mundbilder* by early versus late learners of DSGS reveals that these two groups use *mundbilder* telling anecdotes with equal frequency, but they use them differently (Table I-2) (Boyes Braem, this volume, chap. 1). First, late learners have a much greater percentage of instances

TABLE I.2.   *Distribution of mundbilder in DSGS*

Mundbilder Ratio	Early Learners	Late Learners
a. 1 mundbilder : > 2 signs	10%	2%
b. 1 mundbilder : 2 signs	39%	23%
c. >2 mundbilder : 1 sign	6%	26%
d. Total signs with mundbilder	79%	79%

where there are more than two *mundbilder* per sign than early learners, and, in reverse, early learners have a greater use of instances where one *mundbild* occurs across more than two signs than late learners. Second, Boyes Braem argues that for early learners of DSGS one use of *mundbilder* is to mark prosodic constituent boundaries, called "prosodic binding," while another use is to mark a specific style of signing—i.e., signing by a hearing person, called "constructed signing." Late learners often use this same type of sign-to-mundbilder ratio as a normal conversational-style, therefore it constitutes a higher percentage overall (Table I-2). Examples of "prosodic binding" and "constructed signing" use of mundbilder by early learners are given in examples (5) and (6).

   (5) Mundbilder used as prosodic binding style in early learners (≥2 signs : 1 mundbilder);

German gloss for manual component	ICH	GEHEN-ZU	ICH	ARBEITEN	INDEX (v)	GEHEN-HIN (v)
mouthing		ge_	_he	a-rbei_	_te_	_en

Eng.:'I went to where I work.'

   (6) Mundbilder used in "constructed signing" style in early learners (≥2 mundbilder : 1 sign).

German gloss for manual component	INDEX (Kind)	POSS (Mutter)	KIND	VERGANGENHEIT	ESSEN	WAS?
mouthing		Ihr	Kind	vorher	essen	was

Eng.: 'What did your child eat before?'

Phonological Adaptation of Loan Signs in ASL, in BSL, and in LSQ

Since Battison's analysis of ASL loan signs (1978), we have known that ASL can restructure fingerspelled words and incorporate them into the

TABLE I.3.   *Mechanisms for restructuring fingerspelled words*

1.		movement restructuring (i.e., addition of movement)
	a.	directional morphology (ASL, LSQ)
	b.	movement enhancement (ASL, LSQ)
	c.	use of syllabic letters (ASL, LSQ)
	d.	movement insertion (LSQ, LSQ)
2.		handshape restructuring (i.e., assimilation or deletion of handshape)
	a.	merger or assimilation (ASL, BSL, LSQ)
	b.	deletion (ASL, BSL, LSQ)
	c.	alignment (ASL, LSQ)
3.		place restructuring (BSL)

grammar of ASL as loan signs. Cross linguistically, the restructuring involves some or all of the characteristics outlined in Table I-3.

There is a one-handed alphabet in LSQ and ASL versus a two-handed alphabet in BSL; therefore, the restructuring of borrowings reflects constraints on word formation in one- and in two-handed signs. The additional principles of Symmetry and Dominance that restrict how complex a two-handed sign can be are evident in the BSL manual alphabet and in loan signs derived from it.

LSQ and ASL, two closely related sign languages with almost identical one-handed manual alphabets, exhibit language-specific grammatical differences in their fingerspelled loan signs. I quote Miller (this volume, chap. 5): "Whereas fingerspelled loans in ASL appear, in the unmarked case, to restructure the fingerspelling sequence from the edges in, LSQ adopts a different default strategy, retaining only the first two letters and restructuring them in an oscillating short movement with an identical finger set in both handshapes." This difference can be expressed as a different ranking of two phonological constraints. There are also a number of phonological constraints that operate both in LSQ and in ASL, and these operate in very similar ways (Table I-4).

There are also constraints that operate in both languages but appear to have different ranking. The effect is a different output form for a given type of input word. The constraints at work here are called ALIGNMENT constraints, because they line up a category of phonological units (in this case handshapes) with a category of morpho-syntactic units (either words or stems). We can see the effects of this difference in a loan sign with the same input form in LSQ and ASL—i.e., 'apartment' (7c). Notice that in the ASL output, ALIGN-L and ALIGN-R are both respected, while in the LSQ output, only ALIGN-L is respected.

TABLE I.4.   *Constraints on borrowed words in ASL and LSQ*

1. Constraints that function similarly in ASL and LSQ
    a.   Selected Fingers Constraint (sf) (Brentari, 1998; Mandel, 1981)
        i.   one selected fingers group per word.
        ii.   Hand-internal movements involve only selected fingers.
    b.   Two-type constraint (2-hs; from Perlmutter, 1992) There may be no more than two
         handshapes per lexeme.
    c.   Peripherality Constraint (max-ap; Brentari, 1998) Handshape changes that occupy
         syllable peaks maximize aperture change.
2. Constraints that function differently in ASL and in LSQ
    a.   align(l) (Brentari, 1998) Align initial handshape of stem with left edge of stem
    b.   align(r) (Brentari, 1998) Align final handshape of word with right edge of word

(7) Examples of restructuring in ASL and LSQ

 a.   ASL borrowings   b.   LSQ borrowings
      SOCIAL <u>W</u>ORK   *<u>VE</u>UVE*
      <u>C</u>URRICULU<u>M</u>   *<u>S</u>HERBROO<u>K</u>*
      <u>P</u>ROGRA<u>M</u>   *<u>AF</u>FAIRES*
      <u>A</u>PARTMEN<u>T</u>   *<u>AP</u>ARTMENT*
 c.   Contrast between outputs of APARTMENT in LSQ and ASL

LSQ:<u>AP</u>ARTMENT

/APARTMENT/	ALIGN -L	2-HS	MAX-AP	SF.a	ALIGN -R
☞*AP*					*
APT		*		**	

ASL: <u>AP</u>ARTMENT_

/APARTMENT/	ALIGN -L	ALIGN -R	2-HS	MAX-AP	SF.a
☞APT			*		**
AP		*			

CONCLUSION

From these cases, one can see the wide range of possible mechanisms sign
languages use to borrow elements from a surrounding spoken language.
There are system-internal and system-external reasons for the shapes that
these forms take. For example, the typological profile of the target language is a system-internal motivation for the change in grammatical category of *op* and *door* from Dutch to SLN. The system-external motivation
of ease of perception could be at least partially responsible for the
ALIGNMENT constraints at work in LSQ and ASL; it is easier to identify
a word by the letters at the margins than by letters in the middle of the
word. Attitudes about the language of the hearing are another possible
system-external factor. Within the Canadian and European Deaf commu-

nities represented in this study, there is a positive feeling toward their corresponding spoken language and towards lipreading, whereas in the United States this is less true.

The bilingual nature of sign language communities and their coexistence alongside their spoken language neighbors make them fertile ground for research on the interpenetration of languages with widely divergent grammatical structures.

ACKNOWLEDGMENTS

This work was funded in part by NSF grant #9420873; I am grateful for their support. I would also like to thank the participants of the Linguistic Society of America's Linguistic Institute (1995) for helpful discussion on these issues and Laurinda Crossley for help in preparing this manuscript for production.

REFERENCES

Berruto, G. (1995). *Fondamenti di sociolinguistica.* Roma, Italy: Laterza.

Battison, R. (1978). *Lexical borrowing in American Sign Language.* Silver Spring, MD: Linstock Press.

Ebbinghaus, H. (1998). Theoretische sprachauffassung and sprachliche wirklichkeit. *Das Zeichen* , *43*, 84–91.

Dozier, E. (1956). Two examples of linguistic acculturation: The Yaqui of Sonora and Arizona and the Tewa of New Mexico. *Language, 32*, 146–157.

Ebbinghaus, H., & Hessmann J. (1996). Signs and words: Accounting for spoken language elements in German Sign Language. *International Review of Sign Language Linguistics, 1*, 23–56.

Grosjean, F. (1982). *Life with two languages: An introduction to bilingualism.* Cambridge, MA: Harvard University Press.

Grosjean, F. (1992). The bilingual and bicultural in the hearing and in the deaf world. *Sign Language Studies, 77*, 307–320.

Grosjean, F. (1999). The bilingual's language modes. In J. L. Nicol & T. D. Langendoen (Eds.), *Language processing in the bilingual.* Oxford, England: Blackwell.

Hasselmo, N. (1970). Codeswitching and modes of speaking. In G. Gilbert (Ed.), *Texas studies in bilingualism* (pp. 179–210). Berlin: de Gruyter.

Haugen, E. (1950). The analysis of linguistic borrowing. *Language, 26*, 210–231.

Itô, J., & Mester, A. (1995a). Japanese phonology. In J. Goldsmith (Ed.), *A handbook of phonological theory* (pp. 817–838). Oxford, England: Blackwell.

Itô, J., & Mester, A. (1995b). The core-periphery structure of the lexicon and constraints on reranking. In J. Beckman et al. (Eds.), *University of Massachusetts Occasional Papers 18: Papers in Optimality Theory* (pp. 181–210). University of Massachusetts, Amherst: Graduate Linguistic Student Association.

Lane, H., Hoffmeister, R., & Bahan, B. (1996). *A journey into the Deaf-World.* San Diego, CA: Dawn Sign Press.

Lovins, J. (1974). Why loan phonology is natural phonology. In A. Bruck, R. A. Fox, & M. W. LaGaly (Eds.), *Papers from the annual meeting of the Chicago Linguistic Society, Vol. 2: Parasession on Natural Phonology*. Chicago, IL: Chicago Linguistic Society.

Lucas, C., & Valli, C. (1992). *Language contact in the American Deaf community*. San Diego, CA: Academic Press.

Mandel, M. (1981). *Phonotactics and Morphophonology in American Sign Language*. Unpublished doctoral dissertation, University of California, Berkeley.

Padden, C. (1998). The ASL lexicon. *Sign Language and Linguistics, 1*, 35–53.

Padden, C. (1991). The acquisition of fingerspelling by deaf children. In Siple & S. Fischer (Eds.), *Theoretical issues in sign language research: Psychology* (pp. 191–210). Chicago: University of Chicago Press.

Padden, C., & Humphries, T. (1988). *Deaf in America: Voices from a culture*. Cambridge, MA: Harvard University Press.

Paradis, D., & Lacharité, D. (1997). Preservation and minimality in loanword adaptation. *Linguistics, 33*, 379–430.

Perlmutter, D. (1992). Sonority and syllable structure in American Sign Language. *Linguistic Inquiry, 23,* 407–442.

Poplack, S., & Meechan, M. (1998). How languages fit together in codemixing. *International Journal of Bilingualism, 2*, 127–138.

Poplack, S., Sankoff, D., & Miller, C. (1988). The social correlates and linguistic processes of lexical borrowing and assimilation. *Linguistics, 26,* 47–104.

Rickford, J. R. (1987). *Dimensions of the Creole continuum: History, texts, and linguistic analysis of Guyanese Creole*. Stanford, CA: Stanford University Press.

Romaine, S. (1992). *Language, education, and development: Urban and rural Tok Pisin in Papua New Guinea*. Oxford/New York: Oxford University Press.

Sandler, W., & M. Nespor. (1999). Prosody in Israeli Sign Language. *Language and Speech, 42,* 143–177.

Schermer, T. (1990). *In search of language: Influences from spoken Dutch on Sign Language of the Netherlands*. Eburon, Delft, The Netherlands.

Wempe, K. (1997). Nur wo abschied gonommen wird, gibt es platz für neues leben [It is only where a departure exists that there is a place for new life]. *Das Zeichen, 42,* 516–526.

Wilbur, R. B. (1994). Eyeblinks and ASL phrase structure. *Sign Language Studies, 84,* 221–240.

1

Functions of the Mouthing Component in the Signing of Deaf Early and Late Learners of Swiss German Sign Language

Penny Boyes Braem

ABSTRACT

"Mouthings" are unvoiced pronunciations of German words, produced along with manual signs by deaf signers of DSGS. At first glance, it is reasonable to suppose that these mouthings primarily represent an intersentential code-switching to, or borrowing at the lexical level from the deaf signer's other language, German. Although lexical code-switching as well as borrowing do explain the function of many of the mouthings in the spontaneous signing of three early and three late learners of DSGS in this study, further analyses of the data have indicated that the situation is often much more complex. Because these deaf bilinguals' two languages are communicated in different modalities, the spoken word, which has a primarily denoting function in the oral language, can in the silent mouthings of sign language, where the hands are the primary channels of denotation, take on nonlexical functions as well. This is particularly the case for the early learners, for whom the uses of mouthings seem to be more thoroughly grammaticized, with a larger range of systematically used subtypes: lexically and grammatically, stylistically to mark a particular kind of signing, "constructed speaking," and prosodically, to mark boundaries of grammatical phrases and prosodic groups. For lexical items involving mouthings, criteria for distinguishing between codeswitches, nonce borrowings, and established borrowings are proposed.

INTRODUCTION

Swiss German Sign Language (DSGS)

Swiss German Sign Language (Deutschschweizerische Gebärden-sprache, henceforth referred to as DSGS) is used by an estimated 4000-5000 deaf persons living in the German-speaking cantons of Switzerland. (Deaf persons living in the French and Italian-speaking cantons have their own, separate sign languages.) DSGS is composed of five related dialects; there is no standardized version of the language. The tradition of schooling deaf children only in the oral language is still quite strong in German Switzerland and has influenced not only the spoken and sign language skills of Swiss deaf persons, but also their attitudes toward these languages. Deaf adults in German Switzerland live in a bilingual situation in which one of their languages–German–is actively furthered and positively viewed both by hearing and by deaf persons, whereas their other language—DSGS—has only recently been exposed to much public attention, is insufficiently researched, and is still viewed as a dispensable evil by a large number of hearing authorities responsible for deaf education as well as for medical and family counseling. (cf. the Appendix for a more detailed description of the sociolinguistic situation of sign language and its deaf users in German Switzerland).

Mouthing and DSGS

The "mouthings" discussed in this report refer to the voiceless pronunciation of German words or word parts that accompany the production of manual signs. For example, in DSGS the manual sign *MUTTER*[1] ('mother') is always accompanied by the mouthed word *Mutter.* In the sign language sentence, the mouthed element sometimes has the same or similar meaning as a manual sign; in other cases it modifies or is completely different from the simultaneously produced manual sign.

   The component called "mouthing" that is analyzed here does not include all the forms that the mouth can make in sign language, but only includes those forms that clearly stem from the spoken language. Other uses of the mouth that are not based on the spoken language, and are not part of this study, are referred to here as "mouth gestures" and include

---

[1]Glosses provided in the surrounding spoken language (e.g., DSGS glosses given in German) are indicated in upper case italics. (see further discussion on the "Notational Conventions" page, given in the front of this volume.)

what have been termed in the literature "nonmanual adjectives and adverbs," or nonmanual components of "multichannel signs."[2]

The mouthing component derived from spoken language has attracted more attention from researchers of some sign languages than of others, leading to the impression that mouthing is indeed a more important linguistic factor in European sign languages. Studies of mouthings in European sign languages include those by Schröder (1985) for Norwegian Sign Language, Schermer (1990) for the Sign Language of the Netherlands, Ebbinghaus & Hessmann (1994, 1995, 1996) for German Sign Language, and Pimiä (1990) for Finnish Sign Language.

There are several possible reasons why mouthing seems more significant for DSGS than has been reported, for example, for ASL. One reason is that most Swiss German deaf persons do not customarily use fingerspelling, the principal technique for incorporating lexical items from the oral language into many other sign languages, including ASL. The lack of a standardized form of DSGS also has the consequence that, in this small country, one's conversation partner quite likely is using a different sign dialect from one's own. In this sociolinguistic situation, mouthing can serve as a redundant marker of a lexical meaning that might have different forms in the manual signs of other dialects. Finally, given the bilingual living situation of the Swiss German deaf population, heavily weighted as it is by educational policy and by general positive language attitudes of deaf as well as hearing persons toward the oral language, it is not surprising that mouthing of German words has become an important element in the signing of deaf Swiss Germans.

Research Questions

For this study, the principal research questions concern the status of mouthing in sign language: In what situations are mouthings instances of

---

[2]An example of a "nonmanual adjective or adverb" (or "mouth gesture") would be the "square" mouth form that adds the meaning of 'intensely or with difficulty' to a manually produced verb. When combined with the sign TO-WORK, for example, the combination would be translated by the phrase 'work hard.' Compare Baker & Cokely, 1980, and Baker-Shenk, 1983, for ASL examples; Coerts, 1992, for nonmanual grammatical markers in Dutch Sign Language; Vogt-Svendsen, 1983, for Norwegian Sign Language; Pimiä, 1990, for examples in Finnish Sign Language. Some mouth forms seem to be based on facial expressions that are used by hearing as well as deaf persons for nonverbal communication of the speaker's physical or emotional state. An example of this is the dropped jaw mouth form ('ash') as an expression of surprise, shock, or fear. In signed texts, this can be used to indicate the nonverbal state not only of the signer but also of a character in the narrative being signed. The accompanying manual sign is held or quite often dropped altogether, resulting in a kind of pantomimic island inserted into the sign string. The function of these kinds of mouth forms seems analogous to the facial expressions and gestures that accompany spoken narratives presented in a dramatic style.

codeswitching between the oral and sign languages and when so used, in what environments and for what purposes does this codeswitching occur? To what extent are mouthings permanently integrated loan elements, or borrowings, in DSGS, and at what levels of the language do these borrowings function? To approach these basic questions, this study began with an analysis of data from spontaneous signing of three early and three late learners, all deaf, of DSGS. The first part of this report is therefore a description of the mouthings found in the data. In the last section, an attempt has been made to interpret these data by means of a theoretical model for code-switching and borrowing.

Subjects, Data Collection, and Coding

To investigate these questions, data was analyzed from a study of three early and three late deaf learners of DSGS.[3] The comparison of the data of these two subject groups is helpful, because it clearly shows that the functions of mouthings are very dependent on who is producing them. The data used for this mouthing analysis are from the first 4 minutes of each subject's unrehearsed short narrative about a personally experienced accident. The audience for these narratives consisted of the other five deaf subjects, most of whom already knew each other. Filming was done in the Deaf Center in Zurich, with no hearing persons present during the filming. The subjects were aware that their signed stories would be used for research purposes.

At the time of data collection, all early and late learners had been using sign language in their daily lives for more than 10 years, and all are fully integrated into the local deaf community. The early learners were all born profoundly deaf, had deaf relatives, and had attended schools for the deaf. They learned sign language from their relatives and from other children at the school for the deaf that they attended. The late learners have more varied backgrounds: Two had lost their hearing between the ages of 6 and 7; the third has been severely hard-of-hearing from birth and attended a strictly oral school for the deaf where signing was not allowed, even in the dormitories. All three late learners mastered sign language as

---

[3]This data is from the Swiss National Science Foundation-sponsored projects Nr. 11-28770.90 and 11-36347.92, " An exploratory study of how age of acquisition affects forms of sign language used by the deaf in German Switzerland" (1991–1995), carried out by the Forschungszentrum für Gebärdensprache in Basel by Boyes Braem, Tissi and Jauch (Boyes Braem, 1995).

adults, after they had completed their basic schooling. German is thus the first language and DSGS a later second language for all three.[4]

Two deaf coworkers (both early learners of DSGS) transcribed the German words that they thought were being mouthed by the videotaped subjects, paying attention to how the mouthed element was distributed over the flow of manual signs. When not otherwise noted, the mouthing was transcribed as a complete German word. If the mouthing was clearly a reduced form of the word, the deaf assistants noted the part of the word which they judged to have been actually produced.

DATA ANALYSES

The small number of informants (six) and the fact that the data is composed of short anecdotes means that all the observations based on the analyses of this data are necessarily tentative. However, both informant groups, but especially the early learners, performed quite uniformly on the aspects of mouthing that were studied, which suggests that the major findings of this study could be investigated further using only early learners.

Initially, several different aspects of the mouthing data were analyzed. The four following kinds of analyses are briefly described in this section: frequency of mouthing, forms of mouthing, coordination of mouthing and manual components, and coordination of mouthing and manual meanings.

Frequency of Mouthings

Because the oral language was their first, and for many years their only, language one original hypothesis of this study was that the late learners would accompany more of their manual signs with mouthings than would the early learners and that these mouthings would primarily represent code-switching to German.

This hypothesis was disproved by a first analysis of the data that showed that both the early and the late learners accompany approximately the same, quite high, percentage of their manual signs with mouthings. Figure 1.1 shows the percentage of all manual signs that are accompanied

---

[4]One of the deafened late learners did attend a school for the deaf for a few months of first grade where she was exposed to some signing. However, she then transferred to a school for hard-of-hearing children where no signing was used and where she completed the rest of her education. She reports that she feels she learned DSGS only after age 16 from deaf friends.

by mouthing over the first 4-minute stretch of the spontaneous narrative signing. The three early learner subjects accompany an average of 80% of their signs with mouthings; the late learners, an average of 76%. Thus the first quantitative finding was that both groups of learners accompanied nearly four fifths of their signs with mouthings, although the late learners showed more individual variation than did the early learners.

The high percentage of signs accompanied by a mouthing component found in this study is partly due to the coding method used. Signs were counted as being accompanied by mouthing even if the mouthed element was only part of a German word accompanying two or more successive manual signs. Thus, in the signing of the early learner in Example (1) that follows, each of the six manual signs was coded as being accompanied by a mouthing or mouthing segment. In this case, however, only three mouthings were involved, as they have been co-produced (or "stretched") over two or more manual signs. (The English translations of all DSGS examples can, of course, only give a general idea of how the original German mouthings are spread.)

(1) Early learner data: 3 mouthings stretched over 6 manual signs (English translation: 'I went and did it quickly in about one minute.')

German gloss for manual component	*SCHNELL-MACHEN*	*UNGEFäHR*	*EIN*	*MINUTE*	*ICH*	*SICH-BEWEGEN-Bein*
German mouthing	*schne_*	*_ll*	*ei_*	*_n Mi_*	*_i_*	*_nute*

English gloss for manual component	DO-QUICKLY	APPROXIMATELY	ONE	MINUTE	I	LOCOMOTION -legs
mouthing translation	*quick_*	*_ly*	*o_*	*_ne Mi_*	*_i_*	*_nute*

Example (2) is from the signing of a later learner. In this sentence, five manual signs are also accompanied by mouthings, but here a different mouthing is produced for each manual sign, giving a total of five mouthings.

Although both the early and late learners accompany a high percentage of their manual signs with mouthings, further analyses indicate that the two groups often use different forms of mouthings, in different ways, for different purposes.

(2) Late learner data with 4 mouthings matched to 4 manual components (English translation: '[she] said, please stay quiet.')

German Gloss for manual component	₃SAGEN ₁	BITTE	RUHIG	BLEIBEN
German mouthing	sagen	bitte	bleibe	ruhig

English Gloss for manual component	₃3AY ₁	PLEASE	QUIET	STAY
mouthing translation	say	please	stay	quiet

Forms of Mouthing

Phonological Reduction of Mouthings. Another initial hypothesis of this study was that the early learners would tend to use more monosyllabic mouthings as well as "reduced" mouthings (forms in which

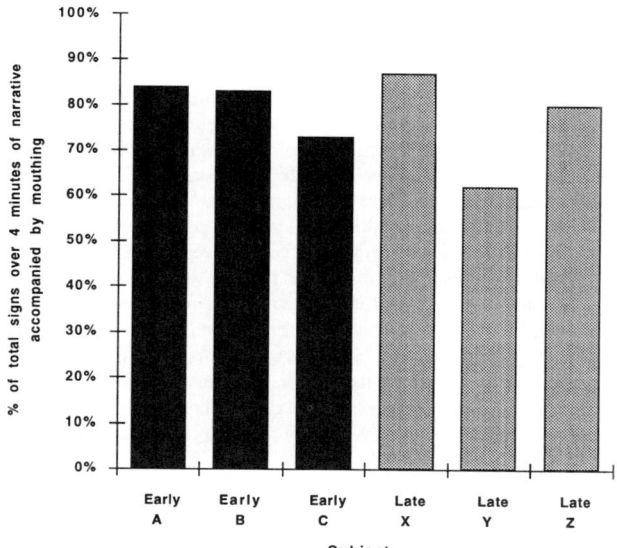

FIG. 1.1. *Percentage of manual signs accompanied by mouthing over 4-minute stretches of spontaneous signed narratives for early and late learners.*

only the first part of polysyllabic words are produced), whereas the late learners would tend to mouth forms more like those of standard German, specifically more polysyllabic and nonreduced forms. Although there was technically some difficulty in seeing if a mouthing was a reduced form, when only obviously reduced forms were compared, it was found that they represented only 1% of the total mouthings of both subject groups.[5] All the reduced forms represent polysyllabic words, but only a small number of polysyllabic words in this data are reduced in mouthing. The reduced forms seem to be primarily of frequently occurring mouthings. For example, *gehörlos* ('deaf')is usually reduced to *gelos*.[6]

Both learner groups also tended to reduce words that had adjectival or adverbial meanings (*mühsam, unsympathisch, plötzlich, komisch, möglich;* Eng.: 'tiring,' 'unlikable,' 'suddenly,' 'funny/strange,' 'possible') rather than nouns. The only obvious reductions of nouns in this data were for the name of a local deaf school, *Wollis(hofen)*, and a repeated reference to the police, *Poli(zei)*.

---

[5]Ebbinghaus and Hessmann (1995) found 9.5% reduced words in their mouthing data of DGS. Schermer (1990) found 7% reduced words in the Sign Language of the Netherlands. The lower percentage found for DSGS in this study is probably related to the methodology in which "doubtful" cases of reduction were counted as full forms. There were several difficulties in trying to decide if a mouthing was actually produced as a reduced form or if the full form was produced, but in such a way that the endings were visually unclear. Outside of labials (m, p, b) and vowels, most parts of mouthed words are difficult to see, as they involve invisible actions of the tongue and the glottis. Thus, in the following mouthings, the final parts in parentheses can be produced so as to be almost invisible: *sof(ort), wi(chtig), fe(rtig), me(hr), Stu(nde), de(nken), helf(en), Schu(ld)*. (Eng.: ' immediately,' 'important,' 'finished,''more,' 'hour,' 'think,' 'help,' 'guilt.') Especially in the mouthings of the early learners, it was often difficult to decide, for example, whether a mouthing such as *helfen* was produced as a reduced form (only *help*) or whether the participant simply articulated the final morpheme *en* with minimal internal mouth movements that made the final morpheme less perceptible. As it was difficult to judge whether mouthings of words with such "less visible" endings were full or reduced, the doubtful cases were always coded as being complete forms. Easier to judge as being reduced forms were words of two or more syllables in which the vowel in the second syllable involved a visible change from that in the first, like *ge(rade), wes(halb), kom(isch)*. (Eng.: 'straight' or 'right away,' 'why,' 'funny' or 'strange'). One clear difference between the participant groups was that the late learners seemed to take more care in their enunciation of the mouthings, which made it easier to judge whether they were using complete or reduced forms. Ebbinghaus and Hessmann (1995) made the interesting observation that there might be more reductions on verbs than nouns in their data, as a reduction of a German verb does not impair the understanding of the meaning as does the reduction of a noun. They also argued that it doesn't matter how much the form is reduced if the form can be reconstructed by the perceiver in the context in which it appears.

[6]Deaf informants have informally observed that one motivation for this reduction of the mouthing *gehörlos* ('deaf') to *gelos* is so that the mouthing will have the same number of components (two syllables) as the simultaneously produced sign, which moves between two locations (the ear and the mouth). Other sociolinguistic motivations for this sign are discussed in Boyes Braem et al. (2000).

Inflections on the Mouthings. Mouthings of the early learners were usually forms of German lexical items that are uninflected for plural, tense, and case. The verbs are usually either in the infinitive form or first person singular for frequently occurring verbs such as *gehe* ('I go'). This often results in mouthings that are not inflected as they would be in a corresponding German sentence. This is particularly true for irregular forms, for example in the mouthing *vergessen* ('to forget') where a German sentence would require the third person singular, present tense *vergisst*.

One exception to the previously noted conventions are past participle forms for some very frequently used verbs. For example, all three early learners used the mouthing *gesagt*, the past participle of *sagen* ('to say'). Two of the early learners even produced the full German construction for the first person in their mouthing, as a kind of frozen construction: *habe gesagt*. Most of the other past participles mouthed in the early learner data appeared without the auxiliary *haben*.

In the late learner data, many more past participles of verbs were used than by the early learners.[7] Also conjugated forms of the auxiliary *haben* were more prevalent, although these sometimes occurred without a following past participle, for example in *habe Umfall (gehabt)*; have accident ('had').

Coordination of Mouthing and Manual Components

There are several different ways in which mouthings and manual signs can be coordinated. As the kind of coordination is an important difference in the early and late learner data, as well as for the different functions of the mouthings, the following types of coordination are described in more detail:

- mouthing alone with no accompanying manual sign;
- one mouthing matched to one manual sign;
- several mouthings produced with one manual sign; and
- one mouthing stretched over two or more manual signs.

---

[7]Past participles forms that occurred in the late learners' data were *gemacht, gemerkt, geweint, geholfen, gesehen, gefahren, aufgeschrieben, aufgestanden, gebracht, gebremst, gehalten, gemacht, geplaudert, gestanden, gewonnen, heimgegangen, and hinuntergefahren* (Eng.: 'made,' 'noticed,' 'cried,' 'helped,' 'seen,' 'gone,' 'written down,' 'stood up,' 'used,' 'braked,' 'stopped,' 'made,' 'gossiped,' 'agreed,' 'won,' 'gone home,' and 'driven down').

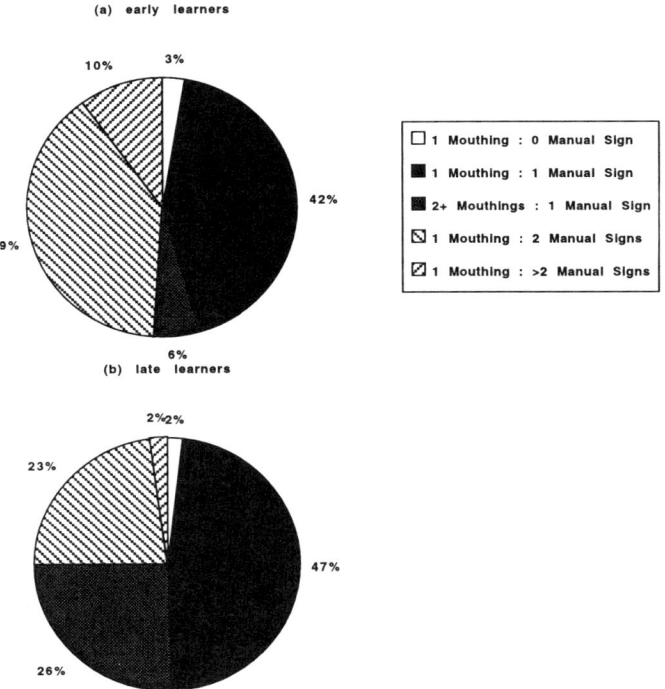

FIG. 1.2.   *Techniques for coordinating mouthings and manual signs used by (a) early learners and*
(b) late learners.

Figure 1.2 shows the proportions in which the two subject groups used these different coordination techniques.

Mouthing With No Accompanying Manual Component. Unaccompanied mouthings turned out to be very rare in the data of both early and late learner subjects (3% of the early and 2% of the late learners' mouthings). Both groups produced unaccompanied endings of mouthings to complete the production of longer polysyllabic words. All categories of words seemed to appear as unaccompanied mouthings by the late learners. The early learners tended to use unaccompanied mouthings more restrictively, for example for negation (*nein, nicht*), an occasional conjunction (*und*), as well as for constructed speech of hearing persons (cf., the section titled "Constructed Speaking").

One Mouthing With One Manual Component. The type of coordination most frequently used by both groups matches one mouthing to one manual component, accounting for 42% of the early and 47% of the late learners' mouthings.

Several Mouthings With One Manual Component. Producing two or more mouthings simultaneously with one manual component accounted for 26% of the late learners' mouthings but only 6% of those of the early learners. Here again, the early learners seemed to use this technique in a more constrained way than did the late learners. Early learners used multiple mouthings most often with set German phrases, such as *was machst Du?* ('What are you doing?'), *nicht schlimm* ('not bad'), and *am Abend* ('in the evening'). The more frequent production of multiple mouthings indicates that the base language is often German for the late learners, who then try to fit as many manual signs as possible to the mouthed words. To coordinate the more numerous mouthings with the more slowly produced manual signs, the late learner is sometimes forced to match more words to each manual sign.

One Mouthing Stretched over Two or More Manual Aigns. The stretching of one mouthing over two or more signs is a technique used much more often by the early learners (49% of their total mouthings) than by the late learners (25%) For the early learners, the stretching did not necessarily correspond to syllable breaks, but rather occurred over a vowel. A stretching can therefore be produced with monosyllabic as well as with polysyllabic mouthings. (One early learner stretched 45% of the monosyllabic mouthings in his text). Although most stretches were over two signs, there are cases where a monosyllabic mouthing was stretched over as many as four signs. The special use of these stretched mouthings by the early learners for prosodic purposes will be discussed separately in the section titled "Mouthings as Borrowings for Prosodic Functions."

Coordination of the Meanings of Mouthing and Manual Components

An analysis was made of the relation of the meaning of the mouthings to meanings carried by the manual sign and by the nonmanual components of the signing. One of the ways in which the two participant groups differed was whether the mouthing was the sole carrier of meaning in the sentence, or whether the mouthing had a meaning that was supplementary or redundant to that of a manual sign in the sentence. The frequency of these three kinds of relation in the data of the early and late learners are shown in Fig. 1.3.

Mouthings carrying the sole meaning in the sentence made up a larger proportion of the late learners' total mouthings (39%) than of the early learners' (16%). The mouthings of the early learners, on the other hand, were more often used for meanings that are "redundant" to those of the manual signs in the sentence (74% vs. 51% of the late learners). The proportion of mouthings used for meanings that are supplementary to those of the manual signs was the same for both participant groups (10%).

Sometimes the late learners used mouthings as the sole carriers of meaning, even though they have used the conventional sign themselves elsewhere in the videotaped texts. This is an indication that these mouthings represent not code-switching but rather the fact that German, rather than DSGS, is the base, or matrix language. (cf., Example (3).

(3) Late learner use of mouthings to carry sole meaning (English Translation: 'But I will only tell about one accident.')

German Gloss for manual component	*INDEX FINGER*	*ICH*	*EIN*	INDEXa	*UNFALL*	*INDEX FINGER*
mouthing	*aber*	*ich*	*erzähle nur*	*ein*	*Unf_*	*_all*

English gloss for manual component	INDEX FINGER	I	ONE	INDEXa	ACCIDENT	INDEX FINGER
mouthing translation	*but*	*I*	*tell-about only*	*one*	*acci_*	*_dent*

Another indication that the late learner's base language is often German rather than DSGS it the fact that almost the entire meaning of some sentences can be (lip)read (cf. Example (4a)). In comparison, the mouthings of the early learners without the manual signs carry only a part of the meaning of the sentence (cf. Example (4b)).

(4)   Typical mouthing sequences of late learners (a) and early learners (b).

a. Mouthings alone from a late learner, signed sentence meaning 'I had to fetch the mail and had to ride with the bike from the company, back and forth every morning and every afternoon, four times a day.'

German mouthing	muss	von der	Firma	mit	dem Velo	fahren hin und	zurück	jeden	Morgen	und	Mittag	viermal	im pro Tag
English translation	must	from the	firm	with	the bicycle	ride to and	fro	every	morning	and	after-noon	four times	in the per-day

b. Mouthings alone from an early learner, signed sentence meaning 'I quickly went to the balcony and hung up the wash, very quickly, about one minute. I came back.'

German mouthing	ich	schne_	_ll	Ba_	_lkon	wa	_schen	schne_	_ll	ei_	_n Mi_	_i_	_nute
English translation	I	qui_	_ck	ba_	_lcony	wa_	_sh	qui_	_ck	o_	_one mi_	i_	_ute

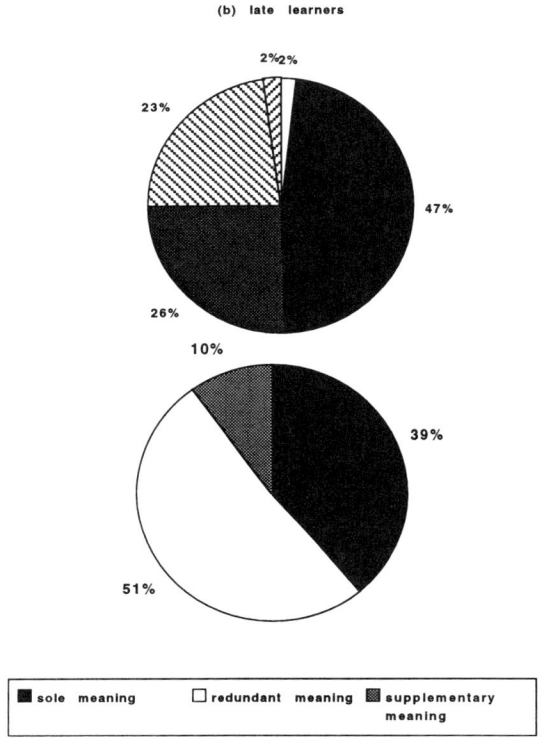

FIG. 1.3. *Mouthings as sole, redundant or supplementary carriers of meaning in the data of early learners (top) and late learners (bottom).*

To say that the meanings of the Mouthings are "redundant" with those of the manual signs is actually not quite accurate. The complete meaning of a lexical item in one language rarely completely overlaps with all the meanings of an item in another language. Here, redundant means that the mouthing and the manual sign belong to the same lexical category and have roughly one meaning in common. A comparison of the mouthings of the early and late learners shows, however, how broad the scope of redundant meaning can be. The late learners often used a much wider variety of semantically related mouthings to accompany a sign. For example, to accompany the sign *sagen* ('to-say/tell'), the early learners consistently used the mouthing *sagen*. In contrast, in some situations, the late learners might have used a word such as *melden* (report). For the sign WIE-GEHTS? (how are you?), both in the sense of a common greeting and as a serious inquiry about someone's health or state, the early learners used the same mouthing *wie gehts?* for both situations, whereas a late learner mouthed *nichts passiert?* ('Nothing happened?') for the inquiry about someone's state after an accident.

The different ways in which the meanings of mouthings are related to the meanings of manual signs is the theme of the remainder of this chapter. Hypotheses are made about the functions these mouthings might have for the two groups of signers. For the late learners, it is argued that the primary function of the mouthings is a lexical one, often representing code-switching to German. For the early learners, some mouthings can serve a lexical function either as code-switching or as a borrowed element. In addition, the structures that have been analyzed to date have provided evidence for grammatical, stylistic, and prosodic purposes of mouthings in the early learners data. An example of the grammatical use of mouthings is seen in the system of reference of DSGS; the stylistic use of mouthings occurs in so-called "constructed speech" in which deaf persons render into DSGS how a hearing person talks. A prosodic use of mouthing occurs when a signer expresses emphasis by adding a mouthing element to a manual sign. Another prosodic function of mouthings in the early learners data is performed by the "stretched" mouthings that indicate prosodic boundaries and domains.

Mouthings as Code-Switches to German for Lexical Purpose

Further analyses were made on the data that indicate that the signers clearly code-switched to German for lexical purposes out of two different kinds of motivations: to fill lexical gaps in the sign language itself, and to fill lexical gaps in an individual signer's production.

To Fill Lexical Gaps in the Sign Language. One of the most obvious functions of mouthing is that of denoting meaning. If a mouthing is the sole carrier of a meaning in a particular sentence (i.e., there are no manual signs with that meaning in the sentence), it, in most cases, would represent an obvious code-switch to the signer's other language, German.

This kind of code-switching can be seen in many of the early learners' mouthings for concepts for which there is no conventionalized sign in DSGS; that is, to fill lexical gaps in the language. These mouthings denote primarily nominal concepts that are either proper names or nouns not commonly used in the local deaf culture. Signers of other sign languages, such as ASL, use the fingerspelled form of word from the spoken language for this purpose.

Both the early and late learners of DSGS sometimes hold the index finger to the chin to draw special attention to this use of mouthing as a code-switch. Code-switch mouthing was articulated by the early learner more slowly and clearly than for other kinds of mouthings in their data.

To Fill Lexical Gaps in an Individual's Production. As indicated in example (3), the late learners used mouthings that are the sole carriers of meaning in a sentence more than twice as much as did the early learners (39% for the late learners vs. 16% for the early learners). In contrast to the early learners, the late learners used mouthings as sole carriers of meanings for a wide variety of word categories. The late learners' code-switching, however, seemed often to be for meanings for which they seemed not to know a sign, although a conventionalized sign for that concept may exist in the language. This "second language learner" motivation for the use of code-switching mouthings is not surprising, given the fact that the late learners seem to have a smaller sign vocabulary than the early learners. The late learners had an average of 99 different sign types in the first 4 minutes of their stories, as compared to 153 sign types in the corresponding early learners' data.

Mouthings as Borrowings
for Lexical and Grammatical Functions

The mouthing of a word accompanied by a manual form may not represent a clear "code-switch" but rather an incorporation of the borrowed word into the lexicon of the language. The term "borrowing" will be discussed in more detail in the section titled "Discussion." For the moment, the term is used here in the sense of Thomason and Kaufman's (1988) definition: "The incorporation of foreign features into a group's native language by speakers of that language: the native language is maintained but is changed by the addition of the incorporated features"(p. 37). The candidates for borrowed forms found in this data were found in the following situations:

- to avoid homonyms of manual forms;
- to further specify the basic meaning of the manual component;
- to modify the meaning of adjectives, adverbs and a modal;
- to negate the modal 'can';

- to specify nominal notions in verbs clauses;
- to name the possessed referent in possessive noun phrase constructions;
- to distinguish between word and sentence level meanings.

To Avoid Homonyms of Manual Forms. For some manual signs, a simultaneous mouthing often seems to be obligatory to avoid homonyms with signs having the same manual component. For example, the manual sign *GLEICH* ('same') is combined with the mouthing *Bruder* ('brother') and the same manual sign is produced with the mouthing *Schwester* ('sister'). In one DSGS dialect, one manual form can mean 'license plate,' 'subtitle,' or 'football team,' depending on the accompanying mouthing.

To Further Specify the Meaning of the Manual Component. Sometimes, the mouthing will function not to distinguish between meanings, but rather to make more precise the meaning of the manual component. For example, the mouthing of *Zettel* ('note') adds precision to the simultaneously made manual sign for 'paper'; the mouthing *Skischuh* ('skiboot') further specifies the meaning of the manual sign for 'shoe.'

The homonym-avoiding and meaning-specifying functions of mouthings have been reported for several other European sign languages (cf. for example, Ebbinghaus, 1998; Ebbinghaus & Hessmann, 1994, 1995, 1996; Pimiä, 1990; Schermer, 1990).

To Modify the Meaning of Adjectives, Adverbs and a Modal. For the early learners, the addition of a mouthing to a sign can be a means of modifying the intensity of the concept.

A mouthed adverb can add an intensification to another meaning carried by the manual sign. For example, the sign GUT (good) accompanied by the mouthing *sehr* (very). If, in addition, the manual component is inflected manually for 'intensive' (by changing the movement to include an initial hold and then a large movement), the result would be an even greater intensification of the meaning, 'extraordinarily good.'

The repetition of a mouthing with the same meaning as the manual component can also convey an intensification. For example, one early learner made the manual sign meaning 'more' with no repetition, and accompanied it with the repeated mouthing *mehr mehr mehr* ('more more more') resulting in the augmentative meaning of 'more and more.' Although the mouthing here stems from the German word, its repetition to indicate intensification is a sign language device.

When produced with no mouthing, the sign normally glossed as *MÜSSEN* ('must') actually has the weaker meaning of *sollen* ('should'). If the mouthing *müssen* is coproduced, the meaning of the construction is that of stronger obligation, 'must.' Late learners, in contrast to the early learners, for the meaning of 'should' used the mouthing *sollen* alone or with the sign meaning 'must.' Early learners used this construction only when they were producing constructed speech of persons communicating in the spoken language.

To Negate the Modal 'Can'.   DSGS does have conventionalized manual signs for negation, as well as conventionalized nonmanual facial signals, specifically the tilting or shaking of the head. However, sometimes an early learner will signify a negative with a mouthing alone, usually the German word *nicht* (not). This use of mouthing alone for negation is produced with no sign for negation appearing in the same sentence and with no negative head markers. This use of the *nicht* mouthing alone in the learners' data occurred primarily together with the manual sign for the modal 'can,' resulting in a manual + mouthing construction meaning 'can not.'

The only other occurrences of the mouthing *nicht* occurring alone seem to be in particular styles of discourse, which are discussed further in the section titled "Mouthings as codeswitches for stylistic functions."

To Specify Nominal Notions in Verb Clauses.   In DSGS, verbs denoting self-movement, including polymorphemic verbs with classifier handshapes, are usually not accompanied by mouthings that denote the meaning of the verbal element (i.e., 'walk,' 'lie down,' 'move upward,' etc.). The mouthings or mouthing segments that do co-occur with movement verbs in this data tended rather to specify more precisely nominal notions (such as agents, patients, locations, sources or goals of the movement) or adverbial modifiers. For example, one early learner signed 'the doctor approached me' with a polymorphemic verb meaning '+move-self+approaching+single agent' accompanied by the mouthing *Doktor*, which identified the single agent. Another early learner, trying to explain that the path he was describing was actually a sidewalk, used a polymorphemic verb meaning to walk with a mouthing indicating who is walking, resulting in the construction: 'LOCOMOTION+by foot'+ *people*. The sentence in Example (5), meaning 'I walked up to the second floor (where I was shocked; six doctors were waiting for me),' is an example of a mouthing that identifies the goal of the movement verb. In this sentence, the polymorphemic verb is a complex of morphemes meaning 'move-self+by foot+in upwards direction.' The precise goal of the movement, 'floor' is indicated only by a mouthing, with no corresponding manual sign in the sign string.

(5) *Early learners' use of mouthing to indicate the goal of a polymorphemic verb of locomotion in the sentence: 'I walked up to the second floor (where I was shocked; six doctors were waiting for me).'*

German gloss for manual component	SICH-BEWEGEN +Bein+aufwärts	ZWEITE	ICH	SICH-BEWEGEN +Bein+aufwärts	ERSCHROCKEN
German mouthing		zwei_	_te Sto_	_	_ck

English Gloss for manual component	LOCOMOTION +by foot+upward	SECOND	I	LOCOMOTION +by foot +upward	SHOCKED
mouthing translation		se_	_cond sto_	__	_ry

To Name the Possessed Referent in Possessive Noun Phrase Constructions. The mouthing often functions as a borrowed element carrying the sole meaning in possessive noun phrase constructions in the early learners' data, particularly in indicating family relations (for example 'my father'). In these constructions, the pronoun indicating the "possessor" is a manual sign (POSSESSIVE) orientated toward the spatial locus of the possessor, and meaning 'my,' 'your,' 'his,' and so forth. The "possessed" referent is usually not indicated at all by a manual sign but only by a simultaneously produced mouthing for the relative. Thus, although there is a conventionalized sign meaning 'father,' the construction of the phrase meaning 'my father' would be produced as in (6):

(6) *Possessive noun phrase construction in DSGS in a construction meaning 'my father.'*

manual sign	POSSESSIVE$_1$
mouthing	*Vater (Father)*

To Distinguish Between Word and Discourse Levels of Meanings.
Sometimes the mouthing can indicate at what level the manual sign
functions. For example, the manual sign *FERTIG* ('finished'), when
accompanied by the mouthing *fertig* or *schon* ('already') functions at the
morphemic level as a perfect tense marker for a verb, as in *GESTERN ICH
BUCH LESEN FERTIG + schon* (YESTERDAY I BOOK READ
FINISHED + *already;* I have read the book yesterday). If the same sign,
FERTIG, is combined with no mouthing or the mouthing *dann* ('then'),
the sign functions at the discourse level to indicate boundaries between
sequences of related events, as in *GESTERN ICH BUCH KAUFEN
LESEN FERTIG + dann ARBEIT SCHREIBEN.* ('Yesterday, after I had
bought and read the book, I wrote the paper.')

Mouthings as Borrowings for Discourse Functions

The mouthings discussed in the previous sections are either the sole carriers of a particular meaning in a sentence, or they give meanings that are
supplementary to the basic meaning of a manual sign in the sentence.
However, as indicated in Figure 1.3, a surprisingly large proportion (74%)
of the early learners' mouthings have meanings that are the same as that of
the accompanying manual component (or a sign elsewhere in the sentence). This is puzzling because if the manual components can carry the
meaning by themselves, why bother adding a redundant mouthing? One
possible motivation has already been mentioned: As DSGS signers very
often are in situations where they are communicating with a person who
uses another sign dialect (often one's own husband or wife), the redundant
use of mouthings may be a measure to avoid misunderstanding the manual
signs of the other dialect. However, these sociolinguistic factors alone
cannot account for the very frequent and persistent use of redundant
mouthings observed in the early learners' data.

Additional analysis has indicated that, especially in the early learners'
data, mouthings also can function at the discourse, prosodic, and stylistic
levels of the language. These other functions of mouthing no doubt contribute to the large proportion of early learners' mouthings that, at the lexical level, have meanings redundant with those of the manual signs in the
signed sentence.

In this section, two kinds of discourse level functions are discussed: to
help establish linguistic reference, and to add stress.

To Help Establish Linguistic Reference. One of the most important functions of mouthing among the early learners seems to be the clear identification of new referents in the discourse. There are numerous techniques for making linguistic reference in DSGS, including manual signs for proper names,[8] nouns, and noun phrases, the use of spatial techniques (coordination with the sign, the direction of eye gaze or both to a spatial locus that has been identified with a referent), and the use of "character identifying" facial and body expressions. Fingerspelling is not commonly used for this purpose in DSGS. As in spoken languages, in DSGS, different combinations of referencing techniques are used at different levels of the discourse, depending on whether a referent is being newly introduced, repeatedly referred to within an episode, or reintroduced in a later episode (Boyes Braem, 1992). The early learners in this study introduced all new referents and reintroduced all participating characters in new episodes by combining a namesign or a nominal sign or nominal sign phrase with a mouthing for the same referent and often an indication of a spatial locus for this referent. An example of the resulting construction for the first mention of a referent would be a sequence such as the following: GIRL+*girl* LITTLE ANNE+*Anne* INDEX (spatial locus). There was a quite striking regularity to the early learners' use of this combination of semantically redundant techniques for establishing first mention of a referent. When the early learners did use a mouthing alone for a referent, it was usually at a lower level of the discourse structure, within subsequent scenes of an episode, after the referent had been introduced and identified with the usual combination of redundant techniques.[9]

The late learners did not consistently combine a mouthing with manual techniques for a new or reintroduced referent. This indicates a second

---

[8]Reference to proper names in DSGS is interesting, as until recently very few such references made use of the finger alphabet, either in the spelling out the whole name, or in "initialized" name signs. Sometimes names of persons are indicated by a name sign accompanied by the forename and family name being pronounced together without voice (for example, *Heinz Schreiber*). Some deaf persons in German Switzerland have no name signs at all, but are referred to by a voiceless mouthing of their names followed by some kind of physical description of the person (cf. Tissi (1993) for a more complete description of name signs in DSGS).

[9]The combining of several these devices for establishing or reestablishing identity of a linguistic reference has been reported for other sign languages (cf., the discussion of discourse devices used in Swedish Sign Language in Ahlgren & Bergman, 1990, 1994). However, the conventional use of mouthing to establish reference in this combination has not, to my knowledge, been reported for other sign languages.

language learner problem in mastering the DSGS referencing techniques appropriate to different levels of the discourse. Some late learners used mouthing as the only means of identifying an intended referent. These cases seem to be examples of interference from their first language—that is, an over-reliance on German words alone to establish reference.

To Add Stress. A stressed or focused lexical item in DSGS is usually indicated by its placement in the final position in the sentence (as Wilbur, 1990 noted is the case for stressed items in ASL). However, the use of a mouthing with a meaning redundant to the manual component also seems to be able to add stress, particularly to manual components that do not necessarily occur in final position. The effect of this kind of stress is not so strong as a final placement would be. The use of mouthing for adding lexical stress seems to occur more frequently with manual adjectives and adverbials (for example, KURZ+*kurz*, AUCH+*auch*, VERRÜCKT+ *verrückt* / (SHORT+*short*, ALSO+*also*, CRAZY+*crazy*).

Mouthings as Borrowings for Prosodic Functions

The use of mouthing in this DSGS data for prosodic functions involves the use of what has been described as stretched mouthings, mouthed words that are produced over two or more successive manual signs. It is not being claimed here that these stretched mouthings are the sole prosodic markers in sign language. Facial and body markers also have an important prosodic role in sign languages.

In the early learners' signing, however, these stretched mouthings seemed to act as an additional suprasegmental for binding sequences of manual signs. This form of prosodic marking did not occur with all kinds of sequences. Stretched mouthings found in this data seem to have the following prosodic functions: to bind constituents of noun phrases, to bind verbs and their subjects, and to bind larger prosodic units.

To Bind Constituents of Noun Phrases. Stretched mouthings as prosodic markings occurred often with manual components that involve the use of spatial techniques that are common in sign languages but impossible in spoken languages. For example, in noun phrase constructions of a nominal sign followed by an indication of the spatial locus for that referent, the mouthing for the referent tended to be stretched over both signs (7).

(7) Mouthing stretched over noun sign and a spatial index sign

English gloss for manual component	MANN	INDEX $_a$
mouthing translation	Ma_	_nn

The mouthing also tended to be stretched over phrases that involved a nominal referent and the DSGS person classifier, a sign that can be repeated in horizontally slightly shifted locations to indicate plurality (see (8) below).

(8) Mouthing stretched over a noun and a plural indicating a sign in a construction meaning 'six doctors.'

German Gloss for manual component	SECHS	DOKTOR	PERSON +(plural)
mouthing	sechs	Do_	_ktor

English gloss for manual component	SIX	DOCTOR	PERSON +(plural)
mouthing translation	six	Do_	_ctor

Both this example and the MANN INDEX construction in (7) seem to be cases of a stretched mouthing binding a nominal with a free form morpheme inflection. This might be an equivalent of the marking of a prosodic word.

To Bind Verbs With Subjects. One component of the polymorphemic verb, the handshape, can refer to a class of referents, such as 'large vehicles', 'single thin vertically orientated objects,' and so forth. The exact referent was normally identified elsewhere in the sentence or discourse passage by a noun sign. Often these signs occurred before the verb, in which case the mouthing accompanying the manual component was also stretched over the following verb. In Example (9), in a sentence meaning 'the car moves,' the mouthing *Auto* begins accompanying the manual component AUTO and is stretched over the polymorphemic verb SICH-BEWEGEN (locomotion).

(9) Mouthing stretched over a noun and a polymorphic verb in a
*   construction meaning 'the car moves.'*

German Gloss for manual component	AUTO	SICH-BEWEGEN+Fahrzeug
mouthing	Au_	_to

English gloss for manual component	CAR	LOCOMOTION+vehicle
mouthing translation	Ca_	_r

The stretched mouthing also seemed for some of the early learners to act
as a kind of prosodic binding for phrases in which the manual pronoun *ICH*
('I') is repeated. In the sentence of an early learner (10), the first instance of
ICH functions syntactically as the subject of the verb. The resumptive pronoun at the end of the sentence does not seem to have this semantic function.

(10) Mouthings stretched over resumptive pronouns in the sentence
*   meaning 'Maybe I did not pay attention.'*

German gloss for manual component	ICH	NICHT	AUFPASSEN	ICH
mouthing	vielleicht	nicht	aufpa_	_ssen

English gloss for manual component	I	NOT	PAY-ATTENTION	I
mouthing translation	maybe	not	pay-a_	_ttention

Whatever other linguistic function these resumptive pronouns may
have,[10] it is interesting that in the DSGS data, each is prosodically bound to

---

[10]The addition or reduplication especially of the pronoun "I" occurs fairly often in DSGS, even when
the pronoun is not stressed or focused. Wilbur (1994) has suggested that for ASL, unstressed pronouns
in final position fall into the category of extragrammatical pronoun clitics. Both Wilbur and Bos
(1994) think that this kind of pronoun copy might be a kind of proto subject agreement marker. The
DSGS data reported here, however, indicates that on the prosodic level, an unstressed phrase-final
pronoun might also be motivated by a need to add temporal length to the final unit, so that this unit
will be more temporally balanced with the preceding unit. (Boyes Braem, manuscript)

the preceding sign by means of a stretched mouthing. In a separate analysis of the data for this study, it was found that these resumptive pronouns were also accompanied by another type of prosodic marking, a rhythmic horizontal swaying of the torso that typically accompanied certain kinds of discourse structures. When resumptive pronouns occurred at the end of sentences, the torso would tend to reverse direction and move toward a "neutral" central position, indicating the end of a larger prosodic phrase (Boyes Braem, 1999).

To Bind Larger Prosodic Units. The sign sentence in (11) has two stretched mouthings. The first, *gehe,* ('go') binds a resumptive pronoun. The second mouthing, *arbeiten* ('work'), is stretched over a succession of three manual components: a verb, an indexical locus, and a verb. (WORK, INDEX[for workplace] GO [direction workplace]).

(11) Mouthing stretched over verb sequences in sentence meaning 'I went to where I work.'

German gloss for manual component	ICH	GEHEN-ZU	ICH	ARBEITEN	INDEX (v)	GEHEN-HIN (v)
mouthing		ge_	_he	a-rbei_	_te_	_en

English gloss for manual component	I	GO-TO	I	WORK	INDEX (forward)	GO-THERE (forward)
mouthing translation		go_	_o-to	wo_	_o_	_rk

Another example of a mouthing stretched over a larger unit is found in Example (5) (discussed earlier in the section titled "To Specify Nominal Notions in Verb Clauses"). The meaning of this example is, 'I walked up to the second floor (where I was shocked; six doctors were waiting for me).' Here, the mouthing *Stock* (floor) begins with the pronoun 'I' and is stretched over a repetition of the verb ('walk up') and into the following sign ('shocked') conveying the signer's state at what she found on the second floor (six doctors waiting for her). The boundaries of this stretched mouthing do not correspond with single phrase or clause boundaries, but instead seem to mark a larger discourse structure unit.

Another example of the stretching of mouthing over larger discourse units is shown in the sentence in (12), where the word *nervös* ('nervous') is both reduced (*nerv*) and stretched over into the beginning of the next sentence (*ICH DENKEN;* 'I think').

(12) Mouthing both reduced and stretched over several signs in sentence meaning 'I was also nervous, like I was lucky, I was nervous and kept quiet.'

German gloss for manual component	ICH	GLEICH	NERVöS	ICH	DENKEN	GLEICH	GLüCK	ICH	NERVöS	ICH	SCH-WEIGEN	ICH
mouthing	ich	au wie	ner_	_v_	_v	wie	Glü_	_ck	nerv_	v		

English gloss for manual component	I	SAME	NERVOUS	I	THINK	SAME	LUCK	I	NERVOUS	I	KEEP-QUIET	I
mouthing	I		ner_	_v_	_v	like	Lu_	_ck	nerv_	_v		
translation	I	also like										

Mouthings as Codeswitches for Stylistic Functions

The early learners would often use code-switches to German for the following specific stylistic functions: constructed speaking, narrative emphasis, and perspective.

Constructed Speaking. Early learners tended to use mouthings in a special way for a style of discourse that is termed here "constructed speaking." This can be reported speech of a hearing person or the report of a deaf person who is using speech to communicate with a hearing person. These are not citations or "direct speech," but rather constructions of a conversation involving a nonsigning person.

In this style of discourse, there were far fewer stretched mouthings than were generally found in the early learners' signing, and there are more mouthings without any accompanying sign, more multiple mouthings per sign, and more matching of one mouthing with one manual sign. The resulting sentences are similar to what late learners used in all forms of discourse.

Sometimes the mouthed word in constructed speaking was conjugated as it would have been in spoken German, which (except for some perfect participles, models, and frequently used verbs) is usually not the case for other forms of early learners' mouthing. Although the order of the signs in the sentence does not necessarily follow that of German, other German grammatical rules are followed. For example, in constructed speaking, the possessive is indicated not by the normal DSGS device of combining the manually expressed possessive pronoun with a mouthing for the possessed (as with *MEIN+Vater* described earlier), but rather by successive signs plus mouthings for both, as in the sentence in (13):

(13) Constructed speech of a doctor asking a mother, Was hat Ihr Kind vorher gegessen? ('What did your child eat before?')

German gloss for manual component	INDEX (Kind)	POSS (Mutter)	KIND	VERGANGENHEIT		ESSEN	WAS?
mouthing		Ihr	Kind	vorher		essen	was

English gloss for manual component	INDEX (child)	POSSESS (mother)	CHILD	PAST	EAT	WHAT?	
mouthing translation		your	child	before	eat	what	

It is also in constructed speech that the early learners used the mouthing *nicht* ('not') but with no other manual or facial signals for negation, in combination with concepts other than 'can not' (discussed in the section titled "To Negate the Modal 'Can'"). For example, in the mother's response to the doctor's question concerning how much her child had eaten that morning, the construction *VIEL+nicht* (MUCH+ *not*) occurred. Another signer, in a story about a car that ran into him, reported his conversation with the hearing driver of the car, in which the signer proclaimed that he, himself, is not guilty. The manual+ mouthing construction here was *SCHULD+nicht schuld* (GUILTY+*not guilty*).

The constructed speaking style can sometimes lead to complicated coordination of the manual and the mouthed components of the sentence. In Example (14), an early learner reports what her hearing neighbor said to her. Here the word order of the mouthing is that of German, whereas the order of the signs is that of DSGS.

(14) Constructed speaking in which the German word order of the mouthing is opposite that of the signs.

German gloss for manual component	*₃SAGEN₁*	*BITTE*	*RUHE*	*BLEIBEN*
mouthing	*sagen*	*bitte*	*bleibe*	*ruhig*

English gloss for manual component	*₃SAY₁*	PLEASE	QUIET	STAY
mouthing translation	*say*	*please*	*remain*	*quiet*

Another stylistic device related to spoken German is the repeated mouthing *dädädädädä* or *bäbäbäbäb*. This is mouthing based on how hearing people look, from the perspective of a deaf person, when they're producing a continuous stream of sentences.

In the constructed speech style of early learners, sometimes mouthings of some conjunctives, nonspatial adverbs, and adverbial prepositions occur, for example, *und, darum, weil, aber, als, doch, auch, durch, für, von, also* ('and,' 'therefore,' 'because,' 'but,' 'as,' 'yet,' 'also,' 'through,' 'for,' 'of/from,' 'thus'). These mouthings are all accompanied by a manual component that consists of an upheld index finger that makes a small downward, inward curving arc movement. This manual component seems to be a semantically empty manual accompaniment to the mouthing. The early learners in this study used this kind of manual + mouthing construction primarily in special kinds of discourse, in particular when representing the speech of hearing persons. The motivation for their use thus seems to be more stylistic than grammatical. This is in contrast to the late learners, who tended to use these constructions with the arcing index finger throughout their signing, in all forms of discourse.

Narrative Emphasis and Perspective. Another function of mouthings that have redundant meaning is to add emphasis or a special perspective, for example, to draw attention to some aspect of the narrative. An example of this is in a sentence signed by an early learner in a story where she is sitting in a hospital waiting room and the doctor who has just operated on her child comes toward her (15).

(15) 'Someone approached me, the anesthesiologist walked in, approached me.'

German gloss for manual component	$_a$SICH-BEWEGEN$_1$	NARKOSE	DOKTOR	LAUFEN	$_b$SICH-BEWEGEN$_1$
mouthing	j_	_mand Na_	_rkose	Do_	_ktor

English gloss for manual component	$_a$LOCOMOTION$_1$	NARCOSIS	DOCTOR	WALK	$_b$LOCOMOTION$_1$
mouthing translation	so_	_meone Na_	_rcosis	Do_	_ctor

Throughout most of the production of the first sign, a polymorphemic verb indicating an approaching person, the signer produced no mouthing, but her facial expression indicated that of a person stolidly waiting for many hours in a hospital waiting room. Towards the end of the production of this sign, the signer began to mouth *jemand* (someone), followed by *Narkose Doktor* (anesthesiologist). The dramatic effect is that of the portrayed person's growing awareness of the identity of the person who is approaching.

DISCUSSION

Overview of the Functions
of Mouthings in DSGS

The data presented in the previous sections indicate that mouthings in DSGS seem to have a number of different functions. A distinction has been made between mouthings that are "sole carriers" of meanings and those that have meanings that are redundant and related to the meanings of manual sign in the same sign, phrase, or clause construction.

At the discourse level, redundant mouthings help to establish new or reintroduced referents. It has been argued in the section titled "Mouthings as Borrowings for Prosodic Functions" that mouthings that are redundant and also stretched over two or more signs seem to function as prosodic markers binding elements into larger grammatical and prosodic units. The early learners of DSGS often used mouthings as sole carriers of meaning for concepts for which there is no sign (often proper names), that is, to fill in lexical gaps in the language itself. As presented in the section titled "Mouthings as Borrowings for Lexical and Grammatical Functions" indicate, there are also some instances of mouthings used by the early learners that carry the sole meaning but seem to function as more stable borrowed elements in specific grammatical constructions. These instances include the mouthings that specify nominal notions in verb clauses (e.g. LOCO-MOTION+by foot+*second floor*), the mouthing of *nicht*(not) that regularly negates the sign modal meaning CAN, the mouthing of the possessed in possessive noun phrase constructions (MY+*father*), and the use of mouthings to modify the intensity of some adjectives and adverbs (GOOD+*very*). The early learners also used mouthings as sole carriers of meaning in the constructed speaking style of signing.

The Deaf late learners sometimes used sole carrier mouthed German words for concepts for which a sign does exist in the language, but that they perhaps don't know or can't readily access. These seem to be instances of inadequate language acquisition or momentary interference from their first language, German.

The Status of Mouthings:
A Linguistic and Political Problem

The use of mouthings for lexical functions, especially redundant or related meaning mouthings, touches directly on important questions about the linguistic status of mouthings. In which cases are they codeswitches to the spoken language and when would they be better described as borrowings, or as more permanently integrated loan elements in the language?

The question of the status of mouthings not only is of theoretical interest to linguistics and has important practical consequences for sign language lexicographers, but it can also evoke high emotional and political interest in wider circles. One indication of this interest is the number of articles and letters to the editor that have appeared in several issues of the German sign language journal *Das Zeichen* in 1997 and in 1998. This public debate on the linguistic status of mouthings in German Sign Language was touched off by comments made by H. Leuninger, a generative grammar linguist from Frankfurt, in an interview with the editor of the magazine.[11] Among other comments, she made the following statements: "I can imagine no systematic linguistic theory which could offer a plausible explanation for the (phonological) connection of mouthing and manual sign" (Wempe, 1997, p. 524); "So long as this vocabulary [of DGS] is not developed, I use a mouthing. If I continue to do this, the sign language vocabulary will naturally not develop"(p. 535). The next issue of the journal published a strong reaction from Ebbinghaus (1998), who warned of the possible consequences of statements that imply that mouthings are not a true part of the sign language:

> In the end, by stating that the true DGS signer uses no, or at best few, German words brings into question the language competence of every deaf person who, in normal signing, uses German words. Of course, this strikes at the core of one's self-identity as an authentic member of the Deaf Community. And what Deaf person would willingly let himself be labeled as someone who, out of sheer habit, perpetuates the means of his own suppression by hearing persons? (p. 90).

The argument that mouthings in sign language represent an intrusion from the spoken language, which very likely will fade away as the language is allowed to develop, also underlies Schermer's (1990) study of mouthings in SLN.

---

[11] All translations of quotations from *Das Zeichen* from the original German into English were done by P. Boyes Braem.

In an earlier large-scale study of mouthings in DGS, Ebbinghaus and Hessmann (1994, 1995, 1996) noted that when modern research on sign languages was begun in the 1960s and 1970s, many linguists felt "under pressure" to show that this form of language was independent of the spoken language. Describing elements from the spoken language, such as mouthings, as integral components of sign language could give the impression that sign language by itself is somehow inadequate. Ebbinghaus and Hessmann rejected the argument that mouthings are merely lexical stopgaps that would, or should, fade away as soon as possible. They argued that the mouthings occur so often and so regularly that the theory that they are largely redundant is highly unlikely. If they were merely redundant, one would expect that they would be used unsystematically, which their research indicates is not the case.

However, they also do not think that one can treat mouthings as phonological components of the sign, for no matter how often and consequently a mouthing appears with a manual element, they say that it is not possible to know specifically which of several possible mouthings will occur. For example, one manual sign in DGS can occur with the German mouthings meaning 'butter,' 'marmalade,' and 'color'; another manual form occurs with mouthings meaning 'know,' 'believe,' 'aware-of,' and 'memory.' For this reason, Ebbinghaus and Hessmann (1995) argue that German Sign Language and other sign languages should be seen as heterogeneous systems in which mouthings and manual signs are clearly different elements. The relationship between these elements can, however, be described. They present a theory based on the perception of this visual language in which manual signs and mouthings reciprocally provide the context for the perception and interpretation of each other. This linguistic mixing of basically separate elements occurs, they suggest, because of the multichannel production possibilities of signed languages.

Although Ebbinghaus and Hessmann's (1995) main argument against a future disappearance of mouthings from DGS is based on a theory of perception, they also mentioned as another factor the social function of mouthings "in the communication between the different worlds in which deaf persons live" (p. 58).

In the remainder of this discussion section, it will be argued that it is these sociolinguistic factors, specifically bilingualism and a daily contact language situation that are of utmost relevance to the question of the status of mouthings in sign languages. Most deaf signers in European and in North American countries are bilinguals, making daily use of both their national signed and spoken languages in intense language contact situations.[12] Several concepts and theories that have been discussed in the literature of spoken language bilingualism are examined to see how they might apply to the phenomenon of mouthings in sign language.

Relevant Findings From Spoken Language Bilingual Research

Language Mode and Base Language.   In all bilingual discourse, it is generally agreed that one language is more basic than the other. Myers-Scotton (1993), for example, referred to the more basic language as the "matrix" language. She defines the matrix language as the one with more morphemes in the discourse sample and in the situation in which the samples were collected, also the more "unmarked" language, or the language most expected in that situation. Her term for the other language in the sample is the "embedded language." The base language has also been referred to in the literature as the "host language" or "recipient language."

Grosjean has argued in several places (1992, 1995, 1997, 1999) that, in addition to the concept of "base language," a control or assessment of the bilingual's "language mode" is also necessary. This language mode represents the level of activation of the languages involved in the discourse. The levels of activation can be thought of as a continuum ranging from a largely monolingual mode (when the interlocutors share only one language) to a largely bilingual mode (when the interlocutors share two or more languages). At the monolingual end of the continuum one language is highly activated and the other is highly—but never completely—deactivated. At the bilingual end, both languages are highly activated. Between the two poles, there are intermediary modes of activation of the languages involved. The base language in this model is the more highly activated of the languages and is the main language of processing.

In the collection and analysis of any bilingual material, it is thus essential that both the base language and the language mode be either controlled or clearly identified. Grosjean has pointed out (1999) that getting monolingual mode data from individuals can be jeopardized by small

---

[12]European deaf persons are considered here as being bilingual in the sense that Grosjean (1992) defined the term: bilinguals are those people who use two or more languages (or dialects) in their everyday lives. This includes people who have spoken skills in one language and written skills in the other (a situation that is akin to the Deaf who sign one language and read and write the other), people who speak two languages to varying degrees of proficiency (and who do not know how to read or write them), all the way to people who have complete skills in their two (or more) languages. (p. 308) For a discussion of American deaf signers in contact language situations, see Lucas & Valli (1989).

things, such the subjects simply being aware that the experiment they are participating in involves bilingualism, or by an experimenter's pretending to be monolingual but signaling by nonverbal behavior an understanding of the other language. Other factors cited by Grosjean (1999) as potentially influencing language mode are the following:

- Interlocutors (language proficiency, usual language of interaction, kinship relation, socioeconomic status, attitude toward language mixing, etc.)
- Situation of the interaction (location, presence of monolinguals, degree of formality and of intimacy)
- Content of the discourse (topic, type of vocabulary needed)
- Function of the interaction (to communicate information, to request something, to create a social distance between the speakers, to exclude someone, etc.)

Codeswitches, Nonce and Established Borrowings, Loanwords.
Codeswitches and borrowings are generally considered to be two different kinds of language mixing, involving different processes: codeswitching is an alternation between languages; borrowing is an integration of lexical items from one language into another (Grosjean, 1995). In codeswitching, the other-language element maintains both the content and form that it has in the original "donor" language. In borrowing, the morphological and phonological form of the element conforms to the recipient language's linguistic patterns (Poplack & Sankoff, 1984).

Borrowings, if they reoccur within the discourse of the bilingual community, are considered "established borrowings." Some forms can be one-time occurrences, but if they have the linguistic patterning of the recipient language, would still be considered borrowings, in this case "nonce borrowings."[13]

Codeswitches and borrowings occur almost exclusively in discourse of bilinguals. When an established borrowing used by bilinguals is

---

[13]I am grateful to F. Grosjean for pointing out this distinction between nonce and established borrowings. In earlier literature, these elements have been referred to as "speech" and "language" borrowings respectively (cf. Grosjean, 1982). Poplack and Meechan (1998) described nonce borrowing as follows: "Nonce borrowing differs from codeswitching, and resembles established borrowing in all but its extralinguistic characteristics of recurrence and diffusion" (p. 136). "nonce borrowings pattern exactly like their native counterparts in the (unmixed) recipient language, and not like elements of the language of their etymological origin" (p.137).

adopted by the monolingual community, it becomes a "loan word" in the language of that community as well. An overview of these different types of second language elements is shown in Table 1.1.

For linguists more interested in describing the structure of a language than in the language behavior of bilinguals, and especially for lexicographers of the language, the distinctions between these different types of elements are very important. From any corpus of data, one would want to describe the established vocabulary of the language, including the loan words, but not necessarily the codeswitches and borrowings used primarily in bilingual discourse. Relevant here is the following advice about making these category distinctions, which Poplack and Meechan (1998) stressed is important in spoken language research:

> Insofar as codeswitching and borrowing are based on some principled combination of elements of the monolingual, that is unmixed, vernaculars of the bilingual community, it is important to have as explicit an idea as possible of the nature of these vernaculars before concluding that a codemixed element takes aspects from one or the other or both. (p. 130)

Researchers of DSGS would find it difficult to follow this advice, for not only is there often no existing description of the sign vernacular, but, more crucially, there is no monolingual community of users of the language. All Swiss German signers are bilingual in both German and in DSGS, and there is no area of the country, no foreign "mother country," not even an educational institution where only DSGS is used for communication. Distinctions between established borrowings and loan words made on the basis of comparisons to the language of a monolingual community are impossible in DSGS. It is therefore proposed that phenomena that fit the criteria for established borrowings for sign languages such as DSGS also be considered to be permanent lexical items of the language.

TABLE 1.1. *Some distinctions between codeswitches, borrowings, and loanwords in spoken languages*

Contact Phenomenon	Linguistic Patterning	In Discourse of Community	Frequency of Occurrence
codeswitch	donor language	bilingual	non-recurring
borrowing			
nonce	recipient language	bilingual	non-recurring
established	recipient language	monolingual	recurring
loanword	recipient language	monolingual and bilingual	recurring

Most Mixed Discourse Involves "Lone Elements" That Are Major-Class Content Words.   According to Poplack & Meechan (1998), in all the spoken language bilingual corpora that have been studied, mixed discourse consists largely of single (or lone) elements that are usually major-class words (nouns, verbs, and adjectives) embedded in the syntax of the recipient language. Of the major-class words, nouns occur most frequently in codemixing of all languages.

In the data of this sign language study, most of the mouthings of both the early and late learners also fall into major-class categories (nouns, verbs, adjectives and adverbs.) (cf. Fig. 1.4). In the early learners' data, the least used categories of mouthings are conjunctions, locative and temporal prepositions, all non major-class words.[14]

The data from this study, together with similar findings from studies of other sign languages (Ebbinghaus & Hessmann, 1994, 1995, 1996; Pimiä, 1990; Schermer, 1990), thus provide evidence that signed languages do follow one of the basic principles for the structures of codeswitching and borrowing found for spoken languages, namely that the majority of lone elements are major-class content words, primarily nouns.

Most Lone Other-Language Items Are Borrowings, Not Code-switches.   An entire issue of the *International Journal of Bilingualism* was devoted to reports of studies that focused on lone other-language items in five languages (Turkish, Persian, French, Ukrainian, and Igbo) with English. All studies used the same quantitative (variationist) methodology, which is independent of any one theory of codeswitching.

A common finding in all these studies was that most lone items from the other language were borrowings, not codeswitches:

> Whatever the linguistic properties of the language pair examined, ranging from typologically distant to nearly identical, and the diagnostic employed—phonological, morphological, or syntactic—lone other-language items overwhelmingly surface with the *patterns* of the language in which they are incorporated. This is evidence that they have been borrowed into that language, despite the lack, in some cases, of any dictionary attestation or diffusion within the community." (Poplack & Meechan, 1998, p. 136)

---

[14]The German copula *sein* (to be) was nonexistent in the early learners' data The use of the auxiliary *haben* (to have) was limited to some cases of the first person, present tense form in a few commonly used phrases that seemed to function as a unit in a frozen form (*habe gesagt*; 'have said').

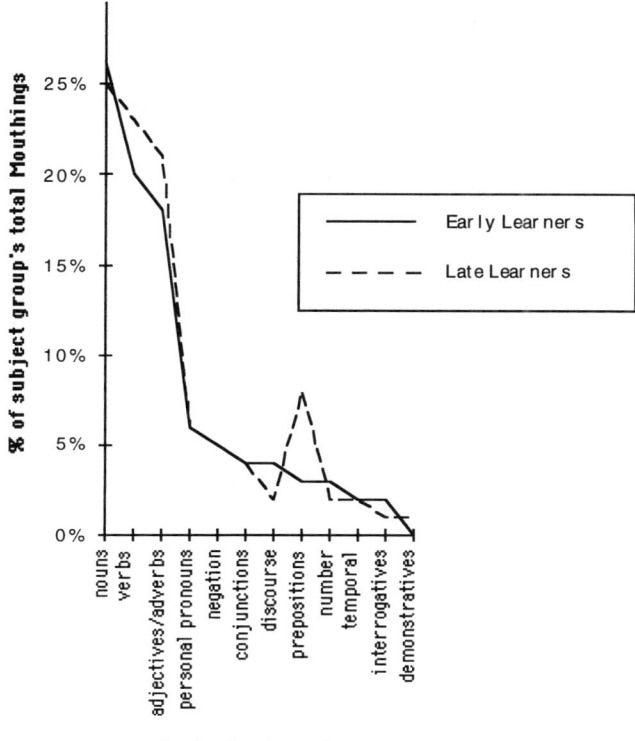

FIG. 1.4.   *Lexical categories represented by the mouthings of early and late learners.*

Whether most mouthings used by early learners are also considered borrowings and not codeswitches depends to a great extent on how well the two categories can be discriminated from each other. In the following section, some criteria for identifying borrowings and codeswitches in spoken languages are described and examined as to their possible application to the mouthing data in sign languages.

Discriminating Borrowings From Codeswitches

Linguistic Patterning Criterion.   One criterion for measuring the integration of other-language material into a recipient language is the phonological, morphological, and syntactic adaptation of the item to the linguistic patterns of the recipient language, as indicated in the previous quotation from Poplack and Meechan (1998).

The DSGS mouthing data in the present study are not from a sufficiently large corpus to enable the use of the quantitative methodology that has been used in many spoken language bilingual studies. However, the mouthings of the early learners include very few instances of morphological inflections on nouns and verbs. When an inflection was made on the sign, (for example, on verbs to indicate grammatical person, number, case, manner, time aspect; or on nouns to indicate number, form specification), it was carried out by special manual techniques involving changes of the parameters of the manual component (handshape, location, movement, orientation). In addition, many inflections involved the mouthing being replaced by a mouth gesture.

Many inflections on signs in DSGS, however, are for meanings for which German words are not inflected. For example, the DSGS sign meaning 'to clean up' (putzen) is, in the uninflected form, accompanied by the German mouthing *putzen*. The sign can be inflected for manner ('to clean up strenuously') by a rapid repetition of the manual component with an accompanying specific mouth gesture. There is no corresponding inflection for manner on the German verb *putzen*.

A first task is therefore to identify "conflict sites," or those functions that are comparable in the two languages, but have different markings (Poplack & Meechan, 1998, p. 132). Both DSGS and German do have inflections for grammatical person, number and case on some verbs, as well as number on some nouns. Here, however, the fact that the two languages are produced and perceived in two different modalities (aural–acoustic vs. visual–corporal) places some restrictions on comparisons.

For example, the marking of person, number and case on "agreement verbs" in DSGS is done by using space, whereas in German an affix is used. The German verb *schicken* ('to send') marks the second person singular form with the affix *-st* (*schickst*). In sign language the same function is marked by moving the sign from the spatial locus for the second person. The accompanying German mouthing in this case often remains a kind of base, or "bare" form: *schick*. In some instances, however, the mouthings do seem to be inflected with an appropriate German affix, a kind of double marking of a function, using inflection techniques from both languages simultaneously. The fact that sign language has the hands and face as well as the mouth as possible articulators make this simultaneous marking possible. However, it is often difficult to determine from videotaped data whether the spoken language marking has really been produced, as the appropriate German affixes often involve consonants or vowels that are not easily visible on the lips (e.g. *-n, -st, -t*. Cf. the discussion of visibility of mouthings in footnote 5).

Another potential conflict site for German and DSGS is the plural marking on nouns. Again, this is in practice difficult to measure due to the less visible forms of the most common German affixes for plural (*-e, -en,* as in *Berg, Berge,* 'mountain,' 'mountains'). A frequently used technique for indicating plural in DSGS, as in many sign languages, is to repeat rapidly the sign for the noun in closely adjacent locations, often accompanied by a single mouthing stretched over all repetitions, or by a rapid repetition of the first part of the mouthed word. In both cases, the German word in the mouthing becomes temporally distorted, making it even more difficult to determine whether or not affixes have been used.

In the end, whether or not an appropriate German affix is produced with any particular mouthing might depend more on individual variables (particularly, how well the signer knows German, which can vary greatly from person to person), as well as whether the signer is more in a sign language monolingual mode or more in a sign-spoken language bilingual mode. To discriminate between mouthings that are borrowings and those that are codeswitches, the criterion that is more important than the simultaneous production of spoken language markings is the clear production of the appropriate sign language (manual and nonmanual) inflections for the item. If the sign language inflections are produced, the item is categorized as a borrowing. Mouthing+manual constructions that occur only once and involve no sign language patterns would be considered clear codeswitches.

Frequency Criterion. In spoken language discourse, the frequency with which an other-language form is used is considered an indication of its degree of integration into the language (cf. for example, Hasselmo, 1970). Myers-Scotton (1993), uses the following working rule for determining whether a form has appeared sufficiently frequently to qualify as a borrowed form: When a form occurs three or more times in different conversations in a corpus of a minimum of twenty hours of conversation, it is considered a borrowed form.

When all the so-determined borrowed terms are eliminated from the corpus, the remaining forms are considered by Myers-Scotton (1993) to be potential codeswitches, because according to her theory codeswitches are essentially nonrecurring spontaneous forms. This definition of codeswitch forms does not take in account the existence of nonce forms, which have the linguistic patterning of the recipient language but do not reoccur.[15]

For the sign language mouthing data, the following frequency criteria is proposed: Established borrowings are those mouthing + manual constructions that occur three or more times in a large corpus of spontaneous conversations. The constructions that are candidates for established borrowings could be checked in elicitation sessions, in which signers are asked to name objects in pictures, using complete sentences, and are asked if they know any other signs for the object. (This methodology is similar to that used by Poplack and Sankoff (1984) to determine Spanish-English borrowings by Puerto Ricans living in New York City.)

The data collection methodology for conversations and elicitation sessions should include controls that insure that the interlocutors are towards the monolingual end of the language mode continuum and that sign language is the base language. In this situation, the other language, German, would not be totally deactivated, here in the sense that the bilingual signer has a knowledge of German. However, the mouthings would be being processed not as German words, but as sign language lexical items.

Displacement of Old Items, Creation of New Items Criteria. Another criteria for measuring how much an item is integrated into another language is the degree to which it displaces an equivalent item within the recipient language (Poplack & Sankoff, 1984, p.128).

For many sign languages, however, the use of mouthings seems to function not so much as a displacement of already existing manual signs, as rather a means of creating new signs. This would apply particularly to those structures in which the mouthing's meaning has a supplementary relation to the meaning of the manual component (e.g., the DSGS group of signs in which a manual component meaning 'drugs' is combined with German mouthings meaning not only 'drugs', but also 'to take drugs' and 'drug-dealer').

When a sign is first coined, the signer is probably in an intermediary language mode where the base language is DSGS but German is also activated, to access the German words to be produced with manual signs for the new lexical item. The new mouthing + manual construction corresponds to a nonce borrowing, as it would pattern linguistically like sign

---

[15]F. Grosjean (personal communication) has also pointed out the problem that nonce borrowings present for Myers-Scotton's definition of codeswitches.

language items but not necessarily reoccur in a large corpus. This does not mean the nonce wouldn't reoccur within the immediate discourse situation, for example a particular conversation about a particular topic. However, it would not reoccur in other conversations with other persons at other times. Nonce borrowings that do not reoccur in different discourses would not become established and thus would not be considered loan words in the language.

This use of mouthing in DSGS as a productive device to created new, semantically related signs is not unlike the use of the finger alphabet in ASL in "initialized signs" (e.g., in the signs for 'group,' 'family,' 'association,' which differ only in their handshapes, which are the finger alphabet handshapes for -G-, -F-, and -A- respectively). There seems to be little doubt among linguists or ASL users, that newly coined "initialized signs" in ASL, if used regularly within the community, often become over time established and even "dictionary-attested" signs (e.g., WATER). In principle, there is no reason why the analog mouthing + manual constructions in DSGS couldn't over time also be consider to be fully integrated into the community's language. The fact that many Swiss deaf signers often report that they couldn't imagine their sign language without mouthings may reflect the individual signer's sense of a high degree of integration of mouthings both as established borrowings and as a highly productive device for coining new lexical items. This sense of the integration of mouthings may also be one reason for the high emotions generated by the published debate on mouthings in Germany.

The several criteria discussed her for determining the status of mouthings used for lexical purposes are summarized in Table 1.2.

CONCLUDING REMARKS

The data presented here indicate that mouthings in DSGS can function at several different levels of the linguistic structure: for establishing reference in discourse, for the prosodic marking of different kinds of units, and for denotating (as part of a lexical item or in a grammatical construction with a noun or verb).

To begin to untangle the problem of determining the status of mouthings in lexical items as codeswitches or borrowed forms, an examination was made of how some findings and methodologies stemming from research on spoken language bilingualism can be applied to sign language. It has been argued here that the use of spoken language forms should be seen as a productive device for coining new signs in the DSGS community, and that some of these mixed forms go on to become established borrowings in the community. Firmly established borrowings should be considered part of the sign language lexicon.

This does not mean that the use of mouthings can't become less important to future generations of DSGS signers. A move away from using mouthings would depend on many factors. One of these would be the changing status and use of sign language within the both the signing and nonsigning communities. It could be that the younger generation would want to clearly signal the separation of sign language from the spoken language by trying to avoid mouthings as much as possible. This kind of young deaf person is represented by the person who contributed the following to a German deaf website in December 1997:

> If we sign with mouthings, the hearing people think—look there, sign language doesn't exist without mouthing, it is dependent on the oral language. We want to show with sign language that without mouthing it's a full-fledged language, equal to the spoken language and not dependent on it. (Ebbinghaus (1998) p. 86, translation from the German original by Boyes Braem)

To avoid using mouthings, one could turn to other techniques for coining new lexical items, among which might be an increased production of initialized signs, a technique not available to the older generations of Swiss German deaf who use no fingerspelling. There could also be a greater tendency to borrow signs from other sign languages, particularly for the technical terms and specialized vocabularies that become increasingly necessary as deaf persons gain access to higher forms of education. Whether these signs borrowed from another sign language would be accompanied by a German mouthing (which is obviously not present in the form of the sign in the donor language), would be an interesting research question.

The coming generation of deaf signers, however, will also include, at least in German Switzerland, more and more persons who have been given cochlear implants at a very young age and have been integrated into hearing classrooms, with no sign language at all in their environment. A growing proportion of the next generation of deaf persons will be late learners, for whom German is the first language (cf. the Appendix). For these later learners, codeswitching to German will be a ready option, as will be accessing their spoken language for the production of new signs.

TABLE 1.2. *Categories of mouthings in sign languages: codeswitches, nonce borrowings, and established borrowings*

Codeswitch	Nonce Borrowing	Established Borrowing/ Loanword
a one-time occurrence across the corpus;	a one-time occurrence across the corpus	frequent and regular occurrences accompanying a specific manual form in a large corpus of several different informants
can be produced with no accompanying manual component	is not produced without a manual component	is not produced without a manual component
the exact mouthing cannot be predicted	the exact mouthing cannot be predicted	the exact mouthing form, or small set of forms, can be predicted
the semantic patterning of the mouthing will be that of the spoken language, sometimes a highly inflected German form	the mouthing will usually not be a highly inflected German form	the mouthing will usually not be a highly inflected German form
might accompany inflected forms of the manual component (as a kind of simultaneous production of inflected forms from both languages)	when accompanying an inflected manual form, is usually stretched, repeated or replaced by a mouth gesture	when accompanying an inflected manual form, is usually stretched, repeated or replaced by a mouth gesture
can displace an existing sign	does not displace an existing sign, but is rather used to create a new nonce sign for concepts for which there is no existing single sign in the sign language	is the existing sign in the sign language
if produced with a manual component, its production is not reported by signers to be obligatory	if produced with a manual component, its production is not reported by signers to be obligatory,but may be necessary to be able to understand the intended meaning	its production is reported by signers to be obligatory with specific manual components in specific contexts (for example, when the uninflected form of the sign is required)
is not part of the mental lexicon of sign language	is part of the mental lexicon of the spoken and of the sign language	is part of mental lexicon of the sign language, i.e. the lemma for that concept includes one (or a limited set) of mouthings which accompany the uninflected form as well as socio-pragmatic values keyed to particular contexts.
is used more when the signer is at the bilingual mode of the language mode continuum and sign language is the base language	is used more the signer is at an intermediary or bilingual mode and sign language is the base language	is used in all modes on the continuum when sign language is the base language.

APPENDIX

The Sociolinguistic Situation of Sign Language in German Switzerland

The relatively few deaf persons in German Switzerland (ca. 5000) are scattered throughout the 18 Swiss German-speaking cantons. There is no central gathering place for the deaf in German Switzerland, although the recent concentration of several educational and service groups concerned with deafness and sign language in one building in Zurich may turn this meeting place into such a center.

The five dialects of DSGS have developed historically around the five regional deaf schools (in Basel, Bern, Zürich, St. Gallen, and Luzern), where the deaf children typically learn their sign language from other children in the dormitories. Although sign language has always been used outside the classrooms in all but the most strictly oral private schools, there have been no adult deaf role models in the dormitories, much less in the classrooms, until very recently. Currently, most schools for the deaf in German Switzerland are attempting to integrate as many of their pupils as possible into hearing classrooms. There is also very strong support within hearing pedagogical circles to encourage cochlear implants for young deaf children in the belief that this technology will wipe out deafness in the foreseeable future. As a result of these trends, residential schools, which traditionally have been the place where most deaf children have learned sign language, are fighting drastically declining enrollments. The deaf school in Basel recently shut down its residential program. Because entrance to all Swiss universities require a special degree from higher secondary schools (the "Matura"), graduates of schools for the deaf—which are not able to give this degree—have no direct access to higher academic education.

The emphasis that hearing pedagogical and medical authorities in Switzerland have traditionally placed on oral language skills has led many Swiss deaf to take pride in their skills in the spoken language. It was not unusual in the past for deaf parents to use German rather than sign language with their children, even if the children were deaf. Further, the form of oral German that deaf children are taught is "standard High German" and not one of the nonstandardized Swiss German dialects spoken by hearing Swiss Germans (which includes the families of most deaf children whose deafness is not hereditary).

Sign language theater groups have only recently been founded; sign language courses and professional interpreters have been available for less than 10 years. No sign language is used regularly by deaf persons or interpreters on any Swiss German television programs. A half-hour bimonthly program that had involved deaf signers as moderators and presented news of the local Deaf community in sign language was terminated in January, 1999, a victim of cost-cutting at the Swiss German Television. There is currently no dictionary of DSGS, although the Swiss Nationalfonds project for a computer databank of the DSGS lexicon, begun in 1996, is collecting the linguistic data for a future lexicon. All teaching and research on DSGS is currently being done in private institutions; there is no sign language being used in any Swiss university.

Since the late 1980s, the Swiss Deaf Association has been actively trying to create a more positive picture of sign language for the hearing public as well as for deaf persons. There have been no studies done to determine how successful this activity has been in influencing the attitudes of either the hearing or the larger deaf population toward sign language. However, one positive episode in the history of sign language in Switzerland did occur in 1994, when both Chambers of the Swiss Parliament approved a petition proposed by the Swiss Deaf Association, which "recommends sign language for the integration of the deaf and urges its support, together with the oral language, in the fields of education, training, research and communication." This is a morally encouraging first step for the signing deaf community. However, the Minister of the Interior gave the responsibility for the implementation of this postulate back to the individual cantons, where what will count is not the idealistic aim, but rather the comparative political power of different lobbies. The signing Deaf community represents only a very small and unimportant lobby in the country, compared with those groups that oppose any recognition of sign language (many educators of the deaf, doctors, commercial firms doing cochlear implants, hearing aid specialists, as well as associations of parents of deaf children who in the past and still today generally prefer an oral education, sometimes combined with "Cued Speech," for their children [cf. Boyes Braem, Caramore, Hermann, & Shores Hermann (2000) for more details on the legal and sociolinguistic situation of DSGS]).

REFERENCES

Ahlgren, B., & Bergman, B. (1990). Preliminaries on narrative discourse in Swedish Sign Language. In S. Prillwitz & T. Vollhaber (Eds.), *Current trends in European Sign Language Research. Proceedings of the 3rd European Congress on Sign Language Research, Hamburg July 26-29, 1989* (pp. 257–163). Hamburg: Signum.

Ahlgren, I., & Bergman, B. (1994). Reference in narratives. In I. Ahlgren, B. Bergman, & M. Brennan, (Eds.), *Perspectives on sign language structure*. Durham, England: The International Sign Linguistic Association.

Baker, C., & Cokely, D. (1980). *American Sign Language: A teacher's resource text on grammar & culture*. Silver Spring, MD: T. J. Publishers.

Baker-Shenk, C. (1983). *A microanalysis of the nonmanual components of questions in American Sign Language*. Unpublished doctoral dissertation. Berkeley: University of Berkeley.

Bos, H. (1994, September). *Pronoun copy in sign language of the Netherlands*. Presentation at the 4th European Congress on Sign Language Research, Munich, Germany.

Boyes Braem, P. (1992, July). *Techniques of linguistic reference used in narratives by early and late learners of Swiss German Sign Language*. Paper delivered at the XXV International Congress of Psychology, Brussels.

Boyes Braem, P. (1995). *Eine Untersuchung über den Einfluss des Erwerbsalters auf die in der deutschsprachigen Schweiz verwendeten Formen von Gebärdensprache*. Zurich: Verein zur Unterstützung der Gebärdensprache der Gehörlosen.

Boyes Braem, P. (1999). Rhythmic temporal patterns in the signing of early and late learners of German Swiss Sign Language. *Language and Speech* (Special issue on prosody in spoken and signed languages, edited by W. Sandler and M. Nespor.). Vol 42 (Parts 2 & 3 April - Sept. 1999) pp. 177–208.

Boyes Braem, P., Caramore, B. Hermann, R. & Shores Hermann, P. (2000). Romance and reality: Sociolinguistic similarities and differences between Swiss German Sign Language and Rhaeto-Romansh. In L. Monaghan (Ed.) *Many ways to be deaf: International variation in language, identity and ideology*. Hamburg, Germany: Signum.

Caramore, B. (1988). *Die Gebärdensprache in der Schweizerischen Gehörlosenpädagogik des 19. Jahrhunderts*. Hamburg: Verlag Hörgeschädigte Kinder.

Caramore, B. (1990). Sign language in the education of the deaf in the 19th century Switzerland. In S. Prillwitz & T. Volllhaber (Eds.), Current trends in European sign language research. *Proceedings of the 3rd European Congress on Sign Language Research*. July 26-29, 1989, (pp. 23–32). Hamburg, Germany: Signum.

Coerts, J. (1992). *Nonmanual grammatical markers. An analysis of interrogatives, negations and topicalisations in the sign language of the Netherlands*. Amsterdam: University of Amsterdam.

Ebbinghaus, H., & Hessmann, J. (1994). Formen und Funktionen von Ablesewörter in gebärdensprachlichen Äusserungen (Teil I). *Das Zeichen, 30,* 480–487.

Ebbinghaus, H., & Hessmann, J. (1995). Formen und Funktionen von Ablesewörter in gebärdensprachlichen Äusserungen (Teil II). *Das Zeichen, 31,* 50–61.

Ebbinghaus, H., & Hessmann, J. (1996). Signs and words: Accounting for spoken language elements in German Sign Language. In W. Edmondson & R. Wilbur (Eds.), *International Review of Sign Linguistics* (Vol. 1, pp. 23–56). Mahwah,NJ: Lawrence Erlbaum Associates.

Ebbinghaus, H. (1998). Theoretische Sprachauffassung und sprachliche Wirklichkeit. Anmerkungen zu einem Interview mit Helen Leuninger und Pater Amandus im *Zeichen. Das Zeichen* 43, 84–91.

Grosjean, F. (1982). *Life with two languages: An introduction to bilingualism*. Cambridge, MA: Harvard University Press.

Grosjean, F. (1992). The bilingual and the bicultural person in the hearing and in the deaf world. *Sign Language Studies, 77,* 307–320.

Grosjean, F. (1995) A psycholinguistic approach to codeswitching: The recognition of guest words by bilinguals. In L. Milroy & P. Muysken, (Eds.), *One speaker, two languages* (pp. 259–275). Cambridge, U.K.: Cambridge University Press.

Grosjean, F. (1997). Processing mixed language: Issues, findings, and models. In A. M. B. De Groot & J. F. Kroll, (Eds.), *Tutorials in bilingualism: Psycholinguistic perspectives* (pp. 225–254). Mahwah, NJ: Lawrence Erlbaum Associates.

Grosjean, F. (1999). The bilingual's language modes. In J. L. Nicol & T. D. Langendoen (Eds.), *Language processing in the bilingual*. Oxford, England: Blackwell.

Hasselmo, N. (1970). Code-switching and modes of speaking. In G. Gilbert (Ed.), *Texas studies in bilingualism* (pp. 179–210.) Berlin: de Gruyter.

Lucas, D., & Valli, C. (1989). Language contact in the American Deaf community. In C. Lucas, (Ed.), *The sociolinguistics of the deaf community*. San Diego, CA: Academic Press.

Myers-Scotton, C. (1993). *Duelling languages. Grammatical structure in codeswitching*. Oxford, England: Clarendon Press.

Pimiä, P. (1990, July). Semantic features of some mouth patterns in Finnish Sign Language. In S. Prillwitz & T. Vollhaber, (Eds.), Current trends in European Sign Language research. *Proceedings of the 3rd European Congress on Sign Language Research*. Hamburg, Germany: Signum.

Poplack, S., & Meechan, M. (1998). How languages fit together in codemixing. *International Journal of Bilingualism. 2*(2), 127–138.

Poplack, S., & Sankoff, D. (1984). Borrowing: The synchrony of integration. *Linguistics, 22*, 99–135.

Schermer, T. (1990). *In search of a language: Influences from spoken Dutch on Sign Language of the Netherlands*. Published dissertation, University of Amsterdam.

Schroeder, O. -I. (1985). A problem in phonological description. In V. Volterra & W. Stokoe (Eds.), *SLR '83 sign language research*. Silver Spring, MD: Linstok Press.

Tissi, T. (1993). *Namengebärden in der Deutschschweizerischen Gebärdensprache*. Zurich: Verein zur Unterstützung der Gebärdensprache der Gehörlosen.

Thomason, S., & Kaufman, T. (1988). *Language contact, Creolization and genetic linguistics*. Berkeley, CA: University of California Press.

Vogt-Svendsen, M. (1983). Wordpictures in Norwegian Sign Language. In *Working papers in linguistics*. Trondheim: University of Trondheim.

Wempe, K. (1997). Nur wo Abschied genommen wird, gibt es Platz für neues Leben. *Das Zeichen,42*, 516–526.

Wilbur, R. (1990). An experimental investigation of stressed sign production. *International Journal of Sign Linguistics, 1*(1), 41–59.

Wilbur, R. (1994). *Stress, focus, and extrametricality in ASL*. Presentation to the Annual Meeting of the Linguistic Society of America, Boston, MA.

2

Making Borrowings
Work in British
Sign Language

Mary Brennan

ABSTRACT

This chapter explores the function of English-based borrowings in British Sign Language (BSL). BSL makes use of three main categories of English borrowings: fingerspelled items; English-based lip patterns, usually accompanying a manual BSL sign; and literal borrowings, where the manual signs used are literal renderings of an English-based structure. The primary focus of the chapter is fingerspelling, but observations are made concerning the relation between fingerspelling and other types of borrowing in BSL. It is recognized that the very term "borrowing" with respect to lip pattern in particular has been brought into question particularly by the work of Ebbinghaus and Hessmann (1996). Therefore, the status of these forms is discussed further with respect to the particular situation of BSL.

INTRODUCTION

The central claim of this chapter is that the full nature of borrowings can only be understood when they are viewed in relation to other components of sign language. In particular, it is suggested that fingerspelling often occurs at a transitional stage in the development of new, nonborrowed forms. Moreover, processes of lexicalization with respect to fingerspelled items are rather more limited than has been implied within the previous literature. Such claims do not, of course, minimize the importance of English borrowings within BSL. However, they do imply that it is unhelpful to view or study borrowings in isolation; to do so is to ignore their interconnectedness with other parts of the language and to distort their pragmatic effects.

FINGERSPELLING IN BSL: TYPOLOGY

Fingerspelling in BSL offers a way of representing the letters of written English. Thus it allows English words to be incorporated into BSL via a visual representation of their written form. The view taken here is that these forms do fit with the notion of linguistic borrowing, and that like borrowings within spoken languages, the fingerspelled forms typically go through a process of assimilation. Although the focus here is on the function of such borrowed forms in the language, some brief observations are made on the formational changes that may occur over time.

BSL makes use of what might be called a primary fingerspelling system, which is two-handed, and a secondary system, which is one-handed. Some type, or indeed more accurately types, of manual alphabet appear to have been available in the British Isles for hundreds of years. Bede, the Northumbrian monk who wrote in the 7th and 8th centuries referred to "some kind of manual speech" that allows the letters of individual words to be expressed so that one "may convey the words contained in these letters to another who had learned this art" (Farrar, 1889; Sutton-Spence, 1994). Sutton-Spence (1994) categorized British manual alphabets into two main types: arthological and dactylogical. She suggested that prior to 1698, most manual alphabets were based on allocating letters to specific areas of the hands or joints of the fingers and then pointing these out in succession: the arthological system (see Fig.2.1).

A remnant of such a system remains in the current manual alphabet in which the tips of the thumb and fingers represent the five English vowels, 'a,' 'e,' 'i,' 'o,' and 'u.' As Sutton-Spence (1994) pointed out, exactly the same forms were described by John Wilkins in 1641 in a work on cryptography. The second category of alphabet makes use of different hand formations to represent each letter.

The earliest record of such a system is "Digiti lingua," an anonymous document dated 1698 (see Sutton-Spence, 1994). The range of potential

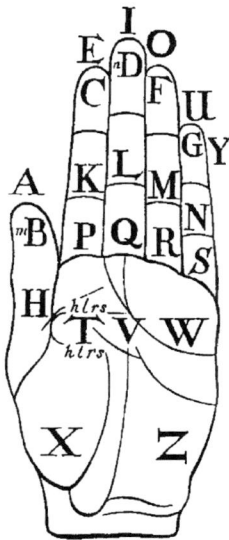

FIG. 2.1.   *An Example of an arthrological system: Dalgarno, 1680.*

hand configurations available allowed there to be a direct relationship between the form of the letter represented and the form of the handshape or handshapes. However, along with other cryptographers of the time, the author of "Digiti Lingua" worked according to two competing principles: the system needed to work practically and, in possible competition with this, the system should allow secrecy. This explains why relatively few of the forms appear to be iconically related to the written letter forms. Nevertheless, many of the forms present in today's manual alphabet can be traced back to "Digiti Lingua." Daniel Defoe's work, "The Life and Adventures of Mr. Duncan Campbell" contains an illustration of a manual alphabet that is very like the one in use today. As Sutton-Spence (1994) argued:

> Thus somewhere between 1698 and 1720 (or possibly 1732) our manual alphabet became fixed in the form we know it. It is unlikely that Defoe was the author of this manual alphabet, and it is more likely that he learned of it from Campbell, or perhaps Wallis. (p. 54)

In the current form of the alphabet (Fig. 2.2) we can see that "iconic" or "motivated" forms include the following: the curved handshape of -C-

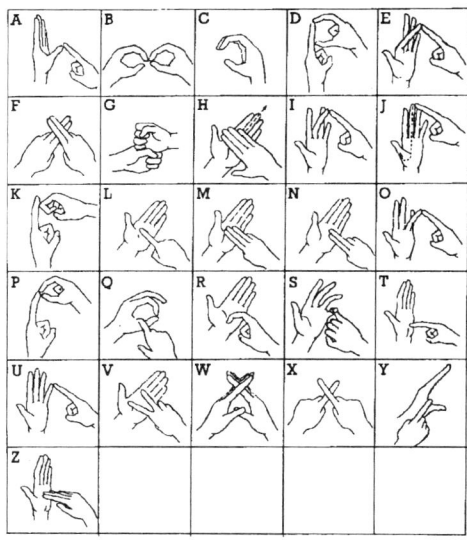

FIG. 2.2.   *British Manual Alphabet.*

imitates the curved form of the letter 'c'; the extended three fingers of fingerspelled -M-, the two extended fingers of -N- and -V-, and the single
extended finger in -L- and -T- reflect the number of uprights in these letters; and the crossed fingers in -X- imitate the crossed stems in the letter
'x.' Other forms, such as -B-, -D-, -G-, -P-, -Q-, and -V- have some dis-
cernible link with the letters they represent.

However, even where there is a clear link between the handshapes and
the letters they represent, this iconicity can be masked in actual use. Illustrations of the British manual alphabet often provide 26 illustrations to
show the forms relating to each letter of the English alphabet. However,
this is somewhat misleading because in everyday use, the individual letters take on different configurations. These changes include primarily
changes of orientation and changes of handshape. Most illustrations show
the nondominant hand with finger orientation up, but frequently the orientation is away from the body. Illustrations of the forms representing English vowels typically show the nondominant hand as a fully open flat
hand. In typical usage, however, the handshape will be influenced by phonetic context: the closed fist with the index finger extended (A with a dot)
may be used as the nondominant hand in -E- and the closed fist with the
little finger extended in -I-. The manual alphabet -B- may exploit two -O-
handshapes, that is where all fingers are extended, bent and touching the

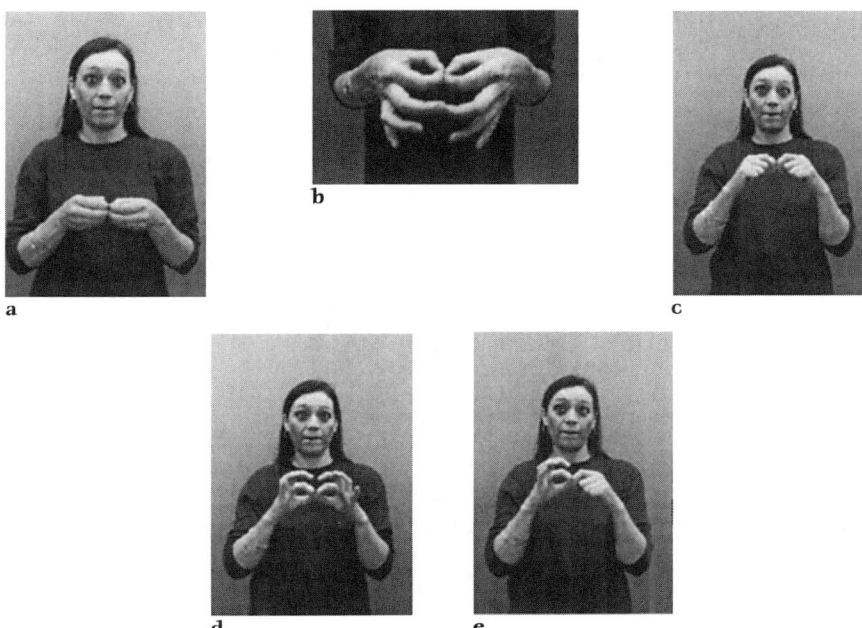

FIG. 2.3.   *Variants of the -B- of the BSL manual alphabet (see text for description).*

thumb tip, as in Fig. 2.3a; it may also make use of two -F- handshapes, where the index finger and thumb are bent and touching at the tips with the other fingers extended, as in Fig. 2.3b; the same thumb index finger configuration may be used, with the other fingers bent into the palm, sometimes called "baby-O" (see Fig. 2.3c). When we add to this the further dimension of changes in orientation (Fig. 2.3d) and mixed forms (Fig. 2.3e) we can see that the single letter -B- is conveyed in a number of different ways—ways that may well diminish the original iconicity inherent in the single illustrated form.

What we have, then, is a system that though created artificially, has been conventionalized and incorporated into the language in quite complex ways. The forms of the hand configurations appear to be influenced primarily by their positioning within fingerspelled words; for example, a consonant may vary in its form depending on whether it is in initial, medial, or final position. It is also possible to predict specific processes of assimilation and deletion within categories of words. These processes may lead to an alphabetic form being so reduced that it takes on the property of a BSL sign.

THE ONE-HANDED
FINGERSPELLING SYSTEM

The main one-handed fingerspelling system that has had an influence upon the lexical resources of BSL is the system used in the Republic of Ireland (Fig. 2.4). Formationally, the Irish alphabet has some forms in common with the American one-handed alphabet. However, several forms use quite different hand configurations. These include -F-, -G-, -H-, -K-, -L-, -P-, -Q-, and -T-. The Irish alphabet has been used primarily within Catholic Deaf communities in the United Kingdom. It seems to have been introduced by priests and members of religious orders working with Deaf people. Although the main Roman Catholic schools for deaf children primarily operated an oral policy for most of the 20th century, it appears that the alphabet was exploited in out-of-school situations, as well as by adults within the adult Deaf communities. Currently, the Irish alphabet appears to be rarely used by BSL signers for fingerspelling complete words or indeed for new lexicalized forms or new initial letter signs. However, within regional Deaf communities, one can see evidence of Irish alphabet origins in a range of signs. These are discussed in the following section.

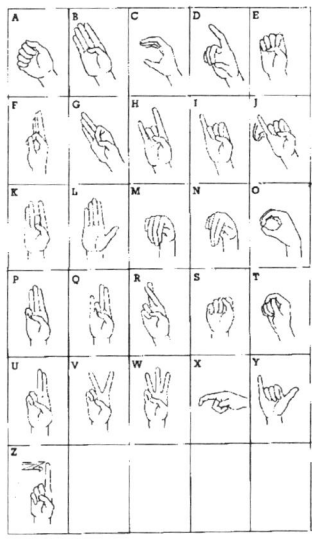

FIG. 2.4.   *One-handed Irish manual alphabet.*

Borrowings and Loan Signs

The use of fingerspelling in sign languages is usually treated as either an example of codeswitching or of lexical borrowing. The use of the term "codeswitching" suggests that the user is operating with at least two linguistic codes, in this case presumably BSL and English—the user would switch from one to another for particular purposes, including specific types of pragmatic effect. The two codes are recognized as being different and as adhering to different types of linguistic patterning. The term "borrowing," on the other hand, is used to refer to the process whereby items, typically lexical items, are extracted from another language and gradually assimilated into the host language. In time, it is likely that such borrowings, usually known as loan words, or in this case loan signs, will not even be recognized as such. English has borrowed massively from other languages, yet speakers are rarely conscious of the origins of such borrowed forms. This is because these forms have taken on the structural properties, particularly the phonological properties of lexical items in the host language.

The seminal work on lexical borrowing in sign languages is Battison (1978). Battison's account has provided a framework and criteria for describing lexical borrowing in sign languages. However, his account is concerned with borrowings from English into ASL. ASL makes use of a one-handed fingerspelling system and Battison has provided an account of the restructuring of these one-handed fingerspelled forms so that they take on the typical phonological properties of ASL signs.

Despite the differences between one-handed and two-handed fingerspelling systems, most writers on BSL have assumed that comparable restructuring rules operate within BSL. Brennan, Colville, Lawson, and Hughes (1984) commented for example that "we can note considerable exploitation of the manual alphabet in the creation of BSL signs. Vocabulary borrowings from English can be modified in such a way that they take on the form and structure of BSL signs" (p. 16). Although it is the case that fingerspellings can indeed take on the structure of BSL signs, this occurs in a rather different way from that suggested by Battison (1978). In one sense it can be argued that British fingerspelling is already more formationally integrated into the sign language than one-handed systems. The two-handed system is articulated in neutral space and shares many formational properties with other signs of BSL: fingerspelled forms can indeed be classified according to Battison's classification of one-and two-handed signs (see Brennan et al., pp. 14–16).

According to Battison, fingerspelled forms are lexicalized when they are "restructured" so as to conform with ASL phonological structure. He suggested that "fingerspelled words undergo tremendous physical changes on their way to becoming signs" (p.16). The processes involved include deletion of one or more handshapes; restructuring of the hand-shapes by assimilation of one handshape to another, that is, one handshape changes to look more like another; dissimilation where one handshape changes to look less like another; locational changes and changes of orientation and movement. Locational changes can be particularly important for as Battison himself points out, **"these loans are no longer restricted to fingerspelling space, but take up other positions in space or on the body, which are found in the articulation of native signs"** (p. 195; author's emphasis). The emphasis given by Battison to this point draws attention to the "advantage" the two-handed system has in occurring within the normal signing space area, in contrast with the one-handed fingerspelling system, which is produced in an area of neutral space restricted for this purpose.

Fingerspellings that have undergone these substantial processes can then be said to be lexicalized in the language; they look like ASL signs. According to Battison, fully lexicalized forms will consist of no more than two (restructured) manual alphabet letters. Examples involving more than two can be regarded as being "in transition," but see evidence in Brentari and Padden (chap. 3, this volume) for forms that stabilize in the more peripheral strata of the lexicon for particular reasons.

Although this criterion has also been applied to BSL it is somewhat misleading. This can be illustrated by a common form that most Deaf informants see as a clear loan sign: #CLUB as in DEAF #CLUB. There are two common forms of #CLUB. When executing the form DEAF CLUB, some signers produce the sign DEAF, which makes use of the tips of the extended index and middle fingers (H handshape) making firm contact with the ear, then the hand moves a short distance away from the signer and the handshape changes so the thumb, index, and middle fingers are all extended and bent, that is, in the form of the -C- handshape, but with the ring and little fingers closed into the fist (Fig. 2.5 left).

Clearly this handshape is expressing the letter -C-, but the handshape has been influenced by the previous hand configuration. An alternate form used both along with DEAF and separately, has the two hands side-by-side in neutral space, with the dominant hand held opposite the nondominant fingers. The nondominant hand is the "flat-B" (i.e., B with a dot) whereas the dominant hand is in the form of the manual alphabet -C-, but

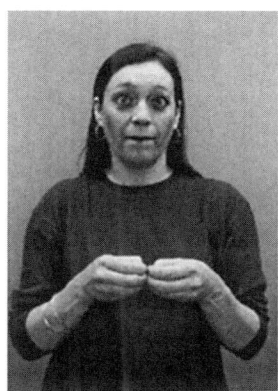

FIG. 2.5.   *The restructured form of #CLUB; initial (left) and final (right) handshapes.*

held so the palm faces left (assuming here right-hand dominance) and the finger, if straightened, would face away from the signer. The dominant hand moves toward the signer so the index finger brushes against the non-dominant hand along the length of the middle finger and part of the palm, then both hands close to two -O- hands and contact as in one realization of the manual alphabet letter -B- (Fig. 2.5 right). What we have then is a kind of approximation of all four letters, but executed with changes of orientation and such fluidity that one cannot isolate the individual letters. The sign appears to the watcher to involve a movement toward the body and a closing action, that is, two salient actions, yet when we know the sign we can recognize the approximation to the fingerspelled letters.

The evidence gleaned from observation and analysis of fingerspelling used within BSL is that relatively few forms, certainly fewer than originally anticipated, undergo the same type of radical reduction that is shown in CLUB and that is required by Battison (1978) for full loans. The most fluent and efficient BSL signers appear to exploit a range of assimilation and reduction processes, so the fingerspelled forms appear fluid and fit in rhythmically with the signing, but these forms may remain longer than two letters or even two salient actions. However, because of the operation of these processes and in many cases the stability of the resultant forms, it would still seem appropriate to treat these as loan signs.

Initialized Signs

A further major category also recognized by Battison (1978) is that of initialized or "initial dez" signs. Some of these may be regarded as fully established. They involve some modification of form and have a stability in the language. The phonological modification may be as simple as reduplication, but this can still be conventionalized into a stable loan sign. Others are "nonce" forms: they are created for the occasion and do not become integrated into the language.

It is worth noting that only one letter of the British manual alphabet is produced by one hand; the letter -C-. This is often said to account for the relatively small number of initialized signs found in BSL. It certainly seems that the single-hand form lends itself to phonological modification more easily than two-handed forms. In particular, the single hand is able to be placed in different locations, including, if appropriate, the other hand, as well as realizing a range of possible orientations and movements. Such flexibility is certainly exhibited in initialized signs exploiting -C- as in the following example:

(1) Initialized BSL forms with the manual letter -C-
CURRICULUM   COMMUNICATION
COPYRIGHT   CONFIDENCE
COURSE   COMMUNITY
COMMITTEE   COFFEE
COLLEGE

The handshape -C- exploited in the British alphabet makes use of the index finger and thumb extended and bent curved. In the Irish and American alphabets, the letter -C- is represented by the form in which all of the fingers and the thumb are extended and bent. In some signs, especially where the hand or hands are located in neutral space, and in two-handed signs where both hands have the same configuration, there is some flexibility between the two forms, with both being generally acceptable. In others, one or the other of the handshapes has been conventionalized. In a few cases it may be possible to treat these as borrowings from ASL or from ISL, but in other cases the origin is less clear. Thus COMMUNICATION requires the full -C- form, whereas CONFIDENCE and COURSE typically use the -G- form.

The potential for creating initialized signs can also, to a much more limited extent, be found in two-handed forms. Here typically the sign is created by adding some type of movement to one or both hands. Examples of well-established initialized signs derived from two-handed alphabet forms include those in (2) and Fig. 2.6. Further examples can be found in the handshape sections of Brien (1992), Sutton-Spence (1994), and Colville (1979, 1984).

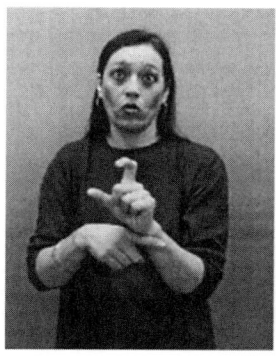

FIG. 2.6.   *Examples of initialized signs: COURSE (left),COMMUNICATION (middle), CONFI-DENCE (right).*

(2)   Initialized signs derived from two-handed alphabet
a.   ENGLAND: the index finger of the dominant "G-hand" moves to and fro against the upper surface of the nondominant index finger).
b.   RUBBER: the bent dominant index finger moves to and fro against the nondominant palm.
c.   VERB: the extended index finger and middle finger in the -V-formation, move to and fro against the non-dominant palm.
d.   FAMILY: the -F- formation of the manual alphabet is maintained, that is, the index and middle finger of each hand are extended and crossed, and articulated as a small horizontal circle in neutral space (see Fig. 2.7).

Sutton-Spence (1994) devoted considerable attention to the nature and role of what she termed Single Manual Letter Signs (SMLS). This category includes those already described previously as initialized signs: these she regards as "established" SMLS. However, she also noted signs that exploit the first letter of an English word in its manual alphabet form, but without further modification. Some of these forms may be regarded as well established within the language particularly within particular registers. Thus such forms as L-A ('local authority'); -Y- ('year'); -W- (week'); -G- ('grandmother'); and T-V ('television'); the last example exploiting the initial letters of a bound and a free morpheme, rather than of words appears well established in the language and is generally quickly identified. However, Sutton-Spence noted 3000 examples of

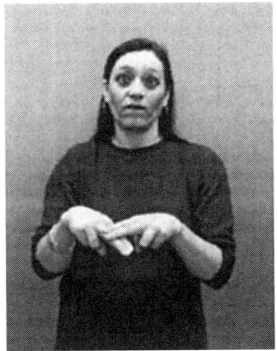

FIG. 2.7.   *The initialized two-handed form FAMILY.*

simple SMLS in her data. This is a surprisingly large number and requires further discussion. It contrasts sharply with the numbers found in Scottish data that form a central part of this account. A very small number of simple SMLS are found within the subset of Scottish data used here. The initialized signs that do occur are almost all well established and involve some type of phonological modification. These include L-A ('local authority'), R-C ('Roman Catholic'), and K-K ('Kilmarnock'). Several examples occur of abbreviated names, for example, D-H ('Donaldson's Hospital'). This is a long-established school for the Deaf, now formally known in English as Donaldson's College and informally as Donaldson's. Although the 'hospital' element has long since been discarded in English, older Scottish signers still use the abbreviated form as the name of the institution, even though a separate sign, not linked to fingerspelling, is also available.

FINGERSPELLING: FUNCTION AND USE

This section explores some of the types of explanations that can be posited to account for the extent and role of fingerspelled borrowings in BSL. Sutton-Spence (1994) has undertaken the most detailed research published in this area to date, although the account presented here will also draw on unpublished work carried out by Colville for the Edinburgh BSL Project (1984). This account additionally makes use of new analyses of both archive material and relatively recent BSL samples available to the author. The main sources of data involving Deaf people are the following: a subset of data from the Edinburgh BSL Project, collected from 1978 to 1986 and selected examples from the Deaf Studies Research Unit, Durham, including BSL lectures, narratives and informal anecdotes, as well as publicly available videotaped materials in BSL.

The specific data chosen from the Edinburgh BSL Project consists of videotaped interactions of six pairs of signers aged between 24 and 70 at the time of the filming. The earliest material used here was filmed in 1979. The interactions involved conversations on topics suggested by the Deaf researcher (i.e., Deaf education and Deaf clubs); conversations following on from stimuli, such as film material, for example, documentary footage relating to Northern Ireland and the Second World War as well as televised activities including a horse show and game show. Participants were filmed in pairs. The situation was artificial in that the participants knew they were being filmed. However, they knew each other, felt comfortable with each other and with the Deaf researchers and often became quite involved and even heated in their discussions. The earliest material, filmed in 1979, was filmed before discussions of the nature of BSL and different types of signing were commonplace within the Deaf community. Thus we might imagine that the data represents signing unencumbered by conscious consideration of the nature of the signing used. A further major feature is that all of the participants were Scottish, although some had spent a significant period of time outside Scotland. This might seem to skew the overall account because Scottish people are said to fingerspell more than others. However, given this general view, it is worth paying particular attention to the functions for which they exploit fingerspelled forms. Moreover, within the samples discussed here, there is nothing like the 10% figure of signs based on the manual alphabet noted by Sutton-Spence (1994) for the "See Hear" data. This will be discussed further in the following paragraphs. The second set of data is newer and includes both Scottish and English signers. This data is primarily in the form of short lecture extracts and discussions involving Deaf staff and Deaf students. Finally, a publicly available videotape of BSL on the subject of unemployment benefits that was aimed at members of the Deaf community was used.

Sutton-Spence (1994) made use of data collected from the weekly television program "See Hear." This magazine program aimed at d/Deaf and hearing-impaired viewers involves a wide range of d/Deaf participants and presenters. An important quantitative finding from the Sutton-Spence study is that an average of 10% of signing within the corpus involved the use of fingerspelling. Such a figure is perhaps higher than might have been envisaged, especially as fingerspelling is often viewed as being more characteristic of signing addressed to hearing participants or influenced by English.

Why do signers make use of fingerspelling? Sutton-Spence (1994) offers the eleven reasons given in (3).

(3) Uses of fingerspelling (Sutton-Spence, 1994)
   a.   to introduce an English word which has no sign equivalent;
   b.   to explain a regional sign that may not be well known;
   c.   to use when a sign equivalent does exist throughout the sign community, but the signer does not know it;
   d.   to accompany a new concept expressed in sign;
   e.   to introduce a sign which is then used for the rest of the discourse only;
   f.   to produce English idioms in codeswitching;
   g.   to use as part of the interpreting task;
   h.   to produce euphemisms;
   i.   for convenience and time saving;
   j.   to use as part of the core vocabulary of BSL;
   k   to represent English acronyms." (p. 208)

In this account, I wish to suggest that Deaf people exploit several strategies. These are not always exploited by BSL or by English interpreters and the rather more erratic use of different types of fingerspelling within certain kinds of interpreting can work against the full expression of communicative intent.

It is suggested here that fingerspelling in BSL is used as a resource both for building the lexicon and for clarifying English discourse in technical areas. Lexicalized fingerspelling-based forms (those to which Sutton-Spence (1994) refers as core vocabulary items) may be used simply as part of the lexical resources of the language and frequently do not express any additional function. However, fingerspelling forms are also used with a **clarifying** function, to provide a further potential for understanding for the addressee: several different types of clarification are noted. Fingerspelling forms can also be used to introduce concepts or technical notions that already have a label in English, but do not have an established label in BSL. It is suggested here that there is, in fact, a dynamic interaction between the use of fingerspelling and the creation of productive forms. Fingerspelling forms also allow explicitly English labels and name forms, including acronyms and abbreviations, to be introduced in the signing: the intention here is to enable the English-ness of the forms to remain apparent.

The Lexical Resource

Sutton-Spence's (1994) category (j) relates to the use of fingerspelled loans from English that "involve core vocabulary" (p. 219). Sutton-Spence gave very few examples in this section, so it is somewhat difficult to clarify exactly what she had in mind. However, she did comment that "Areas of core vocabulary where borrowing from English is highly prevalent include family relationships, and measurements of time and space." (p. 219)

What needs to be stressed here is that there are a substantial number of signs that are used on an everyday basis and that are long established in the language, yet originally derive from English. These signs may be initialized loan signs, simple initial letter forms, fingerspelled signs showing assimilation, and fully reduced fingerspelled forms that we can treat as full loan signs. What is important here is that signers typically choose these forms to express the meanings concerned. In some cases, there is no other option but to use signs derived from English. In other cases, there may be several different options, but all are linked in some way with English. Thus, although some regional forms do exist for the meanings 'mother,' 'father,' 'cousin,' 'grandmother,' 'grandfather,' and so on, in most cases these are forms based on English. Such forms contribute to the core vocabulary of BSL: signers would find it very difficult to avoid using them on an everyday basis. These forms are of two main types: forms associated with specific semantic fields (as indicated by Sutton-Spence[1994]) and forms associated with particular grammatical functions.

This latter group can be exemplified by reference to such forms as I-F; B-U-T; A-N-D; O-R; F-O-R; S-O; B-Y; T-H-A-N; and T-O. There has been a tendency to assume that such forms are used primarily in settings involving hearing people or by Deaf people who use what is sometimes referred to as Sign Supported English. It is usually anticipated that these Deaf people will have attended oral schools or will have been integrated into mainstream settings within their schooling. These forms obviously have a grammatical function in English, expressing, for example, conjunctions and prepositions. In fact they appear to realize similar functions within BSL. It may appear that these forms are redundant in that, for example, conditional meaning is simultaneously being expressed by the borrowed loan sign I-F, as well as nonmanual markers, spatial location and the ordering of signs. Similarly, the contrastive function may be expressed by both fingerspelled B-U-T and by nonmanual marking. Of course, multiple marking of a grammatical function is not at all rare: gender and number are often marked several times within noun phrases, to take just one example.

An examination of the Scottish data reveals that the individual tokens I-F and B-U-T are the most common recurring borrowings in the Scottish data followed closely by A-N-D, S-O and T-H-E-N. Surprisingly, these forms are also common in the recent data. For some signers, BSL signs glossed as AND and BUT are used alongside fingerspelled forms: it has not been possible to find any motivation for the choices involved. It is worth stressing that the frequency of these forms goes against many Deaf persons' own perceptions of their usage. In Appendix II of her study, Sutton-Spence (1994) provides the comments of one consultant on his or her own use of what Sutton-Spence classes as "function words." Sutton-Spence recorded the following comments:

(4) *Deaf individual's comments about fingerspelled forms of function words*
   a. BUT: Another sign. I've seen B-T, but I don't use it.
   b. FOR: Another sign. I only use F-O-R very rarely, if I am angry or to make a strong point.
   c. DO: D-O or -D-, not often, but I do use it, and only as a verb, not as part of a question.
   f. IF: I-F if it was very emphatic
   e. OF: No, I don't use it.
   f. SO: Another sign or S-O, but I don't use S-O, because I think that's very English. (pp.55–56)

Although this is merely one Deaf person's view, it does accord with evidence gleaned by the author from direct interactions with Deaf people during discussions of fingerspelling usage within courses offered at the University of Durham. There was general consensus that these forms are only used in English-influenced styles of signing and that the informants themselves would use them only rarely. However, the evidence from all of the data types suggests that these forms are in common usage across signing varieties. Thus, it would seem that borrowed forms are used not only to express core vocabulary but core syntactic functions as well. Given that these signers also exploit a wide range of non-English BSL grammatical markers, including their complex nonmanual realizations, it seems appropriate to regard them as users of BSL. In fact, the Scottish data referred to here is all taken from Deaf adults with Deaf parents, that is, precisely those who would normally be seen as native signers. Sutton-Spence, Woll, and Allsop (1991) suggested that

> several function words hover on the language boundary of BSL. These include S-O and B-U-T. Our decision to include F-O-R, I-F, B-Y, B-U-T, O-R and T-O in our list of BSL loan signs was based on the decisions of the third author, a fluent native Deaf signer (p. 321).

However, it is argued here that rather than being on the linguistic boundary, these forms are essential elements of BSL structure. It seems that the only reason there could be for querying their status is that they derive from English. As Ebbinghaus and Hessmann (1996) argued with respect to lip pattern, elements that can be "identified routinely and without conscious effort contribute to the stability and flow of communication" (p. 41). The data examined here show that some specific fingerspelled function words are indeed stable features of BSL.

One major function of fingerspelling is to allow English names to be introduced into the signing. These include names of people, places, products, businesses, television programs, and the like. The signer has several different options available in respect to naming. He or she may choose, for example, to allocate a sign name, exploiting BSL strategies for creating such forms. Many of these strategies will be linked with visual encoding, where some visual characteristic of the referent is embedded in the sign name. Other English-based strategies may not involve fingerspelling as such; thus it is relatively common to make use of a simple or compound sign that is linked to the English word; the links may not always be obvious to the non-Deaf participant. Examples include the following: WOLF for 'Wolverhampton'; COW (articulated twice) for 'Cowcaddens'; PRIEST for 'Preston'; FISH for the surname 'Sole'; and BURN for the surname 'Burns'.

Additionally, a range of fingerspelling-based options are available. The signer may fingerspell the full form completely; fingerspell the full form in the first instance and thereafter a shortened version, using initial letters of the forename and surname; fingerspell the title, (e.g., Mr., Mrs.,

Ms., Miss, Dr.) followed by the initial letter of the surname; make use of a mixed form, for example, the sign NEW followed by fingerspelled T-O-N for 'Newton' or the sign BLACK followed by fingerspelled E-T-T for 'Blackett.'

It is fascinating to note that in the Scottish data, full forms predominate. This is the case even where the same name reoccurs again and again. These full forms do usually exploit patterns of articulation found in other fingerspelling, so they appear to the nonsigner to be reduced in length. Thus surnames such as 'Kilgour' and 'Sinclair' will usually be produced with the O-U-R and A-I-R sections involving the dominant index finger making a curved movement in the approximate area of the fingertips relating to the specific vowels, rather than involving separate contact. Although such patterning may be seen as a type of reduction, these forms are classed here as "full" fingerspelling in that they exploit patterns of articulation common to other fingerspelled forms. One possible explanation for the use of full forms lies precisely in the claim that may be regarded as part of "folk mythology" that Scottish signers are fingerspellers. This is normally taken to mean that they include much more fingerspelling in their signing than signers elsewhere in the United Kingdom. However, the evidence from the data examined here demonstrates that Scottish signers, at least in this case, those with Deaf parents, use less fingerspelling, but use more full forms with fingerspelling patterns and very few nonce single letter forms of the type so prevalent in Sutton-Spence's (1994) "See Hear" data. This may link to an expectation on the part of the signer that the addressee will be comfortable with full fingerspelling and that these will be easily read back and understood. Informally, older Deaf people often complain that younger Deaf people cannot fingerspell. Unfortunately, the data set covered here cannot test out this claim. However, there is at least some evidence from comparing the two sets of data, including the Durham material, that where signers use single letter signs, they also appear to make more limited use of productive forms. If this is the case, then the extremely reduced fingerspell form is having to carry a functional weight otherwise shared by full fingerspelling and the productive lexicon. A signer using highly productive BSL may nevertheless exploit such forms. It is clearly important, therefore, in our analyses not simply to note the quantity of fingerspelled usage, but the type. There may also be a mismatch between signers' perceptions of their own usage and what the empirical findings reveal. Thus the perceived association between "English-oriented" signing and the production of fingerspelled forms such as A-N-D and T-H-E-N is not borne out by these data.

Technical or New Concepts

As Sutton-Spence (1994) suggested, fingerspelling forms are used to introduce concepts or technical notions that already have a label in English, but not a widely known label in BSL. However, it is suggested here that such forms do not carry the full burden of meaning. Indeed their function is primarily transitional, given the dynamic interaction between the use of fingerspelling and the creation of productive forms. Where a signer does not exploit the full range of productive morphology, then the fingerspelling may be required to take on a fuller semantic and functional role.

Since the early 1980s there has been an increase in the number of Deaf people involved in teaching other Deaf people. Within the Deaf Studies Research Unit, both internal Deaf staff and visiting Deaf staff have taught a range of courses, particularly in the areas of sign language studies, Deaf community and culture, and the teaching of BSL. Although these courses are typically taught directly in BSL, one frequent feature has been the use of English written forms, on a blackboard, flipchart, or overhead projector. Direct observations of teaching and of videotaped lessons reveal that Deaf teachers and lecturers often start from accounts, even relating to their own language, presented in English. This may change as more and more Deaf people become expert in particular subject areas and as multimedia technology improves access to signed explanations and accounts of signed language. The recently completed CD-ROM BSL Dictionary of Deaf Community and Culture (Brien, Brennan, Collins, Reed, & Thoutenhoofd, 1997), for example, contains for the first time definitions of signs fully expressed in BSL. Tutors thus have the option of referring to a considered account of the meaning of a sign without needing to bring in any reference to English at all. Currently, even where topic areas link directly to the Deaf community, written accounts are frequently used as a starting point. This produces a particular type of interaction between English-based forms.

The following comments are linked specifically to one particular videotaped lecture aimed solely at a Deaf student audience that can illustrate usage in this area more fully. The lecturer is a child of hearing parents in her thirties. She is a well-known lecturer and tutor and has worked as a presenter on "See Hear" and indeed has been active in television for many years. She is regarded as a highly proficient user of BSL.

The lecturer is presenting an overview of an article by Charlotte Baker-Shenk (1986) entitled "Characteristics of Oppressed People." The idea is to present an account of the main characteristics suggested by Baker-Shenk, but using illustrative examples from the British Deaf community rather than those provided by the author. The lecturer presents each characteristic in turn. In every case a clear English lip pattern accompanies the signing. In almost every case, some fingerspelling is used. In fact, what emerges is a very definite pattern of presentation: the fingerspelled form or mixed fingerspelling and signing form is presented along with lip pattern; this is then typically followed by several different signed forms that aim to encapsulate the meaning of the supposed new concept. None of these forms is accompanied by lip pattern. We can see the pattern at work in the following examples:

The signer fingerspells the full form of the English word 'ambivalence' with lip pattern that gives equal stress to each syllable. This is then followed by MEANS AMBIVALENT. The latter sign makes use of two "A" hands twisting alternately to and fro. This is followed by a further explication: MEANS UNSURE followed by yet another paraphrase: DEAF HEARING, PULL ONE WAY THEN THE OTHER. While lip pattern accompanies the sign MEANS and the signs DEAF and HEARING, there is no lip pattern accompaniment to the verb forms (ARE) AMBIVALENT, (ARE) UNSURE, PULL ONE WAY THEN THE OTHER. What is suggested here is that the signer clues into two major resources available to the watcher or the learner: access to English through lip pattern and fingerspelling and, particularly important, the productive lexicon, especially that which exploits metaphor-based morphemes. The productive forms appear to be offered as possible, but not yet definitive, BSL labels for the concept presented. The signer is, in effect, providing a series of synonyms or near-synonyms. In the case of "ambivalent," each metaphor-based sign is providing a slightly different perspective or view of ambivalence. This same pattern is continued throughout the lecture. Thus in presenting the concept of "horizontal violence," the signer fingerspells H-O-R-I-Z-O-N-T-A-L, with an accompanying lip pattern, but then signs VIOLENCE using a two-handed form in which the two -I- hands twist toward and away from each other alternately: this sign is sometimes glossed as VIOLENCE, FIGHT, or QUARREL INTENSELY. In this particular case, the signer accompanies the form with a very clear lip pattern, in which emphasis is given to each vowel (except the silent final e), that is, 'vi-o-lence.' However, the sign is followed by three further forms that use BSL non-manual intensifiers, including stretched lips, and which are modified so as to show many individuals fighting or working against each other. All of these signs exploit the opposition set of metaphoric spatial relation suggested by Brennan (1990; 1992).

In several cases, the signer uses what seem to be potentially confusing mixtures of fingerspelling and sign in presenting the central English-based labels. For the term "self deprecation," the signer produces the sign SELF, along with lip pattern and follows this with D-E-P-R-E-C-A-T-I-O-N in full fingerspelled form. "Basic distrust of self" is signed as follows (5):

(5) *Codeswitching in a single BSL sentence*

BLS gloss		BASIC	SUSPICIOUS/ DISTRUST		TRUST		ME
fingerspelling	B-A-S-I-C			D-I-S-T- R-U-S-		O-F	
mouthing	*basic*			*trust*		*of*	*me*

Thus the fingerspelled B-A-S-I-C is followed by the sign BASIC, which is followed by fingerspelled D-I-S-T-R-U-S-: rather than completing the fingerspelled form, the signer produces the sign TRUST (made with the little finger edge of the dominant hand against the nondominant palm), as if the full sign TRUST replaces the final -T- of trust. This is followed by fingerspelled O-F and the sign ME. The lip pattern is timed primarily to co-occur with the fingerspelled items. The sign glossed above as SUSPICIOUS/DISTRUST makes use of the -I- handshape (little finger extended from the closed fist) in a repeated movement away from the body. The sign is accompanied by stretched lips and eye-gaze away. It could be argued that this sign is the primary carrier of the BSL meaning: the other elements are doing the job of presenting the English label. The signer appears to be influenced by ease of articulation and efficiency, that is, exploiting signs that already exist in the language to express the English label.

Sometimes it is as if in the process of fingerspelling the signer realizes that a corresponding sign already exists and is ready to somewhat distort the fingerspelled form to produce the sign. Thus in a later example, "magical belief in the power of the oppressor," the signer fingerspells M-A-G-I-C-A-L but then adds the sign MAGIC so quickly that one can barely make out the end of the fingerspelled form.

All of the previous examples are linked with the presentation of what is viewed as a possible new concept with an unfamiliar English label, taken from a written English source. The motivation to explicate the English version as quickly as possible is demonstrated both in the eagerness to curtail fingerspelled forms where signs are available and in the tendency to present not just one but several explicatory synonyms. Further synonyms, repetitions, or both of the earlier examples are then typically presented within the illustrative examples. Thus the explanation of horizontal violence involves several verb forms that could be characterized as part of the productive lexicon: these include such forms as dragging individuals down, pulling people back down to earth, and not letting people become high fliers or part of the elite.

What we seeing here, then, is an interaction between what can be seen as opposite ends of the lexical spectrum. The fingerspelled forms are essentially frozen in that they represent given English words (even though in practice the signer may modify these forms); the productive form makes use of productive morphemes, often put together with distributive, agreement, and aspectual inflections to create meaningful, but possibly new to the signer, forms. The claim that is made here then is that to see fingerspelling as by itself the signer's response to the need to find a BSL equivalent is to ignore the full dynamics of the situation. The signer is simultaneously using what is most BSL-like and most English-like to move both the individual interaction, and we might argue, the language, along.

This can be illustrated further with reference to the development of new technical terms within BSL. I focus here particularly on examples relating to sign linguistics and to sign language generally. One might expect, given the role of fingerspelling in the introduction of new technical terminology to BSL users, that the lexicalization of fingerspelled forms would be a major force in the creation of new terminology. However, what is suggested here is that although borrowings do have an important role in this process, it is the productive lexicon, used in conjunction with fingerspelling, that takes the process forward. Fingerspelling is the support required in the early stages, but it is the productive lexicon that carries the sign creation process through.

If we look at the relatively new linguistic terminology, it is interesting to see how few of the terms that are now in common usage among teachers and students of BSL are actually based on English borrowings as such. Indeed there is some evidence that forms that do relate to fingerspelling are being taken over by other, what I would wish to describe as "motivated" terms. Thus the concept of linguistics is expressed in BSL by two main forms: the first is based on a relatively old sign LANGUAGE, which itself is linked to the meaning 'written language,' that is, the nondominant hand is a Size and Shape Specifier classifier, or a flat surface (paper), with the dominant hand indicating the lines (of writing). The form LINGUISTIC is created by performing the simple directional movement involved in the sign LANGUAGE, but adding to this the curved handshape representing -C- (in this case the full-handed form). However, the sign has been used alongside a sign making use of two -F- handshapes initially contacting then separating. This latter sign appears to be becoming the more popular of the two. It is possible that in this case it is the written connotations of the first sign that work against its continued use with reference to signed language, and even to spoken language, or linguistics. The sign GRAMMAR, using the initial -G- manual alphabet configuration and followed by the same sign LANGUAGE also appears to be used less frequently: it is often replaced by signs based on the old BSL STRUCTURE. Not surprisingly, given the newness of the field to most Deaf people, several different signs are often in use for the same concept. However, in other cases, signs have become well established. In one case the sign has been restructured toward a fingerspelled form. The sign ICONIC was used primarily by sign language researchers in the late 1970s. It had quite wide acceptance among Deaf people involved in research. In this early form, it was a motivated sign, exploiting the V-hand of the sign LOOK in front of the eye, but producing a closing action toward the eye-a form regarded by some as indicating the notion of copying or taking in a visual form. It is now popularly produced by placing the dominant index finger below the eye and then moving the hand away in a short action with the hand configuration changing to a curved-V. In discussing this with Deaf people, it seems that many internalize the sign as 'eye + c,' in a way that appears to match the beginning and end of the spoken form. Although both forms are still in use, the latter form seems to enjoy greater popularity.

Overall, it is suggested here that motivation wins out over English-based borrowings when we look at the development of new terminology. The potential is there to fully lexicalize the fingerspelled forms, but in practice this happens only rarely.

Thus, none of the following relatively new signs in BSL make use of lexicalized fingerspelling: DIGLOSSIA, PIDGIN, CREOLE, MORPHEME, CITATION FORM, TRANSCRIPTION, SIMULTANEOUS MORPHOLOGY (see Brien, 1992, glossary section). In all of these cases, it is highly likely that for many Deaf students their initial introduction to the sign and its meaning was tied in with a link to the English label, and often to specific written references or quotations. It has been possible to observe this process over time and to observe "trial" forms coexisting with both longer paraphrases and fingerspelled forms. The sign "diglossia," for example, has emerged alongside its full fingerspelled form. The sign was derived from Deaf people and from interpreters differentially locating the suggested H or High variety of a language and the L or Low variety of a language. The sign that emerged maintains this differential positioning of the hands, but the lower hand contacts the mid-lower arm of the nondominant articulator, thus refining and conventionalizing the form.

Although the data being examined here does not include as many examples with respect to other specialist areas, examination of the examples occurring suggest that the same is true for such fields as computing and multimedia. The new terminology appears to exploit either classifier- or metaphor- based constructions. COMPUTER MOUSE makes use of the handling classifier, "G"; COMPUTER MEMORY exploits the grasp metaphor; DATABASE employs both a SASS classifier and a deposit metaphor; and CURSOR makes use of the deictic G-hand and the handling classifier -G- indicating the simultaneous mouse activity. The one area where fingerspelling appears to come into its own is in relation to the presentation of English acronyms. Thus it is unlikely that new signs will be developed for ROM and RAM other than the fingerspelled forms. However, interestingly, several signs have co-existed for CD-ROM with the one apparently in most common use, that is, not linked with fingerspelling at all, but rather using two SASSes.

LIP PATTERN AND FINGERSPELLING

This section examines the relation between lip pattern and fingerspelled forms in BSL. Like fingerspelling, lip pattern has typically been associated with English-influenced forms of signing (e.g., Lawson, 1981). However, an overview of a wide range of types of data in BSL shows that lip pattern occurs across the range. There are very few samples within the core data of the Edinburgh BSL Project or the archives of the Deaf Studies Research Unit that do not reveal regular use of English-based lip pattern by signers. Even in sign texts where there is very limited use of fingerspelling, as in some personal anecdotes, stories, and jokes, lip pattern is frequent. In fact, in texts where fingerspelling is absent, lip pattern takes on a clarifying function.

It is suggested here that for the majority of signers, **lip pattern co-occurs with fingerspelling.** There are some exceptions, but certainly in the data examined there is a very regular pattern of co-occurrence. The following sets of examples are taken from a public information videotape issued by the Benefits Agency and produced by the BDA (Benefits Agency, 1994). The video, "Out of Work? A Guide to Social Security Benefits." is aimed at ordinary members of the Deaf community and is presented in BSL with English subtitles. It is presented by a recognized BSL user who is also a very well-known television presenter. Deaf actors play the parts of out-of-work Deaf people. The aim of the tape is to provide clear information on different types of benefits available to those who are unemployed. The tape shows the same type of patterning as that described previously in relation to technical linguistic terms: fingerspelling is used to introduce the particular categories of benefit, but this is typically followed, and occasionally preceded by explanatory signs, including productive forms. It is particularly noticeable that lip pattern relating to the English word or words being fingerspelled always accompanies the fingerspelled item, but typically is not used for the explanatory signs in the immediate context. However, lip pattern is used to a considerable extent across the signed text. Thus the following items are all fingerspelled and accompanied by lip pattern (6):

(6) Items that are fingerspelled and accompanied by a lip pattern
S-O-C-I-A-L S-E-CU-R-I-T-Y   G-I-R-O
I-N-C-O-M-E   R-E-N-T
G-R-A-N-T

In each case the full lip pattern accompanies the fingerspelling. In several cases, accepted fingerspelling abbreviations or initialized signs are used, but in each case the form is accompanied, not by mouthing of the individual letters, for example, *es-es* to accompany S-S, but by the full English expression, that is, in this case *social security*. Other examples in the data include the following (7):

(7) Abbreviated signs accompanied by full-word lip patterns
N-I   lip pattern: *national insurance*
C-A-B   lip pattern: *citizens advice bureau*
BUILDING S-O-C   lip pattern: *building society*
BUILDING S-O-C A-C-C   lip pattern: *building society account*
C-A-R-E   lip pattern: *care*

In one example, the lip pattern does not reflect the full English word:

(8) Abbreviated sign accompanied partial-word lip pattern
BENEFITS A-G   lip pattern: *benefits age*
reference: (English Benefits Agency)

The fingerspelled form G-R-A-N-T is preceded and in some cases followed by a sign GRANT that is produced without lip pattern; similarly the standard sign RENT is produced without lip pattern, but is followed by the fingerspelled form with lip pattern. Other explicatory signs can be noted either immediately following or preceding the fingerspelling form, with the lip pattern in each case accompanying the fingerspelled form only. Thus the fingerspelling C-A-R-E with lip pattern *carer* is followed by the sign LOOK AFTER with aspectual marking ('look after over time') and intensifier-stretched lips, eye-gaze toward the object. The fingerspelling R-E-S-T-A-R-T (as in 'restart course, i.e., retraining course) is again accompanied by the related lip pattern *restart* but followed by two explicatory signs, POLISH-UP and ENCOURAGE, each with intensifying nonmanual features and without lip pattern. It is suggested here then that in the typical usage of fluent Deaf signers, lip pattern is a normal and typical accompaniment to fingerspelling.

One major exception to the claim that lip pattern typically accompanies fingerspelling is the group of elderly Deaf people who were educated at a time when fingerspelling was the primary means of communication in school. Several of the Deaf signers filmed by the Edinburgh BSL Project team in the late 1970s and in the early 1980s were in their 70s and 80s at the time of the collection of data. They attended Scottish schools during the first two decades of the 20th century. Research has shown that these signers exploited complex BSL grammatical structure along with considerable use of fingerspelling. Although it has not been possible to reanalyze this material for this study (these signers do not form part of the subset indicated earlier), some general observations can be noted. These signers often use fingerspelling with minimal or even no lip pattern. They may also use nonmanual features, including a head-turn away from the fingerspelling, with eye-gaze averted: these characteristics appear to mark out the fingerspelling as being in some way different from the rest of the discourse. Having said that, the signers also exploit typical nonmanual accompaniments to express additional information.

These signers also often use not just individual fingerspelled words, but whole chunks of English, including full forms of function words. The signers included in the Scottish subset analyzed here were generally too young at the time of filming to have attended school when fingerspelling usage was at its height. However, they would have communicated with signers who exploited fingerspelling at school and their fingerspelling exhibits most of the same patterns of assimilation and reduction. Although, for the most part, these signers exploit individual fingerspelled words within the signed texts, there are some examples of larger English-based chunking. Most are complex noun phrases such as the following (9):

(9) Fingerspelling of entire English phrases
P-O-N-Y-C-L-U-B -G-A-M-E-S
P-O-N-Y -M-O-U-N-T-E-D -G-A-M-E
S-H-O-P-W-I-N-D-O-W-G-L-A-S-S
C-O-N-V-E-N-T-I-O-N-A-L-L-O-C-A-L-S-I-G-N
S-O-C-I-A-L-A-N-D-R-E-C-R-E-A-T-I-O-N-A-L-C-L-U-B
P-I-N-T-O-F-M-I-L-K-F-R-O-M-C-O-W

Although some of these may be influenced directly by labels used in English, others are created on the spot to suit the situation. The examples relating to cows and ponies derive from descriptions of activities shown on film. There was no use of English within the film. The signers used highly productive BSL forms, particularly classifier forms, alongside the noun phrases. There are very few examples in which the English-based chunks cross phrase boundaries, as in (10).

(10) Multiphrasal strings of fingerspelled forms
a.   T-V-R-E-M-I-N-D-M-E
b.   R-I-N-G-F-O-R-A-T-T-E-N-D-A-N-T

Thus even signers who use considerable stretches of fingerspelling within their signing do so while still using lip pattern and also while using a wide range of BSL linguistic features.

The Scottish data used here revealed signers using fingerspelling for similar categories to those found elsewhere in the literature. In accord with previous findings, nouns predominate, with very few verb forms being fingerspelled. The percentages are in Table 2-1.

It should be noted that some of the forms indicated here as adjectives could be functioning more like verbs in BSL. This could therefore increase the overall number of verb forms based on fingerspelling. It appears then that "Scottish fingerspellers" are essentially using finger-spelling for purposes similar to those of other signers. However, they are much more likely to use full forms with assimilation than their English counterparts. The claim that Scottish signers are essentially producing a form of manual English is certainly not borne out by the analysis of a sub-stantial body of Scottish data.

TABLE 2.1.   *Grammatical categories of fingerspelled forms in scottish data*

Grammatical Category	% Subtotal	% Total
Nouns		66.61
place-names	14.34	
days of the week	0.21	
people's names	7.38	
proper Nouns:	3.58	
Verbs		6.96
Conjunctions		37
Prepositions		6.54
Adjectives		10.75
Adverbs		1.2

If we follow through the implications of what has been described previously, then we begin to recognize that fully lexicalized finger-spelling borrowings appear to have a rather limited role in BSL. Such a claim can indeed be supported by comparing the lists of such forms presented by Colville in 1979 and in 1984 to the relatively recent lists presented in Sutton-Spence (1994). In his original 1979 list, Colville presented 36 lexicalized signs representing 16 letters. Sutton-Spence provided a list of modified SMLS occurring in the "See Hear" corpus. She lists 39 examples representing 9 letters of the alphabet. In his later presentation, Colville included 65 examples representing 18 letters of the manual alphabet. However, these lists presented by Colville were based on general observations rather than on data collection as such. Additional examples were codified during the Edinburgh BSL Project. The precise number of examples recorded depends to a large extent on what is regarded as a lexicalized form. In this section I am focusing on what Sutton-Spence described as SMLS with phonological modification. What is surprising about the "See Hear" listing is how many of the forms appear to be long-established, occurring as they do in the earlier listings. The only forms that do not appear in the pre-1984 listings available to me are COMPUTER, CONVENTION, FELLOWSHIP, FINAL, GENERAL, and POSITION. Of course, this nonoccurrence in the Edinburgh listings does not mean these forms were not in use. However, one is struck generally by the lack of new forms. Even the supposedly prolific -C- group is represented in the "See Hear" data primarily by older signs. It would seem then that the full process of lexicalization as described by Battison (1978) and in the later BSL literature (Brennan et al., 1984; Brien, 1992; Kyle & Woll, 1995; Sutton-Spence et al., 1991) has limited realization in contemporary BSL.

INTERPRETERS

The findings reported previously relate to the way in which Deaf fluent users of BSL exploit English borrowings. However, observations of BSL and English interpreters working in courts suggest that interpreters exploit rather different strategies. These observations derive from recent research carried out by the author and a team of researchers within the area of legal interpreting. The project "Access to Justice for Deaf People in the Bilingual, Bimodal Courtroom" examined BSL and English interpreting in the courtroom and in other legal contexts (Brennan & Brown, 1997). The research involved detailed observation of cases in Scotland and in England, videotaping of Scottish courtroom proceedings, interviews with Deaf people who had been involved in the justice system, interviews with BSL and English interpreters, and a survey by questionnaire of interpreters.

This research reveals that court interpreters typically do not exploit the same strategies as Deaf signers. Indeed, we may say that the interpreter often has one key strategy: if there is no directly equivalent BSL sign to an English word or phrase, some form of fingerspelling will be used. Although a few interpreters do exhibit the same monitoring and clarifying strategies as Deaf people, this is relatively rare. The demands of legal interpreting are considerable. The interpreter is dealing with many different types of linguistic complexity. Outsiders often comment on the demands of linguistic terminology. There is no doubt that the specialized usage of certain terms may cause particular difficulty. The verb "to caution," for example, is used in two quite distinct ways in British law. A person may "be cautioned" before being questioned or charged in relation to an offense: here the person is being warned that anything he or she says or signs may be "taken down and used in evidence." However, a person may also be cautioned after an offense. This occurs when it is decided that charges will not be brought, but the person is warned against further misdemeanors. The pragmatic effects of these two different cautions are very different indeed, although both include an element of warning. It might be argued that interpreters should simply allow the context to provide the different intended effects. However, interpreters certainly are concerned that Deaf people will not always be aware of the different implications involved. The strategy of simply fingerspelling the word "caution," a strategy adopted by some interpreters, is of course unlikely to solve the problem. However, this example hints at a wider issue. The interpreter is not only dealing with legal terminology, but with different types of organization of discourse (see Atkinson & Drew, 1979). The interpreter's very presence alters the nature of the discourse (Brennan & Brown, 1997). Moreover, the interpreter is often dealing with highly abstract language and intricate forms of reasoning, as well as colloquial language about day-to-day events. The juxtaposition of the highly abstract and the highly concrete, as often happens in court, is particularly demanding. The findings of the Durham research suggest that even highly skilled interpreters appear to minimize their use of the productive lexicon within the court and even to reduce normal grammatical marking, particularly nonmanual marking, so their signing becomes ungrammatical. Fingerspelling can become a "way-out" for the interpreter; that is, the answer when all else fails. However, as we have seen, while the Deaf signer uses fingerspelling within a complex dynamic interplay of sign forms, the interpreter often uses these forms in a grammatical vacuum. Far from productive signs enabling the Deaf addressee to make sense of the fingerspelling, the rich lexical and grammatical context of native signing is absent. Brennan and Brown (1997) suggested that two key motivating factors affect the interpreter's production: the formality of the court and the interpreter's preconceptions about the Deaf person's linguistic skills. It has been suggested that interpreters at times use what seem to them to be simplifying or clarifying strategies to "help the Deaf person understand." However, because these occur without the support of full and appropriate grammar, the strategies have the opposite effect. In-depth interviews with Deaf persons suggest that such signing results in a form of communication that is often incomprehensible to the BSL user. These informants suggest that rather than being an integral part of the language, the borrowings can appear disjointed and disassociated from the rest of the discourse.

Analysis of borrowings exploited within the courtroom by interpreters reveals that overall there is considerable use of fingerspelling. It has not been possible to calculate percentages in relation to the observed in situ cases, but statistics should be available in the near future relating to videotaped interaction. It has been possible to note that fingerspelling is regularly used for legal terminology, place-names, people's names, and for what are, in effect, literal, nontranslated, manual presentations of "more difficult" English words.

A major feature of fingerspelling borrowings used by interpreters in court is the degree of variability of form. Full forms are sometimes used, but more frequently items are reduced. The inconsistency of usage can be seen with respect to the interpreting of address forms and names. Address forms such as 'Miss,' 'Mrs.,' 'Mr.,' and 'Dr.' can play an important role in signaling formality and attitude. The same is true of the use of a first name alone or a surname alone. However, the form chosen by the interpreter often bears little relation to the choice made within spoken English. Thus interpreters were observed using a variety of versions for the same individual as in (11).

(11) Different forms of introduction using fingerspelling

a.	M-R-S	'Mr. S.'
	D-S	'DS'
	D-A-N	'Dan'
	D-A-N- S	'Dan S'
b.	D-R-G	'Dr G'
	D-R G-R-E-E-N-E	'Dr. Greene'
	D-R GREEN	'Dr. Greene'

It is worth noting that the clarification of what is in the interpreter's mind (given in the previous examples in parentheses) is not available to the addressee. Even where several participants share the same initials or have one initial in common, interpreters have been observed to produce identical abbreviated forms, for example, the same form M-R-S was seen to refer to different defendants where all three defendants (two men and a woman) shared the same initial -S- in their surnames. This was, as might be expected, highly confusing, although as so often happens, the nonsigning legal personnel were completely unaware of the difficulties caused by this.

As we have seen previously, Deaf signers often use fingerspelling of names as a transitional stage to the use of sign names. The research team found that name-signs were less common within the data collected in the courtrooms, although some interpreters would exploit such forms, especially if the addressee also made use of name signs. Thus the team observed the same namesign COMB, even where the lawyer used 'Coombes'—the surname without address form, and 'Mr. Coombes,' the surname with address form—the latter in a rather ironic fashion at times. The interpreter's consistency in this case failed to capture the changing attitudes conveyed by the lawyer. However, generally speaking, interpreters appeared to feel somewhat uncomfortable about using namesigns in such formal settings. Instead pressures of time encouraged interpreters to use abbreviated fingerspelled forms, but without having an overall strategy of reduction.

Interpreters frequently made use of mixed forms for names, that is, part sign and part fingerspelling. However, even within the usage of a single interpreter, these forms were often not used consistently. Forms such as the following, for the names 'Goldman' and 'Butterfield' have all been observed, not simply across a long period of signing, but sometimes in relatively close temporal proximity. The sign is seen as being more efficient in terms of time, but the fingerspelling may come more automatically, hence the mixture (12).

(12) Sign+fingerspelled surnames
a.   GOLD MAN
b.   GOLD M-A-N
c.   G-O-L-D-M-A-N
d.   BUTTER FIELD
e.   BUTTER F-L-D
f.   B-U-T-T-E-R-F-I-E-L-D

The team also observed BSL signs that had some link to the English words being used by interpreters as in (13).

(13) Signs used for surnames
a.   TAILOR   for 'Taylor'
b.   COMB   for 'Coombes'
c.   PAIN   for 'Payne'
d.   BIRD BIRD   for 'Robinson'
e.   HEART   for 'Hart'

In some cases, these forms represented the name sign of the individual within the Deaf community. However, in others, they were used within a trial by all of the interpreters involved, but were new to the Deaf people involved; in others they were created *in situ* by an individual interpreter. Not surprisingly, this at times caused confusion for the Deaf people involved who found themselves being referred to in a totally unfamiliar way.

Perhaps the most striking feature of the use of fingerspelled borrowings in the courtroom is the lack of the follow-up productive forms typical of Deaf usage. However, the formality of the courtroom appears to constrain the interpreter in this regard. Although in ordinary interactions the Deaf person appears to be trying out different possible BSL signs as matches for the English words, interpreters are reluctant to operate in such a way in the courtroom, even though they may do so in other interpreting contexts. Courtroom participants, especially legal participants, expect precision and exactitude. They expect the interpreter to be able to come up with an exact interpretation immediately. The pressure on the interpreter is such that he or she often makes use of strategies that obscure rather than explicate; often reducing the fingerspelling and subsequently omitting any further clarification. We can see this in (14).

(14) *Courtroom interpreting strategies using fingerspelling and lip patterns*

Lawyer:	My Lord
Interpreter:	
lip pattern:	*pee eff*
sign:-	P-F

Here the lawyer is using 'My Lord' as a form of address. The interpreter ignores the form of address and produces the form P-F apparently to indicate that the person speaking is the procurator fiscal, a particular type of legal official within the Scottish legal system. However, the function of the form bears no relation to the function of the words produced by the lawyer. Moreover, this occurs very early on in the case without the interpreter knowing that the Deaf person will understand the reference. The situation is further confused by the fact that the interpreter mouths the labels of the English letter, P-F, rather than the full form, 'procurator-fiscal.'

In the exchanges below which follow on from each other, we see the interpreter producing a misspelling of the English word 'dishonesty': errors of this type are almost inevitable. However, it is the reduction of the English word dishonesty to D-D-H in the second part of this exchange that is yet more problematic. There is no clear motivation for the particular type of reduction that has occurred and there is absolutely no follow-up clarification. The lack of a match between the different elements of the interpreter's signing can also be seen in the following extract.

(15) *Ambiguity caused by overlap of use of a fingerspelled form*

a.	Lawyer:	Mr. Johnston, have you ever been convicted of a crime of dishonesty?
	Interpreter:	
	lip pattern:	*Mr Johnston have you been of like dishonest*
	sign:	M-R- J-T YOU IMPORTANT O-F SOME D-O-S-H-O-N-E-S-T

b. Lawyer: Has he ever been convicted for a crime of dis-
                          honesty
    Interpreter:
    lip pattern: *have you for crime dishonest*
    sign: YOU IMPORTANT C-R-I-M-E D-D-H
c. Lawyer: Is he aware of the Criminal Injuries Compensa-
                          tion Scheme?
    Interpreter:
    lip pattern: *you know about criminal injury*
    sign: YOU KNOW C-R-I-M-I-N-A-L HURT/
                          INJURY MONEY PLAN THAT
d. Lawyer: If the answer is yes, has he put in a claim for
                          criminal injuries compensation?
    Interpreter:
    lip pattern: *have you for crime dishonest*
    sign: THE A-A MEAN YES YES CLAIM C-I
                          MONEY RECEIVE

The lawyer uses the term "Criminal Injuries Compensation Scheme," that is, the English label for a specific scheme carried out under particular legislation. The interpreter initially uses a mixture of fingerspelling and sign to express this meaning. For the second mention of this in the later exchange, the interpreter simply uses C-I. There is some possibility that if the interpreter had initially used the full fingerspelled form, followed by signed forms explaining the term, then the shortened form C-I may have had some meaning. As it is, it seems unlikely that this utterance was meaningful to the Deaf addressee. The form A-A on the other hand is probably understood because it is an established initial letter sign meaning 'answer.'

It is worth noting that during this exchange the lawyer moves from direct second person address to indirect third person address. Within courtroom interactions this often signifies a frustration at what is perceived as the lack of a clear answer. By using the third person, the lawyer, possibly inadvertently, changes the nature of the interpreter's role. Although current indications are that courtroom interpreters do typically accompany fingerspelling with related lip pattern, there is also strong evidence that they exploit simplified lip pattern with respect to other parts of the signed message. In particular, they substitute a more simplified English lip pattern for what they perceive as difficult legal terminology or expression. This again contributes to the lack of textual coherence felt by Deaf participants. Examples of such simplification observed in court include those in (16).

(16) lip patterns reflecting simplification of legal terms and expression

a. *say* for 'claim'
b. *short* for 'brief'
c. *hurt* for 'injury'
d. *say* for 'imply'
e. *think* for 'assume'
f. *talk about* for 'refer to'
g. *give an explanation* for 'offer an explanation'
h. *say* for 'put it to you'
i. *tell off* for 'admonish'

There are thousands of such examples in the data. The interpreter appears to have an internalized sense of what is "appropriate English" for Deaf people. When this has been raised in discussion with interpreters, they often comment that "Deaf people wouldn't use that kind of English" (i.e., they would themselves mouth *tell off* rather than 'admonish'). In many cases, the actual sign used is quite appropriate. In other cases, the sign itself carries a different meaning to that expressed in the spoken language.

Work is still ongoing with respect to the analysis of the data from the courtroom interactions. Certainly the material analyzed to date suggests that although interpreters make considerable use of borrowings from English within the courtroom, they frequently do so in ways that distort rather than explicate the message. By apparently providing what they may regard as a more literal interpretation, they are in danger of obscuring the message. The lack of productive morphology in general in courtroom interpreting means that the English borrowings are having to carry much more semantic weight than in typical Deaf interactions. However, because of the distorted relation between lip pattern and fingerspelling and between sign and lip pattern, full communication of the message is often not achieved.

CONCLUSION

The findings in relation to courtroom interpreting demonstrate all too clearly the importance of understanding more fully how Deaf people themselves exploit borrowings in their own language. Interpreter training can then take account of such findings to develop greater awareness and skills. The current evidence suggests that for Deaf signers, although borrowings, particularly lip patterns, are frequent, they are embedded within a rich structure involving the interplay of the most productive parts of BSL and the most established ones.

ACKNOWLEDGMENTS

The "Access to Justice for Deaf People in the Bilingual, Bimodal Court-room" project was carried out by a team at the Deaf Studies Research Unit, University of Durham, England with funding from the Leverhulme Trust. The members of the research team were: Graham Turner, Maureen Reed, Brenda Mackay, Caroline Taylor, Richard Brown, and Mary Brennan. I am grateful to these and other colleagues in the DSRU, particularly David Brien, Judith Collins, and Ernst Thoutenhoodf for discussions that have contributed to this account. My thanks also to Judith Collins for her willingness once again to model the signs so clearly and to Michelle Robinson for her photography.

REFERENCES

Atkinson, J. M., & Drew, P. (1979). *Order in court: The organization of verbal interaction in judicial settings.* London: Macmillan Academic and Professional Ltd.

Baker Shenk, C. (1986). Characteristics of oppressed and oppressor peoples: Their effect on the interpreting context. In M. McIntire (Ed.) *Proceedings of the Ninth National RID Conference.* Maryland: RID Publications.

Battison, R. (1978). *Lexical borrowings in American Sign Language.* Silver Spring, Md: Linstok Press.

Benefits Agency. (1994). *Out of work? A guide to social security benefits* (Video). London: British Deaf Association.

Brennan, M. (1990). *Word-formation in British Sign Language.* Stockholm: Stockhom University Press.

Brennan, M. (1992). The visual world of British Sign Language: An introduction. In D. Brien (Ed.) *Dictionary of British Sign Language/English.* London: Faber and Faber.

Brennan, M., & Brown, R.K. (1997). *Equality before the law: Deaf people's access to justice.* Durham, England: Deaf Studies Research Unit.

Brennan, M., Colville, M.D., Lawson, L.K., & Hughes, G. (1984). *Words in hand: A structural analysis of the signs of British Sign Language.* Edinburgh, Scotland: BSL Project and Carlisle: British Deaf Association.

Brien, D. (Ed.). (1992). *Dictionary of British Sign Language/English.* London: Faber and Faber.

Brien, D., Brennan, M., Collins, J., Reed, M., & Thoutenhoofd, E.D. (1997). *BSL CD-ROM dictionary of deaf community and culture.* Maarsen, The Netherlands: BSL Computer Services.

Colville, M.D. (1984). *Patterns of fingerspelling.* Paper presented at the Sign '84 conference, Edinburgh, Scotland.

Colville, M.D (1979). *Loan signs from fingerspelled words.* Paper presented at the NATO conference on Sign Language Research, Copenhagen.

Defoe, D. (1732). *The Life and Adventures of Duncan Campbell.* London: E. Curll.

Ebbinghaus, H., & Hessmann, J. (1996). Signs and words: Accounting for spoken elements in German Sign Language. In W. H. Edmondson and R. B. Wilbur, (Eds.), *International Review of Sign Linguistics, Vol. 1.*Mahwah, NJ: Lawrence Erlbaum Associates.

Farrar, A. (1889). Our manual alphabet and its predecessors. *Quarterly Review of Deaf-Mute Education, 2,* 33–41.

Kyle, J.G. & Woll, B. (1985). *Sign language: The study of deaf people and their language.* Cambridge, England: Cambridge University Press.

Lawson, L. (1981). The role of sign in the structure of the deaf community. In B. Woll, J.G. Kyle, & M. Deuchar, (Eds.), *Perspectives on British Sign Language and Deafness.* London: Croom Helm.

Schermer, T.M. (1990). *In search of a language: Influences from spoken Dutch on the Sign Language of the Netherlands.* Rotterdam: Eburon Delft.

Sutton-Spence, R. (1994*). The role of the manual alphabet and fingerspelling in British Sign Language.* doctoral dissertation, University of Bristol.

Sutton-Spence, R., Woll, B., & Allsop, L. (1991). Variation and recent change in fingerspelling in British Sign Language. In *Language Variation and Change, 2,* 313–330.

Woll, B. (1987). Historical and comparative aspects of BSL. In J. G. Kyle, (Ed.), *Sign and school.* Clevedon: Multilingual Matters.

3

Native and Foreign Vocabulary in American Sign Language: A Lexicon With Multiple Origins

Diane Brentari and Carol A. Padden

ABSTRACT

This chapter examines the composition of the ASL lexicon with particular reference to the status of the types of words containing fingerspelled letters. There are four major findings of this research. First, along with morphologically based diagnostic tests, we found that major divisions within the lexicon emerge based on the handshape inventories of different types of words. Second, the native and non-native components are composed of subcomponents; neither the native nor non-native lexicon is a single homogenous set of signs. Third, the non-native component is divided into strata according to the word-formational operations involved and the proximity to the core. Fourth, items in the non-native component are not necessarily on a predetermined path toward the core. Although ASL has had close contact with English since its beginning, the mechanisms for borrowing English elements into the language are constrained, systematic and expressed within the grammar of ASL.

INTRODUCTION[1]

This chapter examines the composition of the ASL lexicon with particular reference to the status of the types of words containing fingerspelled letters. To date, studies of the ASL lexicon have focused on certain sets of vocabulary, notably verbs of motion and location, agreement and plain verbs (Fischer & Gough, 1978; Klima & Bellugi, 1979; Padden, 1988, T. Supalla, 1985), adjectival predicates (Klima & Bellugi, 1979), and derivational forms (Klima & Bellugi, 1979; T. Supalla & Newport, 1978). Mentioned only in brief are signs said to be borrowed from English such as initialized signs and loan signs derived from fingerspelling. For our purposes here these will be referred to as "non-native" or "foreign" vocabulary.

This marked division between native and foreign vocabulary in ASL is most likely due to two reasons. First, there appears to be ideological anxiety about the presence of foreign elements in a natural sign language. Sign linguists have labored long and hard to demonstrate that sign languages are not codes for spoken languages; the inclusion of foreign vocabulary would seem to detract from the strength of this position. Second, there is more generally a shortage of unitary analyses of diverse lexicons, or lexicons where vocabulary derive from more than one origin.

Itô and Mester (1995a, b) have proposed a model of the Japanese lexicon that is based on principles that are directly relevant to an analysis of the ASL lexicon. In Japanese, the Yamoto forms (or native vocabulary) constitute the native subcomponent; the Sino-Japanese, derived from the Chinese ideographic system, foreign, and mimetic subcomponents are peripheral. Itô and Mester (1995a, 1995b) argued that many of the constraints that hold for the native subcomponent cease to hold or are weakened in systematic ways in the peripheral subcomponents. They also predict that the subcomponents of the lexicon do not behave as nonoverlapping entities within the grammar, but rather that principles of the core are weakened in peripheral subcomponents; peripheral subcomponents do not add or strengthen a constraint; and the subcomponents should be identifiable by differences in segmental inventories and exploitation of constraints. These predictions are empirically supported by forms in ASL.

Our goal here is to explore a range of foreign vocabulary in a signed language and demonstrate that there are ways of accounting for them without undermining the fundamental independence of a natural sign language. At the conclusion of this analysis we briefly review the implica-

---

[1]Portions of this work appear in Brentari (1998) and Padden (1998).

tions of a lexicon reanalyzed in this manner for larger issues of sign language description.

There are four major findings that have emerged from this research. First, along with morphologically based diagnostic tests we find that major divisions within the lexicon emerge based on the handshape inventories of different types of words. Second, the native and non-native components are composed of subcomponents; neither the native nor non-native lexicon is a single homogenous set of signs. Third, the non-native component is divided into strata according to the word-formational operations involved and to phonological proximity to the core component of the native lexicon, based on how well a strata conforms to a set of well-formedness constraints. Fourth, items in the non-native component are not necessarily on a predetermined path of relexicalization from the periphery to the core; on the contrary, we find that some items in the most peripheral subcomponent are quite stable, and these remain deliberately foreign.

The structure of the ASL lexicon we are proposing is given in Fig. 3.1. The native lexicon includes the polymorphemic predicates, often called classifier predicates (Part 2) and the "core" lexicon (Part 3); the foreign or non-native vocabulary (Part 1) are words that contain fingerspelled letters. Our analysis shows that each more peripheral stratum of the non-native component obeys fewer and fewer phonological constraints that hold in the core component. Part 3 overlaps with Parts 1 and 2; the analyses presented here make clear how this is so.

The polymorphemic/iconic component (Part 2), is made up of: bound roots and a variety of types of affixes that can be put together to form classifier predicates (T. Supalla, 1985)—verbs of motion and location, size and shape specifiers, and other classifier predicates (e.g., 'two-aircraft-dock-in-outer-space,' shown in Fig. 3.2); spatial verbs, as defined in Padden (1988); the pronominal system; and predicates of locative direction, such as UP, DOWN, THIS-WAY/THAT-WAY, are also included in Part 2. This vocabulary can be defined as "iconic," not in the sense that the forms

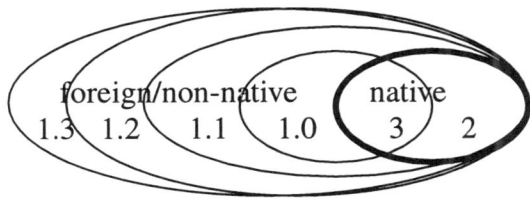

FIG. 3.1. *Components of the ASL Lexicon.*

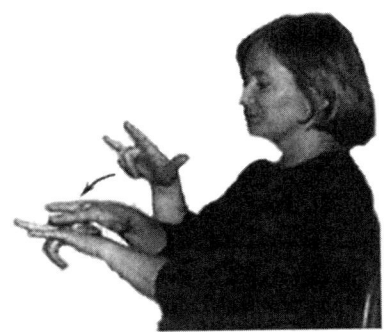

FIG. 3.2.   *A form from the polymorphemic/iconic component of the lexicon (part 2): 'two-aircraft-dock-in-outer-space'.*

are obviously transparent to the naive viewer or continuously vary with the real world, but are understood in terms of their origin in the gestural domain. T. Supalla (1985) described handshapes of ASL verbs of motion as "incorporat[ing] meaning based on salient visual-tactile characteristics of the referent object (p. 184)." Singleton, Morford, & Goldin-Meadow, (1993) found that naive hearing subjects can mimic and report the meaning of ASL verbs of motion and location with 72% accuracy. Their ability to recognize, even mimic, these forms, it can be argued, derives from a common human ability to manipulate gestures for symbolic purposes. Our reference to the term "iconic" is not intended to imply that these forms are "analogic" (i.e., nondiscrete) or nonlinguistic in any way, but rather to capture the fact that these vocabulary originate from the complex gestural resources of human beings (see Goldin-Meadow & Mylander, 1985; Kendon, 1988; McNeill, 1992).

The core lexicon includes the verb categories of plain and agreement verbs and adjectival predicates (e.g., GROUP, shown in Fig. 3.3). New members are added to the core component indirectly by both the fingerspelling system, through a complex set of operations of nativization as discussed in the rest of this paper, and directly by the classifier predicate system.

Non-native forms are those that have a handshape or handshapes whose source is the manual alphabet as well as forms borrowed from other sign languages. In this chapter, we address only the former—those that derive from fingerspelling, such as "loan signs" (first analyzed in Battison, 1978). He proposed calling such signs loan signs because they consisted of handshapes drawn from fingerspelled English words. In this chapter, we expand his initial discovery to include a number of other vocabulary of

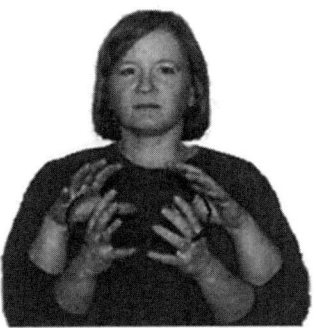

FIG. 3.3. *A form from the core component of the native lexicon (Part 3): GROUP.*

similar origin. Our analysis includes, in addition to loan signs, name signs (first described by S. Supalla, 1992), initialized signs (e.g., WATER, shown in Fig. 3.4), abbreviation signs, and sign+fingerspelled compounds. None are especially rare among signers; indeed, they appear frequently in everyday signing, but few descriptions of ASL vocabulary refer to them.

LINGUISTIC DIAGNOSTICS
FOR COMPONENTS
OF THE NATIVE LEXICON

Important to this analysis of the native lexicon are linguistic tests that address: handshape inventories; the morphemic or phonemic status of handshape, movement, orientation and place of articulation (abbreviated

FIG. 3.4. *A form from the non-native component of the lexicon (Part 1): WATER, an initialized sign.*

POA); prosodic structure; the affixation of inflectional morphology to verbs and nouns; and the affixation of derivational morphology to verbs to form nouns. We can determine where a vocabulary item belongs within the native lexicon using these tests.

Morphology

Regarding inflectional morphology, native verbs (in Parts 2 and 3 of Fig. 3.1) are grouped according to the distribution of inflectional verbal morphology that may co-occur with them (Fischer & Gough, 1978; Padden, 1988). Plain verbs and spatial verbs, including classifier predicates, do not inflect for person and number agreement, although spatial verbs allow locative agreement. Agreement verbs inflect for person and number of the subject and object, with varying subclasses of verbs inflecting for agreement with the object only and others with both the subject and object (Askins & Perlmutter, 1995). Plain and agreement verbs accept a variety of aspectual morphology, as do adjectival predicates. Nouns accept plural affixation in the form of reduplication of the stem.

Regarding derivational morphology, derived nouns with verb counterparts are frequent in native vocabulary (Supalla & Newport, 1978)—for example, PUT-ON-HEARING-AID:HEARING-AID; SIT: CHAIR; GO-BY-TRAIN: TRAIN. In most cases the pairs are distinguished by a smaller, restrained, reduplicating movement on the noun. The rule is productive with many pairs, but some native verbs have no noun counterparts, for example, LOVE or LAUGH (*LAUGHTER).

Classifier predicates and verbs of locative direction (e.g., UP, DOWN) do not inflect for person and number of the subject and object; instead they incorporate locatives that refer to locations of referents. To give a contrasting example, the core agreement verb GIVE inflects for person and number of the subject and object—for example, $_{1sg}\text{GIVE}_{2sg}$, GIVE_{pl}. In contrast, the similar looking classifier verb TO-CARRY-BY-HAND can move between locative points of a donor and a recipient, as well as between locative positions such as to move a book from one point on a table to another point, but it cannot exhibit person or number inflection. It is argued elsewhere that although these two verbs are virtually identical in form, they are members of distinct morpheme classes (Padden, 1988). Classifier predicates do exhibit certain types of distribution classifiers of quantity, such as 'in-a-row' (e.g., 'books-in-a-row,' 'vehicles-in-a-row') or 'scads-of' (e.g., 'scads-of-people'), but this is not plural marking, per se, but rather marking distribution, because the spatial configuration of the items is encoded in these forms.

The ability to exhibit derivational morphology is a characteristic of core forms. There are two types of derived nominals in ASL—reduplicated nominals (T. Supalla & Newport, 1978), and activity nominals (Padden & Perlmutter, 1987). Classifier predicates exhibit neither type of derived nominal, demonstrated in the following examples. Although many lexicalized classifier verbs (those with reduced morphemic complexity) have noun counterparts, for example, TO-FLY-BY-PLANE: AIRPLANE or TO-DRIVE-VEHICLE: CAR, novel classifier structures do not have noun counterparts. 'To-flow-in-liquid-form' does not have a noun counterpart, *WATERFALL, nor does 'to-be-flat-on-ceiling' have one, *CEILING. Further, "activity" nominalizations such as ACT:ACTING, READ:READING (Padden & Perlmutter, 1987) are not possible on novel classifier structures, for example, 'to-flow-in-liquid-form': *'flowing-in-liquid-form.' We can distinguish between classifier structures and core forms in cases where the output looks similar by using this as a diagnostic. The handshape of the core form AIRPLANE can function as a productive, bound classifier morpheme that can be put together in the polymorphemic or iconic part of the lexicon in forms, such as 'two-aircraft-dock-in-outer-space' or 'two-planes-fly-side-by-side'; however, this same handshape is a part of the core stem TO-FLY and the derived noun AIRPLANE (see Fig. 3.5), which can be placed in the core lexicon; because of the existence of this verb and its derived reduplicated nominal, these forms are placed in the core.

Some non-native signs allow aspect and person agreement morphology—for example, 1_{sg}#SAY-NO$_{3sg}$—and some allow aspect morphology—for example, in #SHIT (expletive) [intensive], the first letter is held longer than the other letters exactly like core forms that lengthen the first hold of intensive forms (e.g., GOOD [intensive], BAD [intensive], HURT [intensive]); therefore, the non-native and native components overlap with respect to these morphological criteria. As mentioned earlier, agreement and spatial morphology involves affixing to stems loci that refer to locations of referents. Loan signs accomplish this in either of two ways. In #SAY-NO, the orientation of the palm or fingertips is directed toward the desired object agreement locus, or, in a form such as #BACK, the transitions between the letters can provide the basis for a path movement achieved through phonetic enhancement (Brentari, 1998; Stevens & Keyser, 1989; Stevens, Keyser, & Kawasaki, 1986). In the case of the loan sign #BACK, the transition between the -C- and the -K- involves a flexion of the wrist outward, which is enhanced by the addition of an elbow joint movement outward. The beginning and end of the derived movement provide points of affixation of new spatial loci. All ASL forms, including all

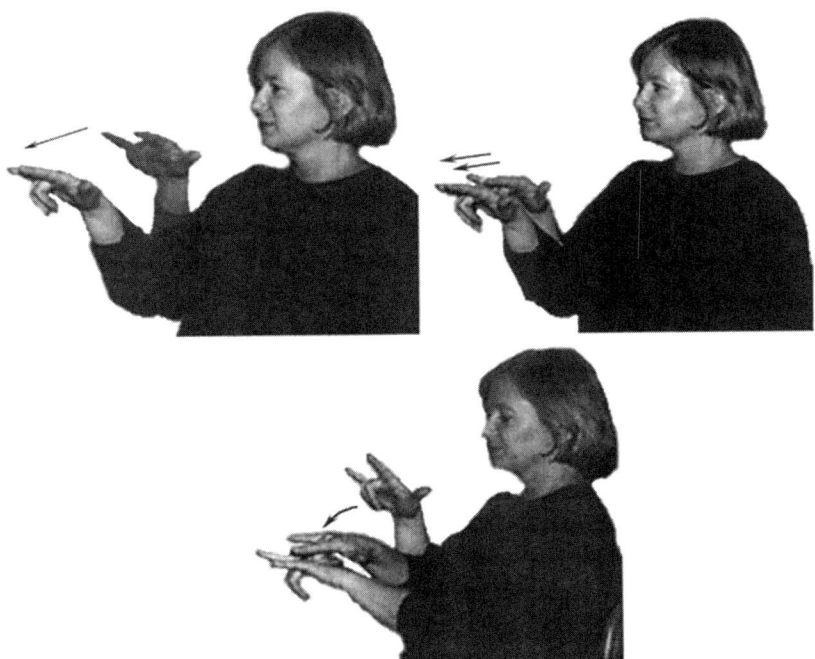

FIG. 3.5.   *The form AIRPLANE (top right) is derived from the core form TO-FLY (top left). In contrast, the polymorphemic form 'two-aircraft-dock-in-outer-space' (bottom) allows no derivational affix.*

fingerspelled forms, can take locative or spatial morphology, clearly seen in contrastive contexts. Fingerspelled words typically occur at a POA at the ipsilateral shoulder. This place can be moved to a different spatial locus in contrastive contexts—for example, B-O-B (left) EAT MEAT; H-A-R-R-Y (right) NOT.[2] These morphological criteria (Table 3.1), plus the phonological criteria in the next section determine the degree of nonnativeness of a form and divide the native lexicon into subcomponents. Often non-native forms allow more types of morphological affixation than do classifier forms. We return to this point at the end of the chapter.

PHONOLOGY

The phonological diagnostics used in these analyses have to do both with the parameters of handshape, movement, and POA, and with constraints

---

[2] There is only one loan sign that takes number agreement (i.e., #SAY-NO), but this may be an accident given the small number of transitive verbs which occur as loan signs.

TABLE 3.1.   *Morphological properties of native lexicon and loan signs*

Component of the Lexicon	Derivational Morphology	Inflectional Morphology			Spatial Morphology	
			agreement			
		aspect	*person*	*number*	*locative*	*quantity/ descriptive*
Part 1 (loan signs only)	?	+	+	+	+	−
Part 2 classifier predicates	−	−	−	−	+	+
Part 3 core	+	+	+	+	+	−

on prosodic structure that hold in the core lexicon and that are systematically weakened in the strata of the non-native lexicon. We address the issue of inventories of phonological elements first and constraints second. The feature geometry in Fig. 3.6 shows how the groups of features being discussed relate to one another in the phonological representation (Brentari, 1998). The handshapes with which we are concerned here are dominated by the hand node. Movement features are all dominated by the Prosodic Features node, and the place of articulation node dominates the place of articulation features. The relevant class nodes for each parameter are circled. Orientation is a derived relation between one of eight hand-parts specified at the hand node and at the place of articulation.[3]

Handshape Inventories.   Itô and Mester (1995a, b) predicted that the components of the lexicon should be identifiable by differences in inventories, and we have evidence for the division between native and non-native components if we compare the handshape inventories of each component (Fig. 3.7). There is evidence for dividing up the lexicon according to handshape inventories from two sources. First, there are restrictions on the combinations of handshapes and movements in initialized and abbreviated non-native signs. For example, if a handshape in a core form retains its status as a classifier, a fingerspelled letter may not be substituted for it. Signs violating such combinatoric restrictions are judged to be ungrammatical by native ASL signers, and many such forms occur in manually coded English systems. Evidence for this restriction is also seen in the ASL name sign system. Name signs are generated to refer to members of the Deaf community and arise via a mechanism for developing "classifier name signs" and "arbitrary name signs" (S. Supalla, 1992). Classifier name signs are generated by combining a bound movement root and a classifier handshape in a POA (often depicting a

---

[3]The orientation referred to here is "inherent" orientation; that is, the contrastive orientation specification of the underlying form.

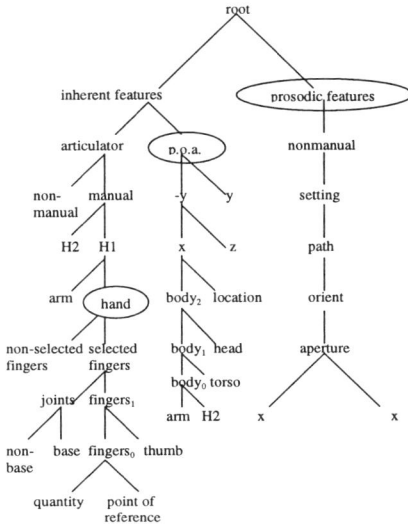

FIG. 3.6.   *Feature geometry of handshape, place, orientation and movement (Brentari,1998).*

salient aspect of the person's habits or personality); arbitrary name signs are generated by combining the first name initial (and sometimes the initial of the last name as well) of the person's English name, given the restrictions on movement and POA described earlier. Native ASL signers reject as ungrammatical name signs that combine bound movement roots of the classifier name signs with handshapes of arbitrary name signs (e.g., *movement root meaning 'limp'+-H- 'Harry') or forms that alter the shape of a fingerspelled letter with a handshape feature with morphemic

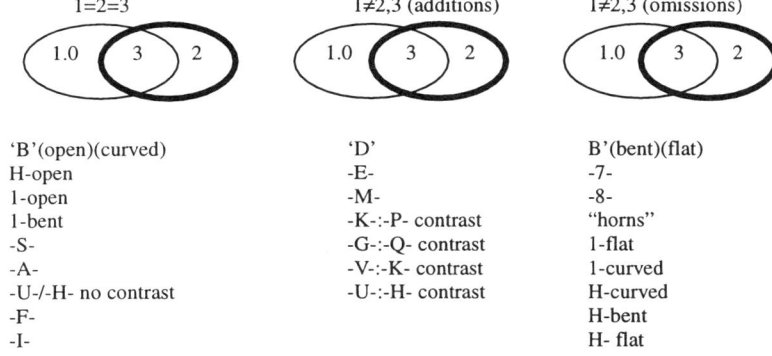

FIG. 3.7.   *Overlap and non-overlap in the handshape inventories of the native and non-native sub-components (1=non-native; 2=iconic (native); 3=core (native)).*

status (e.g., *-H- with bent fingers meaning 'the bent-over-Harry'). In addition to these combinatorial restrictions on forming new words, the handshape inventories used of different components of the lexicon do not overlap in certain areas. ASL handshapes are broken down into three kinds of features: "selected fingers" (Brentari, 1990a, 1998; Mandel, 1981; Sandler, 1989), "joints" (Brentari, 1998; van der Hulst, 1995), and "aperture" (Brentari, 1998; van der Hulst, 1995) and in some cases there are properties of the orientation relation (either of the "hand" node or the "place of articulation" node) that distinguish handshapes (Brentari, 1998; Crasborn & Kooij, 1997). These are defined in (1).

(1) Handshape features
a. "selected fingers": specification capturing those fingers that are able to move or contact the body during the course of executing a sign. Examples of handshapes that contrast in selected fingers features are -G-:-H- and -M-:-N-.
b. "joints": specification that captures the joints of a handshape that may be flexed. The specifications are open (no joints), bent (non-base joints), curved (base and nonbase joints), flat (base joints), and closed (whole hand closed in a fist). Examples of handshapes that contrast in joint features are the three-way contrast -B-:-C-:-E-.
c. "orientation relation": the relation between a specific part of the hand (one of eight possible places on the hand) and the POA. Examples of handshapes that contrast in inherent orientation are -G-:-Q- and -K-:-P-.

There is considerable correspondence among the native components, and there is also considerable non-overlap between Parts 2 and 3 versus Part 1, as (Fig. 3.7) shows. In general, the handshapes shared by Parts 1, 2, and 3 (Fig. 3.7 left) are more simple, whereas those that differentiate (Fig. 3.7 middle) and (Fig. 3.7 right) are more complex. The fingerspelled alphabet lacks handshapes appearing in (Fig. 3.7 right): B-bent, B-flat, H-bent, H-curved, H-flat, 1-flat, 1-curved, and "horns" (i.e., the handshape with the index and pinkie finger extended). These handshapes appear in the classifier system and in core forms. The fingerspelled alphabet also has some handshapes and handshape contrasts that the two parts of the native lexicon do not have (Fig. 3.7 middle). -D-, -E- and -M-, occur as fingerspelled forms, but not in the native lexicon. -K- and -V- are contrastive because of the feature [stacked], but these pairs of handshapes are not contrastive in the classifier predicate system or in the core lexicon. [Stacked] is defined as having the fingers in a global position of a squash racquet grip where the fingers are progressively less closed from the pinkie to the index finger (Brentari, 1998; Greftegref, 1993; Johnson, 1994).

There are also handshapes that are minimally contrastive in the manual alphabet (Fig. 3.7 middle) because of their inherent orientation in space: -K- (palm toward a frontal plane) versus -P- (palm toward a horizontal plane); -U- (palm toward a frontal plane) versus -H- (palm toward a midsagittal plane); -Q- (palm toward a horizontal plane) versus -G- (palm toward a midsagittal plane). In the core and iconic components, these distinctions are neutralized.

Movement and Place Of Articulation (POA) Inventories. Movement and place have different roles according to the component of the lexicon in question. In the iconic part of the native lexicon, movements and place of articulations are generally morphemic—for example, movements: 'S-shaped,' 'square-shaped'; POA: $OBJECT_a$ $OBJECT_b$, where "a" and "b" are referential loci in space. In the core, only inflectional and derivational affixal movements and POAs are morphemic; stem movements and POAs are phonemic.[4]

In non-native forms, there are two ways that POA and movement are employed. One way is typically seen in initialized forms. In these forms the handshape is a letter of the manual alphabet, but the POA, movement and orientation is that of the core lexeme on which the initialized form is based. For example, FINANCES, ECONOMY, and BUDGET are all based on the POA movement and orientation of the core form MONEY. The other way is typically seen in abbreviated and loan signs. In abbreviated signs, the POA is typically that of fingerspelled words—that is, near the ipsilateral shoulder or in neutral space; this single POA is expanded in arbitrary name signs to include a small set of locations—for example, the contralateral shoulder, chin, and ipsilateral forehead. Movement is derived from the transitions between the letters of the manual alphabet used in executing the word. In abbreviated forms, discussed later, the letters used (most often two of them) correspond to letters in specific positions in the English word. Although this is the typical pattern, there are a few loan

---

[4]Thematic transfer expressed as [direction] features on core verbs may be a case of encoding transitivity relations, and as such, may also be a case of morphemic use of movement in core verbs (e.g., RESPECT, SUBSCRIBE, etc.; see Brentari, 1988).

English word. Although this is the typical pattern, there are a few loan signs with displaced POAs (e.g., #SOON, #ALL, from Battison, 1978).

With respect to movements, in loan signs, all of the corresponding letters of the English word are in the input, and the transitional movements between them are made by the wrist or fingers. These transitional movements are subject to an evaluation of sonority (Brentari 1994, 1998). The more proximal the joint the higher the sonority (i.e., from shoulder (high sonority) >> knuckle joints (low sonority)); relatively higher sonority movements are kept and subject to phonetic enhancement, by adding a more proximal joint to the movement (e.g., an elbow movement can be added to a wrist movement). Movements thus derived by phonetic enhancement can form directional movements to which loci of inflectional or spatial reference may affix. Consider the loan sign #BACK. When the middle and index fingers are extended in the -K- the wrist extends in same way as it extends in the core verb SEND. The wrist movement in #BACK is enhanced by adding the elbow. This creates a path movement that can start and end in different places; as a result #BACK often articulated with spatial loci at the beginning and end of the sign (e.g., THEY-TWO SEPARATED, NOW #BACK) The movement and POA characteristics of the components of the ASL lexicon are summarized in Table 3.2.

Prosodic Structure. Itô and Mester (1995a, b) predicted that the subcomponents of the lexicon should be identifiable by differences in the exploitation of phonological constraints. Here we focus on constraints that refer to the ASL syllable and the prosodic word, given in Table 3.3. The number of syllables in a word is equal to the number of sequential, phonological movements it has. All ASL words must have at least one movement, hence words are at least one syllable long (Brentari, 1990a, 1990b, 1990c, 1998; Perlmutter, 1992). Handshape changes in signs have

TABLE 3.2. *ASL movement and POA inventories (N=native; -N=non-native)*

	POAs	Movements
(N) classifier preds	morphemic	morphemic
(N) core	phonemic, morphemic	phonemic, morphemic
(-N) initialized	phonologically derived from core forms	phonologically derived from core forms
(-N) arb. name signs	specified within a small phonological set	specified within a small phonological set
(-N) loan signs	neutral space or derived from core forms	derived from transitional movements

provided some of the strongest arguments for syllable structure in ASL, and as it turns out, are also relevant in the discussion of vocabulary originating or extracted from fingerspelling. When Battison (1978) proposed his constraint on handshape changes in ASL signs, he acknowledged only word-level phenomena: "signs are limited to no more than two such different handshapes" (p. 49). Additionally, ". . . the handshape changes [involve] relative openness and closedness of the handshapes" (p. 52). Moreover, Mandel (1981) and Sandler (1989) refined Battison's observation to express the generalization that most handshape changes involve changes only within the same set of selected fingers. Signs appear not to involve a change from one to another completely unrelated handshape, such as from -8- (middle finger selected) to -1- (index finger selected). Perlmutter (1993) proposed a similar but more general formulation in which there was no reference to which fingers are involved, instead the constraints refer simply to the number of changes permitted at syllable- and word-level. There are no more than two handshape "tokens," or particular instances, forming an allophonic contour in a syllable, and no more than two handshape "types," or distinct handshape contrasts, in a lexeme. Aperture features are involved in allophonic handshape contours, sometimes called hand-internal movements, and they specify whether the joints of a given contrastive handshape are open or closed.

In this analysis, we adopted a version of Brentari's (1998) word-based SELECTED FINGERS constraint and a version of Perlmutter's (1993) 2-TYPE CONSTRAINT. Hand-internal movements, referred to in the PERIPHERALITY CONSTRAINT are changes in aperture setting; that is, given the selected fingers and specified joints of a handshape, allophonic handshape changes involved a change from open to closed or vice versa (Brentari, 1990, 1998).

Within the core lexicon, the sign SEND (Fig. 3.8) is monosyllabic and has two tokens and one type: the -5- (closed) followed by an allophonic -5- (open). The sign GOVERNMENT (Fig. 3.8) is disyllabic, and has three tokens but only one type (i.e., 1-open > 1-bent > 1-open). Both mono- and disyllabic forms have one set of selected fingers and this is evidence that the SF constraint applies at the level of the word. The effect of the two-type constraint is seen in the two-morphemic forms SEND+ 'agent' (Fig. 3.8), which has three handshape tokens at the level of the word, but only two types.

With respect to movement constraints in ASL on words, Coulter (1982) and Perlmutter (1992) have argued that the native lexicon is

TABLE 3.3. *Phonotactic constraints on ASL words*

SELECTED FINGERS Constraints (SF, from Brentari, 1998)
a. One selected fingers group per prosodic word.
b. Hand-internal movements involve only selected fingers.
TWO-TYPE Constraint (2-HS, from Perlmutter, 1992).
There may be no more than two handshapes per lexeme.
PERIPHERALITY Constraint (MAX-AP; Maximize aperture change; from Brentari 1990b, 1998).
Handshape changes that occupy syllable peaks maximize aperture change.
TWO-MOVEMENT Constraint (2-MVT, from Brentari, 1998)
There are at most two movements (i.e., syllables) per prosodic word.
ALIGNMENT Constraints
a. ALIGN(L): initial handshape of stem with left edge of stem.
b. ALIGN(R): final handshape of word with right edge of word.
FAITHFULNESS Constraint
MAX-HS All handshapes in the input must appear in the output.

largely (but not exclusively) monosyllabic. There are monosyllabic, monomorphemic signs such as LIKE, UNDERSTAND, GERMANY, and monosyllabic, polymorphemic signs, for example, agreement verbs such as $_{1sg}$GIVE$_{2sg}$. Smaller in number are polysyllabic, monomorphemic signs that include DESTROY, MAKE-NOTE-OF, and APPOINTMENT. Polysyllabic, polymorphemic signs include some classifier structures, stem+aspectual marking on adjectives, and stem + certain inflections on agreement verbs, for example, dual marking. Importantly, at the level of the prosodic word, there appears to be no more than two syllables allowed, captured by the TWO-MOVEMENT CONSTRAINT, given in Table 3.3.[5]

Foreign words fall into distinct groups according to how they behave with respect to these constraints. Some obey all of them; such forms are in Part 1.0 of the ASL lexicon (1). Some obey none of them; such forms are in Part 1.3. There is some overlap between Part 1.0 and the core (Part 3).

Typology of Non-Native Vocabulary

We define non-native vocabulary in ASL as including, in addition to loan signs first described by Battison (1978), sets of vocabulary ranging from initialized signs and abbreviation signs to sign + fingerspelled compounds and name signs. All share an origin in the American fingerspelling system. The fingerspelled alphabet is a set of names for the

---

[5]Signs with bidirectional movements apparently violate this constraint; further research on this is necessary.

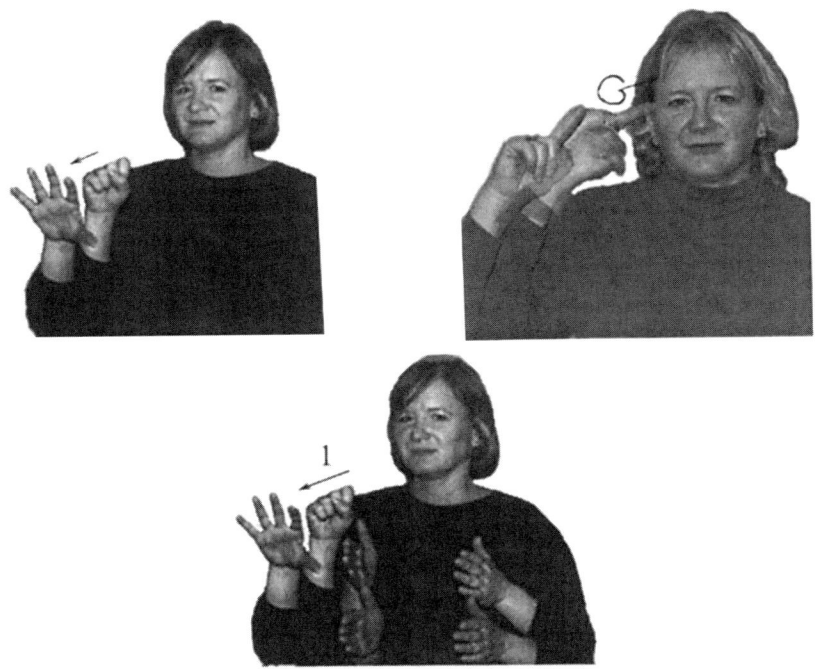

FIG. 3.8.   *The SEND (top left) has two handshape tokens, but one handshape type; GOVERN-*
MENT (top right) three hanshape tokens, but only one handshape type; the word containing SEND
+'agent' (bottom) has three handshape tokens, but two handshape types.

English alphabet, consisting primarily of handshapes, a few of which are
also specified for orientation (e.g., -G-, -Q-, -U-, -H-, -K-, -P-) or for
movement (-J- has an orientation change, and -Z- has a tracing movement). The conventional description of fingerspelling in ASL is that it
constitutes borrowed vocabulary from English and is used to represent
names, places, and vocabulary for which no signs are available. The fact
that fingerspelling has existed since the earliest filmed records of ASL
(Hotchkiss, 1913; Veditz, 1913) and much earlier in Spain (Bonet, 1620)
seems not to have discouraged the popular sentiment that fingerspelling
is English and its presence in ASL is marginal.[6] But as Lucas and Valli
(1992) pointed out, the relation between fingerspelling and English is a
distant one. The system is at least two levels of representation removed

[6]The American fingerspelling system can be traced to an invention by a hearing priest in the seventeenth century, Juan Pablo Bonet (Bonet, 1620), who developed it in the course of his tutoring a young
deaf boy. The system was subsequently appropriated by the Abbe Sicard, a French educator of deaf
children (Lane, 1984).

from English: it is a representation of another representation. More precisely, it is two inventions removed: first, the written invention, followed by the manual, face-to-face invention. Further, its presence in ASL is ubiquitous; fingerspelled words appear as frequently as 7%–10% in the overall vocabulary in everyday signing (Padden, 1991). It has a durable and established niche in ASL. We claim that the long-standing presence of sequences of fingerspelling has made it possible for fingerspelled sequences to become routinized and for words thus derived to become structurally integrated in sign languages.

More globally, the ASL fingerspelling system is one of many similar inventions in sign languages of the world, designed to cross modalities and allow representation of spoken material in visual form, and processes of nativization have been reported for these systems as well. The ASL fingerspelling system is a one-handed alphabetic system also found in European sign languages such as French Sign Language and Swedish Sign Language. The British Deaf community uses a two-handed alphabetic system (Sutton-Spence & Woll, 1993; see also Brennan, this volume, chap. 2), as do Australians and New Zealanders. Deaf Italians use alphabetic fingerspelling for foreign names, but articulate by mouth spoken Italian vocabulary, as do signers of SLN (Schermer, 1990), DSGS (Boyes Braem, this volume, chap. 1), Norwegian Sign Language (Vogt-Svenson, 1984), Swedish Sign Language (Bergman & Wallin, 1998), and German Sign Language (DGS) (Ebbinghaus & Hessman, 1996). In Japanese Sign Language (JSL), there is a manual representation of the syllabic hiragana system. In addition, JSL and other Asian sign languages, including Taiwan Sign Language (Ann, 1995) and Hong Kong Sign Language, have manual character signs, for example, NORTH, and signs that represent Chinese characters (Fok & Bellugi 1986; Fok, Bellugi, van Hoek, & Klima, 1988). Danish Sign Language uses a "mouth-hand system" involving mouth movements coordinated with disambiguating hand configurations (Birch-Rasmussen, 1982).

Because of its origin as an invention for representing English words in alphabetic form, it is as yet unclear how to characterize the form of fingerspelled words in ASL. Obviously, fingerspelling involves a sequence of handshapes that correspond to its sequence in written form. But Akamatsu (1982) and Wilcox (1992) found this description inadequate. From her work analyzing very young signers' fingerspelling attempts, Akamatsu proposed that fingerspelled words have salient "movement envelopes," or characteristic movement shapes at the segmental and word level. Indeed, very young signers can fingerspell and recognize forms they cannot yet read in written form. Wilcox found from kinematic analyses of fingerspelled movements of skilled adult signers that they consistently repeat the same sets of movements across many repetitions of the same word. Less skilled fingerspellers show more variability, demonstrating that skilled, fluent fingerspelling involves knowledge of movement as well as of handshape sequences. We return to the question of the phonological form of fingerspelling in a later section.

Initialized Signs

Among the most frequent and well-entrenched foreign vocabulary items in ASL are initialized signs; for example, WATER, BLUE, PINK, PURPLE, YELLOW, GREEN, FAMILY, and PERSON. The popular definition of initialized signs is that the handshape of a native sign is replaced with one corresponding to the first letter of an English translation (Frishberg & Gough, 1973). However, some initialized signs have no native counterparts, for example, WATER and signs corresponding to color, trait, and status. Instead what appears to be a defining characteristic is that they are members of semantic fields, occupied by several signs varying along a semantic dimension, given in (2).

(2) *Initialized Sign forms (*no native sign)*
GROUP	FAMILY, ASSOCIATION, GROUP, TEAM, SOCIAL, DEPARTMENT
PERSON	PERSON, INDIVIDUAL, CLIENT, HUMAN, SUBJECT
SCIENCE	BIOLOGY, CHEMISTRY, EXPERIMENT
COMPUTATION	STATISTICS, ALGEBRA, CALCLUS, GEOMETRY, TRIGONOMETRY
THOUGHT	THEORY, REASON, LOGIC, MEDITATE
*Color	BLUE, PURPLE, YELLOW, GREEN, BROWN
*Trait	PERSONALITY, CHARACTER, NOBLE, LOYAL
*Status	BACHELOR, SINGLE, TWIN, SENIOR-CITIZEN

Initialization is one of the most productive of word-building processes in ASL, used widely for technical or professional purposes. Many initialized signs often appear in pairs with native signs representing the common and familiar, and initialized signs, the scientific and distant, for example, the native FEELING-DOWN and initialized CLINICAL-DEPRESSION; native SUSPICIOUS and initialized PARANOIA; native SOUND and initialized PHONOLOGY; and native GOVERNMENT and initialized POLITICAL/POLITICS. Initialized signs almost always correspond to the first letter of an English translation of the sign. An exception is the sign SEX/GENDER in which the handshape is the last letter of the word, -X-. Interestingly, there has been further word-building from this particular sign; in the related form, TRANSEXUAL, the contacting root movement has been replaced with a root movement meaning 'to reverse, change.'

As widespread as this particular process of word building has been in ASL, many Deaf people say they are suspicious of initialized signs. Part of the anxiety stems from the fact that sign language reformers of the 1970s (Gustason, Petzfing, & Zawolkow, 1975) proposed substituting large numbers of native vocabulary with initialized signs, an action that predictably met with much resistance in the Deaf community. Yet initialized signs are widespread, even if specific initialized forms from the Gustason and associates' project are disallowed. It should be noted that the rapid growth of new initialized signs used in everyday contexts in the community almost perfectly coincides with the rise of the Deaf professional middle class during this period (Padden, 1990). With the movement of Deaf people away from traditional and low-paying solitary trades into technical and scientific fields of work, new vocabulary for their new work lives was needed. In these contexts, initialized signs are productive means of forming semantic and lexical oppositions between known, intimate, in-group vocabulary with scientific vocabulary (Ramsey & Padden, 1998).

Abbreviation Signs

Except for BULLSHIT, none of Battison's (1978) examples include words that exceed five letters, leaving open the question of how to analyze so-called "abbreviation" signs. Such signs involve reduction of the string of fingerspelled letters to at most two handshapes, as do loan signs. Like loan signs, some take agreement inflection, for example FEEDBACK, which can inflect for person and number of the subject and object; however, unlike loan signs that tend to retain the first and last letters of the origin fingerspelled word, abbreviation signs tend to retain the first and a medial letter. One group of abbreviation signs have a single handshape change and one movement such as a path or brushing movement (3); another involve two contacts (4).

(3) *Abbreviation signs articulated as one sequential movement*
FEEDBACK, VIDEOTAPE, WORKSHOP, WITHDRAW, VICE PRESIDENT

(4) Abbreviation signs articulated as two sequential movements
ṢOCIAL ẈORK, ṢENIOR ÇITIZEN(S), ḄOARD OF ṬRUSTEES,
ḄACKGROUND, ṾIETṆAM(ESE), PROJECT

The second, medial handshape of an abbreviation sign may coincide
with the first letter in the second word of a phrase or a compounded unit,
for example, ỤSHER'S-ṢYNDROME and ẈORKṢHOP, or the second
stem, for example, PROJECT, and ẈITHḌRAW. A few abbreviation
signs involve a first and final letter, for example, ÇURRICULUM. Abbreviation signs, like initialized signs, occupy semantic fields linking clusters
of initialized signs, for example, ṢENIOR ÇITIZEN joins ṬWINS, ṢIN-
GLE; ṾIETṆAM(ESE) joins JAPAN, and ÇHINA, ḴOREA; ṢOCIAL
WORK joins ṬHERAPY, ṚEHABILITATION. For these reasons,
Brentari (1990b) analyzed abbreviation signs as a subtype of initialized
signs, but a number of other abbreviation signs have no such groupings,
for example, FEEDḄACK, ẈITHḌRAW, and ỤSHER'S-ṢYNDROME.
    Aside from the correct assignation of these foreign vocabulary, the
distribution of the two handshapes in abbreviated signs and in initialized
signs are accounted for using the alignment constraints ALIGN(L) and
ALIGN(R) (given in Table 3.3 and repeated here in (5); Brentari, 1998).

(5) Alignment Constraints
a.   ALIGN(L): initial handshape of stem with left edge of stem.
b.   ALIGN(R): final handshape of word with right edge of word.

ALIGNMENT constraints match the beginnings and ends of morphological categories (e.g., stems) with the beginnings and ends of prosodic
categories (e.g., syllables, prosodic words). When the English word(s) on
which the abbreviated sign is based consists of one stem (e.g., ÇUR-
RICULUM), ALIGN(L) will insure that the leftmost letter is used, and
ALIGN(R) will insure that the rightmost letter is used, rather than the second leftmost letter (e.g., *ÇURRICULUM). When the English word(s) on
which the abbreviated sign is based consists of more than one stem or
more than one word, both leftmost letters of the stems are chosen (e.g.
FEEDḄACK, ẈITHḌRAW, ỤSHER'S-ṢYNDROME). This behavior
can be accounted for by ranking ALIGN(L) above ALIGN(R) in the grammar's constraint hierarchy.[7]

---

[7]In Quebec Sign Language (LSQ), the output form derived from the English word 'curriculum' would
be predicted to be ÇURRICULUM, rather than ÇURRICULUM, revealing different constraint ranking of ALIGN(L) and ALIGN(R) (see Miller, this volume, chap. 5).

Name Signs

S. Supalla (1992) noticed that "arbitrary" name signs in ASL constitute an extremely small system of possible forms, constituting a sublexicon. The handshapes are drawn from a limited inventory of fingerspelled hand-shapes in addition to a limited set of permissible movement, location, and orientation elements. In contrast to the "descriptive" name sign system in which names are drawn from the classifier inventory, arbitrary name signs have no classifier elements; instead the signs are formed from combinations of a limited set of arbitrary elements.

Name signs, like initialized signs, employ the fingerspelled handshape corresponding to the first letter of an English name, usually a first name or a last name, and sometimes both. But unlike initialized signs, name signs permit only a few movement elements. One of the authors' name signs, CAROL, is the -C- handshape combined with the shaking movement located in neutral space. Because the inventories are so limited, it is not uncommon for individuals in the national Deaf community to have the same name sign, although typically same name signs are avoided in a local or professional community. Because fingerspelled English names are used widely in the American Deaf community, the problem of name sign similarity is a small one.

Loan Signs

Whereas initialized signs and name signs draw only from the fingerspelled handshape inventory in combination with movement and location elements of the native lexicon, loan signs are entirely derived from finger-spelled words. Nativized loan signs involve extensive restructuring with significant reductions in the movement contour of the origin fingerspelled word. The number of handshapes in the fingerspelled word is typically reduced to two in the loan sign. Battison (1978) listed restructured loan signs whose origin forms ranged from at least two letters up to five letters. Examples are those of two-letter origin, #SAY-NO; three-letter, #JOB; four-letter, #EASY; and five-letter, #WOULD. In his analysis, restructured forms typically retained first and last letters with medial letters deleted or reduced as in #JOB, which has a handshape change -J- to -B-, deleting the medial -O-, and #WOULD, with a handshape -W- to -D-, deleting all other medial letters (Fig. 3.9).

Loan signs fall into a range of word classes, including nouns (#JOB), verbs (#SAY-NO), adjectives (#EASY), conjunctions (#BUT), expletives

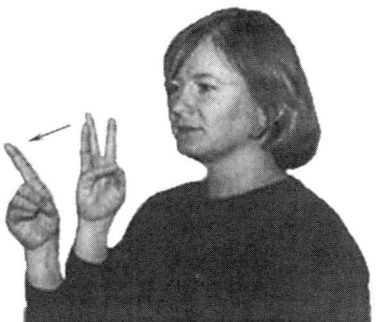

FIG. 3.9.   *The loan signs #JOB (left) and #WOULD (right). Both retain the initial and final letters of the English word and delete the medial letters.*

(#FUCK) and wh-words (#WHAT). Except for very few forms, for example, #BREAD, loan signs' origins as fingerspelled words are still recoverable, despite reduction and resyllabification. Hirsh-Pasek (1981) finds that young signers can report the fingerspelled words from which the loan signs in her sample were derived, which may suggest that loan signs retain not only some of the handshapes but also movements inherent to the full fingerspelled form, which the children can still recognize and, at times, even try to mimic these movements. For example, T. Holcomb (personal communication) observed his young preliterate daughter assigning different movement contours to R-I-C-E and I-C-E ; with R-I-C-E, his daughter used a characteristic circling movement, but with I-C-E, she used an opening and closing movement. Further, the original movements are more salient in emphasized forms.

Locally Lexicalized Loans

When long fingerspelled forms occur in discourse (i.e., more than seven letters), the movements between letters assume regular movement patterns within the discourse after three productions. For example, in a set of video presentations on linguistics, the form M-O-R-P-H-O-L-O-G-Y appears as #MP[HG]Y after the third production (Bienvenu & Colonomos, 1987; Brentari, 1994; examples from Valli & Lucas, 1992 (6)).

(6) Locally lexicalized fingerspelled forms

# letters	1st/2nd production	3rd production	# syllables
6	S-Y-N-T-A-X	S-Y-ø-T-X	2
8	C-U-P-B-O-A-R-D	C-P-[wig]-D	2

8	L-O-C-A-T-I-O-N	[L-I]-O-$\emptyset$-C-N	2
8	M-O-R-P-H-E-M-E	M-P-H-E	2
9	P-H-O-N-O-L-O-G-Y	P-[H-G]-Y	2
10	M-O-R-P-H-O-L-O-G-Y	M-P-[H-G]-Y	2
10	L-I-N-G-U-I-S-T-I-C	L-I-N-G-I-C	2
5	C-H-I-L-D	[C-H]-I-L-D	1

Despite some idiosyncratic variability in such forms, we see that other factors beyond position in the word can influence which letters are deleted or retained. Movements resulting from two-letter sequences are predictably retained because of how salient they are. Letters are potentially deleted if they do not involve a change in orientation from one letter to the next, or, if they occur word medially. A sequence is likely to be retained if if it results in an orientation change (e.g., _G, _H, _P, _X), or if the sequence results in a legitimate handshape contour.

Compounds With Fingerspelled Forms

It is well known that ASL has productive compounding of native forms (Klima & Bellugi, 1979) in which signs combine to form a compound, for example, RED+SQUARE 'brick' and SLEEP+SUNRISE, 'oversleep.' These compounds undergo reduction and simplification of movement from reduplicated to nonreduplicated forms, for example, in BABY+SIT; the reduplicated BABY is reduced to a single movement in the compound.

BABY+SIT joins other compounds of native forms that are "loan translations," or literal translations of English compounds. Examples are DEAD+LINE 'deadline,' TIME+LINE 'timeline,' and HOME+WORK 'homework.' Such compounds are plentiful in everyday ASL, including some that seem semantically odd in ASL, for example, BABY+SIT, which means to 'babysit' and not the phrase 'the baby is sitting.' Despite their loan status, these compounds in all respects behave like compounds of native signs: They constitute a unit and show reduction and simplification of movement.

Because ASL has compounds that permit the loan of meaning as well as of form, the case of compounds that consist of a sign and a fingerspelled word are additional interesting forms (7). As with signed compounds, the forms have lexical integrity; they function as single units and cannot be broken apart without altering the meaning of the combined units. The first list contains compounds where signs constitute the first unit, and the second list, the second unit:

(7) Forms Containing Signs and Fingerspelling

a. Sign + fingerspelled forms

DEAD+E-N-D	'dead-end street'
SUN+B-U-R-N	'sunburn'
PAY+R-O-L-L	'payroll'
SOFT+W-A-R-E	'software'
EYE+T-O-O-T-H	'eyetooth'
CHEAP+S-K-A-TE	'cheapskate'
HARD+W-A-R-E	'hardware'(computer)
SOAP+B-O-X	'soapbox' (for lecturing)

b. Fingerspelled + sign forms

P-R-O-O-F+READ	'proofread'
F-O-O-T+WORK	'footwork'
L-E-G+WORK	'legwork'
B-E-L-L+BOY	'bellboy'
S-T-O-C-K+MARKET	'stock market'

c. Fingerspelled English compounds

B-A-L-L-P-O-I-N-T	'ball-point pen'
L-A-P-T-O-P	'laptop' (computer)
S-K-Y-L-I-N-E	'skyline'
P-I-C-K-U-P	'pickup' (truck)
P-I-C-K-P-O-C-K-E-T	'pickpocket'
W-O-R-K-O-U-T	'exercise/workout'

At first glance, there appear to be no distributional grounds for whether signs appear as first or as second units, or whether English compounds are represented fully or partly in fingerspelling. The patterning does not become obvious until clusters of loan translations are compared as in (8).

(8) Clusters of Loans

a. i. PICK+U-P   'trash pick-up' or 'pick-up bar'
   ii. P-I-C-K-U-P   'pick-up' (truck)
   iii. P-I-C-K-P-O-C-K-E-T 'pickpocket'

b. i. PAINT+B-A-L-L   'paintball' (for war games)
   ii. BLACK+B-A-L-L   'to blackball' (someone)

c. i. TIME+LINE   'timeline'
   ii. DEAD+LINE   'deadline'
   iii. TELEPHONE+LINE   'phone line'
   iv. S-K-Y-L-I-N-E   'skyline'

d. i.   PAPER+WORK   'paperwork'
    ii. HOME+WORK   'homework'
    iii. F-O-O-T+WORK   'footwork'
    iv. L-E-G+WORK   'legwork'

PICK means 'to choose' in (8a.i), but not in (8a.ii–iii). BALL usually means a playing ball held by hand, but in 'blackball' and 'paintball' (8b) the balls are not playing balls nor are they of a size to be held in both hands; a 'paintball' is actually a pellet. Thus BALL is disallowed for meanings varying from the semantic category of the sign BALL. LINE refers to a boundary or a conduit in (8c.i-iii), but not an outline, as in 'skyline,' because the sign translation LINE is disallowed for the latter meaning and the form is fingerspelled to preserve semantic integrity of LINE.

It also appears that pointing classifiers, especially for including those for body parts, are disallowed in compounds. In F-O-O-T+WORK and L-E-G+WORK the body part is fingerspelled (8d.iii–iv).[8] More generally, it appears that there are restrictions on classifier constructions appearing in compounds. WATER+ F-A-L-L is allowed but not *'WATER+liquid-flowing-downwards'; W-I-N-D-S-H-I-E-L-D but not *'WIND+flat-surface-curved'.[9] One possible reason why such compounds are blocked is that the predicate classifier forms lack derived noun counterparts; instead the fingerspelled word is used for the second half of the noun compound. More generally, there are pairs of signs and fully fingerspelled words that stand in either semantic or word class opposition (9).

(9) *Pairs of fingerspelled words and signs in semantic or word class*
     opposition
a.   FREE 'liberated' versus F-R-E-E 'free of charge'
b.   PICK U-P 'to pick up' versus P-I-C-K-U-P 'pick-up' (truck)
c.   WORK O-U-T 'to work out' versus W-O-R-K-O-U-T 'exercise
     workout'
d.   LOVE 'to love' versus L-O-V-E 'love' (noun)

---

[8]The restriction may be that signs articulated below the chest are generally avoided. But pointing is also avoided in other signs; in 'eyetooth' informants report that it is "funny" to point to both the eye, then the tooth; instead the preferred translation is EYE+T-O-O-T-H.

[9]An exception to this are some size and shape specifiers, which appear in RED+'square' ('brick') and 'square'+ZAP ('microwave').

In these cases, fingerspelled words not only convey meaning borrowed from English but coexist with ASL signs in semantic and grammatical distribution. In this sense, fingerspelled words in compounds act as diagnostics of semantic categorization and of word class in ASL vocabulary.

A UNIFIED LEXICON

Using the descriptive generalizations and the proposed phonological constraints given thus far, we can divide the non-native ASL lexicon into systematically distinct groups (Table 3.4). The analysis in this section is expressed using Optimality Theory (Prince & Smolensky, 1993), in which candidate output forms are evaluated with respect to a set of ranked constraints.

Loan signs have representative forms in each of the non-native strata; therefore, they are used as a basis for our analysis. By understanding how the constraints operate in the forms closest to the core, we will be able to apply them consistently to other non-native strata. The constraint tableau for #BREAD is given in (11), using the set of constraints in Table 3.3. At this point, one more constraint needs to be presented, which is a FAITH-FULNESS constraint. FAITHFULNESS constraints do their best to guarantee that the shape of the output matches the input to the greatest extent possible. They militate against deletions from the input form—MAX constraints—or against epenthesis in the output form—DEP constraints. The only FAITHFULNESS constraint we use is called MAX-HS, which requires that all handshapes of the input must also be present in the output; it is given in Table 3.3. and repeated here in (10). FAITH is used instead of the label MAX-HS in the following tableaux.

(10) FAITHFULNESS constraint
MAX-HS: All handshapes in the input must appear in the output.

The tableaux in (11-14) show how the strata of the non-native vocabulary behave with respect to the proposed constraints. A set of possible outputs is listed, but only the one indicated by the ☞ is the optimal one, which best satisfies the ranked well-formedness constraints. The only constraint that must be crucially ranked in the core form #BREAD is FAITH. All of the

TABLE 3.4.   *The non-native lexicon in ASL*

Subcomponent	Description
1.0 « 3.0	Signs that violate none of the rules mentioned in (7)–(10) and (14) and have handshapes that occur in all three components. (e.g., #BREAD, #SAY-NO)
1.0	Name signs, initialized signs, two-letter loans that have a handshape that has a synchronic connection with its English counterpart, but that violate none of the constraints mentioned in this paper. (e.g., TEAM, WAR, WATER, EMERGENCY).[10]
1.1	Some arbitrary name signs, abbreviated signs, initialized signs, two-letter loans. These are forms that violate SF (e.g., VIDEOTAPE, WITHDRAW, WORKSHOP, FEEDBACK).
1.2	Partially assimilated loan signs, three-letter loans. These forms violate SF, MAX-AP, and 2-HS (e.g., #EASY, #SURE).
1.3	Commonly fingerspelled words, sign+fingerspelled compounds. These forms violate SF, 2-HS, MAX-AP, and 2-MVT (e.g., F-R-E-E, S-T-O-C-K-MARKET).

other constraints are unviolated in the output form, -8-[open][closed][11]; the other candidates in (11) are less harmonic in the following ways.

The fully fingerspelled form of #BREAD (the first candidate) has two MAX-AP violations because -B- and -R are both [open] and -E- and -A- are both [closed]. This form contains five, not two, handshapes, thereby incurring three violations of 2-HS. There are three violations of SF.a because although -B- and -E- contain the same selected fingers, -R-, -A-, and -D- cause three changes in selected finger groups. SF.b is violated only once, and ALIGN(L) and ALIGN(R) are unviolated, as is FAITH. Candidates 2 and 3 with unparsed first and last letters incur one less 2-HS and SF.a violation, but they violate and ALIGN(L) and ALIGN(R) respectively. Deleting two of the middle handshapes (candidate 4) eliminates the violations of MAX-AP and 2-MOV, but the violations of SF and 2-HS remain.

---

[10]These signs will have handshapes not found in the core inventory.

[11]Two explanatory remarks about the optimal candidate 7 are in order. One is that the movement realized in the output form is rapidly repeated. The second is that -8- is a conventionalized, shorthand way of notating a handshape with the middle finger selected and nonselected fingers open. The handshape change from [open] to [closed] with this set of selected fingers indicates an output form which changes from having all of the fingers extended (i.e., -B-) to one where the middle finger is flattened, and the index finger and the ring and pinkie finger are extended independently. The extended index finger approximates the -D-.

(11) Constraint tableau for #BREAD (8[open(o)]>[closed(c)]
(nativized form; Parts 1.0 « 3.0)

/BREAD/	2-MOV	ALIGN-LEFT	ALIGN-RIGHT	2-HS	MAX-AP	SF.a	SF.b	FAITH
BREAD	**			** *	**	***	*	
BREA<D>	*		*	**	**	**		*
<B>READ	*	*		**	**	**	*	*
B<RE>AD				*		**	*	**
B-A			*			*		***
B-D						*		***
☞8[o]>[c]								***

The forms with two handshapes (candidates 5 and 6) are quite well formed; B-D incurs only one violation of SF.a. The actual output fares even better, having no violations of the proposed constraints except for FAITH, with a whopping five violations. Notice, too, that the only form with no violations of FAITH is the fully fingerspelled form.

In loan signs with two handshapes (such as #JOB (12)) FAITH is no longer lowest ranked. The output has a violation of SF.a and SF.b, which places the form in stratum 1.1. It is equivalent in structure and number of violations incurred with the #BREAD form of BREAD—candidate 6— that is, J-B has not rid itself of the fingerspelled letters. The output contains one violation of FAITH. The tableau for #EASY (13), a non-native form in stratum 1.2, shows FAITH moving up further in the constraint hierarchy. Violations of 2-HS and SF are what define this stratum. In stratum 1.3, FAITH is ranked above all constraints except ALIGN(L) and ALIGN(R) for example, STOCK in S-T-O-C-K MARKET (14). In this stratum any violation of FAITH will be fatal.

Moving away from the core, each successive stratum ranks FAITH higher in the constraint tableau. In Table 3.5, we can trace the degree of faithfulness to the input of loan signs with respect to the constraints of the core lexicon. It is important to reiterate that forms can be stable members of these strata.

(12) Constraint tableau for #JOB (J-B; non-native, part 1.1; loan sign)

/JOB/	2-MOV	ALIGN-LEFT	ALIGN-RIGHT	2-HS	MAX-AP	FAITH	SF.a	SF.b
JOB				*			*	*
☞J-B					*		*	*

(13) Constraint tableau for EASY (#E-S-Y; non-native, part 1.2; loan sign)

/EASY/	2-MOV	ALIGN-LEFT	ALIGN-RIGHT	FAITH	2-HS	MAX-AP	SF.a	SF.b
EASY	*				**	**	*	*
E-Y			**				*	*
☞E-S-Y			*	*	*		*	*

(14) Constraint tableau for STOCK in S-T-O-C-K MARKET (non-native, Part 1.3; sign+fingerspelled word)

/STOCK/	ALIGN-LEFT	ALIGN-RIGHT	FAITH	2-MOV	2-HS	MAX-AP	SF.a	SF.b
☞STOCK				**	**	**	*	*
S-K			***			**	*	

Initialized and abbreviated signs combine movements of core forms with at most two fingerspelled letters. In (15) we see the tableau for an initialized form with two handshapes—WORKSHOP. The candidate set helps us see a crucial ranking between ALIGN(L) and ALIGN(R). Because of the 2-HS constraint, all of these forms allow for two empty handshape slots in the input, in addition to the path movement from the core form. What we see here is that a two-handshape form incurring one violation of ALIGN(R) is preferred over a form incurring one violation of ALIGN(L) The preferred form chooses the two leftmost handshapes of the two English stems.

TABLE 3.5. *The ranking of FAITHFULNESS in native and non-native components of the ASL lexicon*

Native (1.0)	Non-native (1.1)	Non-native (1.2)	Non-native (1.3)
2-MOV	2-MOV	2-MOV	ALIGN(L)
ALIGN(L)	ALIGN(L)	ALIGN(L)	ALIGN(R)
2-HS	2-HS	ALIGN(R)	FAITH
MAX-AP	MAX-AP	FAITH	2-MOV
ALIGN(R)	ALIGN(R)	2-HS	2-HS
SF(a)	FAITH	MAX-AP	MAX-AP
SF(b)	SF(a)	SF(a)	SF(a)
FAITH	SF(b)	SF(b)	SF(b)

(15) 'workshop'+GROUP (path; non-native, Part 1.1; abbreviated sign)

'workshop'+ GROUP	ALIGN-L	ALIGN-R	2-HS	MAX-AP	SF.a
☞W-S+GROUP		*			*
W-P+GROUP	*				*

DISCUSSION AND CONCLUSION

Forms such as sign+fingerspelled compounds and commonly finger-spelled words constitute the most foreign of all ASL vocabulary. They do not inflect for person or for number, nor do they accept plural affixation. PAINT+B-A-L-L in the plural adds the phrase, 'small round object'+[Redup], but does not itself undergo reduplication. These forms also violate all phonological constraints discussed thus far, except for the FAITHFULNESS constraint MAX-AP. It would appear that without further evidence of resyllabification, or restructuring, that these forms are the least nativized, and reside just inside the boundaries of the lexicon.

The morphological aspects of word formation in the "iconic" versus the non-native vocabulary are worth discussing as a final point. Brentari (1990b) argued that fingerspelled forms are polysyllabic, monomorphemic forms. Handshapes in these forms are not morphemic; instead they are linked with words with English sources. Because of their monomorphemic status, it could be hypothesized that forms derived from fingerspelling are relatively simple morphologically and are therefore freer to accept agreement and aspect morphology than are classifier predicates, which are morphologically much more complex. In contrast, in the iconic component of the ASL lexicon, handshapes (as well as POA and movement) are morphemic. Furthermore, because of this morphological difference between handshapes in non-native forms and in classifier predicates, Parts 2 and 1 of the lexicon stay mainly distinct from one another, and attempts to combine them in name signs or in lexical items are considered ungrammatical by native signers. However, if and when a classifier form enters the core lexicon, which can be tested by the ability to derive nominals or affix inflectional morphology to the form, it becomes a potential candidate for hybridization in initialized signs, abbreviated signs, and compounds. This morphological distinction between Parts 1 and 2 of the lexicon is seen in the separation of the classifier and arbitrary name signs. Finally, when a form, such as FREE, is used differently than its adjectival word class with primary meaning of 'liberated,' it may adopt a fingerspelled variant to express an alternative use—that is, as an affix meaning 'without'—in forms such as SUGAR-F-R-E-E.

What this analysis shows is that, although ASL has had intimate contact with English since its beginning, the mechanisms for borrowing English elements into the language—both morphological and phonological—are constrained, systematic, and expressed within the grammar of ASL.

REFERENCES

Akamatsu, C. T. (1982). *The acquisition of fingerspelling in pre-school children.* Unpublished doctoral dissertation, The University of Rochester, New York.

Ann, J. (1995). *Properties of character signs in Taiwan Sign Language.* Paper presented at the annual meeting of the Linguistic Society of America, New Orleans, Louisiana.

Askins, D., & Perlmutter, D. (1995). *Agreement verbs in ASL.* Unpublished manuscript, University of California, San Diego and University of Rochester, New York.

Battison, R. (1978). *Lexical borrowing in American Sign Language.* Silver Spring, MD: Linstok Press.

Birch-Rasmussen, S. (1982). *Mundhåndsystemet.* Copenhagen, Denmark: Døves Center for Total Kommunikation.

Bergman, B., & Wallin, L. (1998). *The discourse function of noun classifiers in Swedish Sign Language.* Paper presented at the Sixth International Conference on the Theoretical Issues in Sign Language Research, Washington, DC.

Bienvenu, M. J., & Colonomos, B. (1987). *Introduction to American deaf culture, Vol 2: Values,* Burtonsville, MD: Sign Media Inc.

Bonet, J. P. (1620). *Reduction de las letras y arte para enseñar a hablar los mudos* (2 vols.). Madrid: Francisco Beltran.

Brentari, D. (1988). Backwards verbs in ASL: Agreement Re-opened. In D. Brentari, G. Larson, & L. MacLeod, (Eds.), *Proceedings from the 24th Annual Meeting of the Chicago Linguistic Society, vol. 2: Parasession on Agreement in Grammatical Theory* (pp. 16–27). Chicago: Chicago Linguistic Society.

Brentari, D. (1990a). *Theoretical foundations of American Sign Language phonology.* University of Chicago dissertation. University of Chicago Occasional Papers in Linguistics.

Brentari, D. (1990b). Licensing in ASL handshape. In C. Lucas (Ed.), *Sign language research: Theoretical issues* (pp. 57–68). Washington, DC: Gallaudet University Press.

Brentari, D. (1990c). Underspecification in American Sign Language phonology. In K. Hall, J-P. Koenig, M. Meacham, S. Reiman, & L.A. Sutton (Eds.), *Proceedings from the 16th annual meeting of the Berkeley Linguistics Society* (pp. 46–56). Berkeley: Berkeley Linguistics Society.

Brentari, D. (1994). Prosodic constraints in American Sign Language. In S. Gahl, A. Dolby, & C. Johnson (Eds.) *Proceedings from the 20th annual meeting of the Berkeley Linguistics Society* (pp.103-112). Berkeley, CA: Berkeley Linguistics Society.

Brentari, D. (1998). *A prosodic model of sign language phonology.* Cambridge, MA:MIT Press.

Coulter, G. (1982). *On the nature of ASL as a monosyllabic language.* Paper presented at the annual meeting of the Linguistic Society of America, San Diego, California.

Crasborn, O., & van der Kooij, E. (1997). Relative orientation in sign language phonology. In J. Coerts & H. de Hoop (Eds.), *Linguistics in the Netherlands* (pp. 37–48). Amsterdam: John Benjamin's.

Ebbinghaus, H., & Hessman, J. (1996). Signs and words: Accounting for spoken language elements in German Sign Language, In W. Edmondson & R. Wilbur (Eds.), *International Review of Sign Linguistics I* (pp. 23–56). Mahwah, NJ:Lawrence Erlbaum Associates.

Fischer, S., & Gough, B. (1978). Verbs in ASL. *Sign Language Studies, 18,* 17–48.

Fok, Y. Y. A., & Bellugi, U. (1986). The acquisition of visual-spatial script. In H. Kao, G. van Galen, & R. Hoosain (Eds.), *Graphemics: Contemporary research in handwriting* (pp. 329–355). Amsterdam: North Holland Press.

Fok. Y. Y. A., Bellugi, U., van Hoek, K., & Klima, E. S. (1988). The formal properties of Chinese languages in space. In I. M. Liu, H. C. Chen, & M. J. Chen (Eds.), *Cognitive aspects of the Chinese language* (pp. 187–205). Hong Kong: Asian Research Service.

Frishberg, N., & Gough, B. (1973). *Morphology in ASL.* Unpublished manuscript. The Salk Institute, La Jolla, CA.

Goldin-Meadow, S., & Mylander, C. (1985). Gestural communication in deaf children: The effects and noneffects of parental input on early language development. *Science, 221,* 372–374.

Greftegref, I. (1993). *Distinctive features in NTS [Norwegian Sign Language] handshapes.* Paper presented at the Workshop on Sign Language phonology and morphology, Amsterdam and Leiden.

Gustason, G., Petzfing, D., & Zawolkow, E. (1975). *Signing exact English.* Los Alamitos, CA: Modern Signs Press.

Hirsh-Pasek, K. (1981). *Phonics without sound: Reading acquisition in the congenitally deaf.* Unpublished doctoral dissertation, University of Pennsylvania.

Hotchkiss, J. (1913). *Memories of old Hartford* (film). Silver Spring, MD: National Association of the Deaf.

Itô, J., & Mester, A. (1995a). Japanese phonology. In J. Goldsmith (Ed.), *A handbook of phonological theory* (pp. 817–838). Oxford: Basil Blackwell.

Itô, J., & Mester, A. (1995b). The core–periphery structure of the lexicon and constraints on reranking. In J. Beckman et al. (Eds.), *University of Massachusetts Occasional Papers 18: Papers in Optimality Theory* (pp. 181–210). University of Massachusetts, Amherst: Graduate Linguistic Student Association.

Johnson, R. E. (1994). *Handshape features in American language.* Unpublished manuscript. Gallaudet University, Washington, DC.

Kendon, A. (1988). *Sign languages of Aboriginal Australia: Cultural, semiotic, and communicative perspectives.* New York: Cambridge University Press.

Klima, E., & Bellugi, U. (1979). *Signs of language.* Cambridge, MA: Harvard University Press.

Lane, H. (1984). *When the mind hears.* New York: Random House.

Lucas, C., & Valli, C. (1992). *Language contact in the American Deaf community.* New York: Academic Press.

Mandel, M. A. (1981). *Phonotactics and morphophonology in American Sign Language.* Unpublished doctoral dissertation, University of California, Berkeley.

McNeill, D. (1992). *Hand and mind: What gestures reveal about thought;* Chicago: University of Chicago Press.

Padden, C. (1988). *Interaction of morphology and syntax in American Sign Language.* New York: Garland Press.

Padden, C. (1990). Folk explanation in language survival. In D. Middleton & D. Edwards (Eds.), *Collective remembering* (pp. 190–202). Los Angeles: Sage.

Padden, C. (1991). The acquisition of fingerspelling by deaf children. In P. Siple & S. Fischer (Eds.), *Theoretical issues in sign language research: Psychology* (pp. 191–210). Chicago: University of Chicago Press.

Padden, C. (1998). The ASL lexicon. *Sign Language and Linguistics, 1,* 39–60.

Padden, C., & Perlmutter, D. (1987). American Sign Language and the architecture of phonological theory. *Natural Language and Linguistic Theory, 5,* 335–375.

Perlmutter, D. (1992). Sonority and syllable structure in American Sign Language. *Linguistic Inquiry, 23,* 407–442.

Perlmutter, D. (1993). *Handshape, syllables and syllabification in American Sign Language.* Unpublished manuscript, University of California, San Diego.

Prince, A., & Smolensky, P. (1993). *Optimality theory.* Technical Report #2 of the Rutgers Center for Cognitive Science, Rutgers, NJ.

Ramsey, C., & Padden, C. (1998). Natives and newcomers: Gaining access to literacy in a classroom for deaf children. *Anthropology & Education Quarterly, 29,* 5–24.

Sandler, W. (1989). *Phonological representation of the sign.* Dordrecht: Foris.

Schermer, T. (1990). *In search of a language: Influences from spoken Dutch on Sign Language of the Netherlands.* Delft: Eburon.

Singleton, J., Morford, J., & Goldin-Meadow, S. (1993). Once is not enough: Standards of well-formedness in manual communication created over three different time spans. *Language, 69,* 683–715.

Stevens, K., Jay Keyser, S., & Kawasaki, H. (1986). Toward a phonetic and phonological theory of redundant features. In J. Perkell & D. Klatt (Eds.), *Invariance and variability in speech processes* (pp. 426–449). Hillsdale, NJ: Lawrence Erlbaum Associates.

Stevens, K., & Jay Keyser, S. (1989). Primary features and their enhancement in consonants. *Language, 65,* 81–106.

Supalla, S. (1992). *The book of name signs.* San Diego, CA: Dawn Sign Press.

Supalla, T. (1982). *Structure and acquisition of verbs of motion and location in American Sign Language.* Unpublished doctoral dissertation, University of California, San Diego.

Supalla, T. (1985). The classifier system in American Sign Language. In C. Colette (Ed.), *Noun classification and categorization* (pp. 181–214). Philadelphia: Benjamin's.

Supalla, T., & Newport, E. (1978). How many seats in a chair? The derivation of nouns and verbs in American Sign Language. In P. Siple (Ed.), *Understanding language through sign language research* (pp. 91–132). New York: Academic Press.

Sutton-Spence, R., & Woll, B. (1993). The status and functional role of fingerspelling in British Sign Language. In M. Marschark & M. Clark (Eds.), *Psychological perspectives on deafness* (pp. 185–208). Hillsdale, NJ: Lawrence Erlbaum Associates.

Valli, C., & Lucas, C. (1992). *Linguistics of American Sign Language: An introduction.* Washington, DC: Gallaudet University Press.

van der Hulst, H. (1995). The composition of handshapes. *Working Papers in Linguistics,* 1–18. Dragvoll, Norway: University of Trondheim.

Veditz, G. (1913). *The preservation of the sign language* (film). Silver Spring, MD: National Association of the Deaf.

Vogt-Svenson, M. (1984). Wordpictures in Norwegian Sign language. In *Working Papers in Linguistics.* Trondheim:University of Trondheim.

Wilcox, S. (1992). *The phonetics of fingerspelling.* Philadelphia: Benjamin's.

4

Typological and Modality Constraints on Borrowing: Examples From the Sign Language of the Netherlands

Nini Hoiting and Dan I. Slobin

ABSTRACT

Sign Language of the Netherlands (SLN) has borrowed verb particles from Dutch and assimilated them to sign language grammar, using them as semi-auxiliaries in serial verb constructions. Two case studies are examined. The verb particle *door* ('through') is used in SLN as an aspectual marker in combination with verbs that are phonologically blocked from aspectual modulation. The verb particle *op* ('act-on') is used in SLN as an agent-patient marker in combination with verbs that are phonologically blocked from agreement. In both instances, the borrowed item is inflected as an SLN verb (for aspect in the first case, agreement in the second), and is used in combination with lexical verbs that cannot be so inflected. The borrowed items are used as grammatical elements that are consistent with the verb-framed and serial-verb typology of SLN. They do not have the full meanings of the original Dutch elements, but express only those dimensions (temporal or casemarking) that are consistent with the structural demands of SLN. They do not function as full verbs in SLN, but as sorts of auxiliaries. It is proposed that such cases of borrowing are influenced by two major factors: the comparative typology of languages (verb-framed SLN vs. satellite-framed Dutch) and the modalities (visual-manual vs. acoustic). The analysis has consequences for bilingual language acquisition and instruction, as well as the syntactic typology of sign languages.

BACKGROUND: THE HISTORICAL
AND PEDAGOGICAL CONTEXT

The history of SLN begins in 1785, when Henri Daniel Guyot returned to Holland from Paris, bringing the insights of Abbé l'Epée. Along with other European pioneers, Guyot followed l'Epée's advice to build on what we would now call local "homesign" systems, adding structural concepts developed for French Sign Language. By 1790 he had established a school in Groningen (now in Haren) with about a half dozen deaf children. As far as can be ascertained, Guyot's method was eclectic, using sign-supported Dutch to aid literacy, while also allowing for the elaboration of existing systems of gestural communication used by the deaf. The Groningen school was notable in its early employment of deaf teachers.

In the middle of the 19th century, oralism took over. In 1864 the school in Groningen officially designated oralism as the only method of instruction, and after the Milan Convention of 1880 this philosophy dominated in the Netherlands for 100 years. However, documentation suggests that teachers continued to use some sign-supported Dutch throughout the period. There were four schools for the Deaf in the 19th century, each of them providing a nucleus for a Deaf community that must have continued to elaborate a natural sign language—that is, what is currently referred to as SLN. The first Deaf communities in the Netherlands were formed around the schools, and until the rise of oralism, the schools and the communities formed a single entity. However, when the educational establishment turned its back on the use of sign language, independent Deaf associations arose outside of the schools. The first formal Deaf Association was founded in Amsterdam in 1878, and other cities followed. Thus SLN continued as an active language until its formal reacceptance in recent years.

These facts, along with the absence of detailed records of the use and structure of SLN and sign-supported Dutch, make it impossible to determine the historical and sociolinguistic circumstances of Dutch influence on modern SLN.[1] Consequently, in searching for the roots of borrowing from Dutch into SLN, we can only analyze the role of Dutch as reflected in modern SLN. In attempting to reconstruct the situations in which Dutch elements entered SLN, a number of factors must have played a role. We

---

[1]Historical details of the development of SLN (NGT= Nederlands Gebaren Taal 'Netherlands Sign Language') can be found in Hoiting (1981); for a history of deaf education in the Netherlands, see Hoiting, Menke, & Kuik (1990). Tervoort (1953) was the first to document the visual communicative system of deaf children in the Netherlands.

know that fingerspelled Dutch was in use from the beginning of Guyot's school. And, of course, many deaf pupils became literate in Dutch, thereby providing possibilities of borrowing through their own bilingualism. In addition, schools for the Deaf have always included pupils who were deafened after having acquired the spoken language. It should also be noted that until the middle of the 20th century, deaf and hard-of-hearing children attended the same schools. It is also evident that teachers must have introduced various elements of Dutch grammar and lexicon into their ad-hoc instruction using some kinds of gestural communication. The use of various kinds of manually coded Dutch (sign systems) played a role both in introducing Dutch into the manual modality, and in giving rise to contact languages such as those described for ASL and English by Lucas and Valli (1992). All of these avenues were open for the movement of Dutch into SLN, although we cannot document the point-of-entry of any specific element.

In this chapter, we examine two instances of obvious borrowing from Dutch into SLN, indicating ways in which the linguistic system of SLN has assimilated Dutch grammatical elements into its own structural design. Our claim is that verb particles from a spoken language such as Dutch come to serve as semi-auxiliary verbs in a signed language, due to two types of factors: **typological**—the lexicalization pattern typical of signed languages, and **psycholinguistic**—the nature of the manual-visual modality.

TYPOLOGICAL CONSIDERATIONS

We refer to SLN as the **borrowing language** and Dutch as the **source language** (following Moravcsik, 1978). In most instances of borrowing discussed in the literature, emphasis is placed on the influences of the source language on the borrowing language. For example, in Weinreich's (1963) seminal work on "languages in contact" the emphasis is on "the rearrangement of patterns that result from the introduction of foreign elements into the more highly structured domains of language" (p. 1). Moravcsik (1978) defined borrowing as "a process whereby a language acquires some structural property from another language" (p. 99). However, here we wish to focus on ways in which grammatical material from the source language is **adapted** to the typological tendencies of the borrowing language. Rather than making SLN Dutch-like in its grammar, these borrowings take Dutch grammatical morphemes and make them

SLN-like. Therefore we take Thomason and Kaufman's (1988) more neutral definition of borrowing, referring only to "the incorporation of foreign elements into the speaker's native language" (p. 21). However, the sort of "incorporation" analyzed by Thomason and Kaufman involves **accommodation** to the source language—what they refer to as "contact-induced language change" or "interference." By contrast, the instances of incorporation examined here involve **assimilation** of the borrowed elements to the structural tendencies of the borrowing language.[2]

A major determinant of assimilation is the typological contrast between the two languages involved. Dutch and SLN can be characterized as typological opposites in terms of Talmy's (1991) distinction between **satellite-framed** and **verb-framed** languages. Talmy proposed that the languages of the world fall into two types, on the basis of their lexicalization patterns. Here we focus on linguistic expressions in the domains of space and time. Dutch, like all Germanic languages, uses a set of verb particles, or satellites, to express "core notions" of events such as movement in space and time. Satellite-framed lexicalization patterns can be easily demonstrated using English examples:

(1) Satellite-framed language characteristics (e.g., English)
a.   The man went **in** (to the house).
b.   The man went **on** (talking).

By contrast, the Romance languages are verb-framed and use verbs to express such notions, as in Spanish parallels to (1a) and (1b):

(2) Verb-framed language characteristics (e.g., Spanish)
a.   *El hombre **entró** (a la casa).*
     'The man **entered** (the house).'
b.   *El hombre **siguió** (hablando).*
     'The man **continued** (talking).'

---

[2]The cases presented here seem to be relatively rare in the literature on sign language, though we suspect that many more instances of assimilation can be found (see, e.g., Lucas & Valli, 1992, p. 11). The usual assumption, however, is that the influence of the spoken language will lead to accommodation by the signed language to the spoken language. For example, Fischer (1975) proposed:

> When two languages come into contact, there is bound to be an influence in at least one direction, apparently in general from the **more** to the **less** prestigious language. This is a form of linguistic imperialism, really, where the more powerful wins out. English and ASL are two such languages." (p. 11).

Although these "political" factors cannot be denied, the modality of sign language may be a more resilient factor than previously acknowledged.

Slobin and Hoiting (1994) have argued that SLN—and probably all signed languages—are verb framed in their typology.[3] Consider, for example, verbs of movement. The manual modality allows for movement of a gesture in space, which is a natural symbol for movement on the referential plane. Thus a signed language has no need for satellite morphemes such as 'in,' 'across,' 'towards,' 'through,' and the like, because the hand can represent direction by movement, in relation to the establishment of referent locations in signing space. That is, rather than verb–satellite constructions such as 'go in' or 'go towards,' signed languages use directional verbs such as 'enter' and 'approach.' Further, when **manner** of motion is encoded, the two language types have different options. Satellite-framed languages use constructions in which the main verb is a manner-of-motion verb and the satellite encodes direction, such as 'run in' or 'swim towards.' Verb-framed constructions place the manner verb in a subordinate form, such as 'enter running' or in a serial-verb construction, such as 'run enter.' Slobin and Hoiting proposed that signed languages are of the latter type, examining references to movement in SLN and in ASL. (For other discussions of signed languages as serial—verb languages see, for example, Bos, 1994, 1996; Gee & Kegl, 1983; T. Supalla, 1990.) These typological patterns have consequences for the ways in which a language of one type makes use of elements borrowed from a language of another type. As illustration, we offer two examples of the selective use of Dutch verb particles in SLN.

CASE STUDY 1: BORROWING
OF THE DUTCH PARTICLE *DOOR*

In Dutch, as in English, a collection of verb particles, or satellites, function to mark various locative and temporal notions in conjunction with a wide range of main verbs. As a case study, we take the Dutch particle *door*, closely related to the English particle 'through.' As in English, such forms can function as both verb particles (satellites) and prepositions. For example:

---

[3]Most Indo-European languages, with the exception of the Romance languages, are satellite-framed, along with Finno-Ugric and a number of Amerindian languages; verb-framed languages include Romance, Semitic, Turkic, and Bantu languages, along with Korean, Japanese, and others. Serial-verb languages like Chinese and Vietnamese appear to lie between the two types, depending on one's analysis (Slobin & Hoiting, 1994; Talmy, 1991).

(3) Prepositional and verb particle use of door

a.   Locative preposition:
     *Hij reed **door** het park.*
     'He rode through the park.'
b.   Locative satellite:
     *Hij reed **erdoor**.*
     he rode CLITIC-through
     'He rode through (there).'[4]

(4) Temporal/aspectual uses of door

a.   as a postposition
     *Hij werkte de nacht **door**.*
     he worked the night through
     'He worked through the night.'
b.   as a separate verb particle
     *Hij werkte **door**.*
     he worked through
     'He worked on through/kept on working.'

Temporal and aspectual uses are widespread, as in (4). The temporal meaning of *door* is a metaphorical extension of its locative sense of continued forward movement. In its purely temporal use, *door* can be associated with a general verb such as *gaan* ('go'), *maken* ('do/make'), or *laten* ('let') to indicate continuity of a presupposed or established process in discourse, such as the examples in (5):

(5) Temporal/aspectual uses of door *with general verbs*

a.   *Hij ging **door**.*
     he went through
     'He kept on, persisted, continued (doing something).'
b.   *Zij maakte veel **door**.*
     she made much through
     'She went through a lot (of trouble).'

Native users of SLN have undoubtedly been exposed to all of these uses of *door*, both through written Dutch and through the attempts of teachers

---

[4]English satellites can stand alone, without their nominal complements, for example,' 'He rode through'; 'ran in'; 'swam past'. Dutch equivalents require the use of clitic *-er* as a placeholder, as in (3).

to use some form of sign-supported Dutch. It is striking, therefore, that only some of these uses have entered into SLN.[5]

Both the locative and temporal uses are found in Signed Dutch (NmG = Nederlands met Gebaren 'Dutch with Signs'). The form of the sign is a static B-handshape facing the body, crossed by a dynamic B-handshape moving away from the body. Morpheme-by-morpheme equivalents of examples (3), (4), and (5) occur in Signed Dutch; however locative uses such as shown in (3) are not used at all in SLN. Thus we must ask why it is only the temporal uses of *door* that have been borrowed by the natural sign language, although both locative and temporal uses are modeled in the written and signed versions of the spoken language.

The answer is to be sought in terms of the manual-visual modality. Natural sign languages are endowed with an effective means of referring to spatial movement, as noted previously. Sentences like (3a), 'He rode through (the park),' are signed by means of a verb of motion, with a handshape vehicle classifier moving across a 'park' that has been located in signing space. There is no motivation for borrowing a locative term from Dutch to encode the path of motion. Rather, the verb-framed typology of SLN is completely adequate to the task, using native means. The use of the crossed B-handshape sign in such contexts is seen as a redundant and non-native importation from Signed Dutch.

On first consideration, it would seem that SLN would also have no need for the **temporal** senses of *door*. The language provides several types of cyclic repetition to indicate verbal aspect, similar to those described for ASL by Klima and Bellugi (1979, pp. 247–271) and Anderson (1982).[6] For example, the verb TELEPHONE[7] is signed by a Y-handshape held near the ear. Continuative Aspect is marked by three repetitions of an elliptical modulation accompanied by pursed lips and a slight blowing gesture. Habitual Aspect, by contrast, uses a slower elliptical modulation accompanied by gaze aversion, lax lips with protruding tongue, and slowly circling head movement. It appears, however, that a portion of the SLN verb lexicon is not amenable to this sort of aspectual modulation, due to phonological constraints: if a sign has internal movement, it is not possible to superimpose an elliptical movement over the

---

[5]The findings are based on data provided by several native signers of SLN in the northern provinces of The Netherlands (Groningen, Friesland, Drenthe, Overijssel).

[6]To our knowledge, there are no written analyses of aspect in SLN. However, work with SLN informants makes it clear that the sorts of aspectual modulations discussed in this chapter are part of the grammar of the language.

[7]Lexical items in capital letters are glosses of SLN items.

inherent movement of the sign; if a sign includes body contact, elliptical movement is also blocked. It is precisely in such instances—and only such instances—that SLN borrows *door* as an aspectual particle. That is, a lexical element is borrowed to perform a function that is already present in the language, but that cannot be inflectionally expressed on all verbs.

Taking the verb WORK as an example of the first type, the source language models are as shown in (6). However, SLN users do not simply sign the equivalent of *door* in such constructions. Rather, the crossed B-hand-shape sign, or THROUGH, is itself treated as a sort of verb, in consonance with the verb-framed typology of SLN. The evidence for this claim is the fact that THROUGH receives the same aspectual modulations as a verb such as TELEPHONE in the example discussed previously. The verb WORK is an example of the first proposed phonological constraint: it consists of parallel opening and closing of two flat O-handshapes (downward palm orientation and forward finger orientation).

(6) *Dutch models for analogous SLN sentences*
  a. CONTINUATIVE:
      Hij werkt door.
      he works through
      'He's going on working (at the moment).'
  b. HABITUAL:
      Hij werkt altijd door.
      he works always through
      'He always works on and on.'

The continuative sense of (6a) and the habitual sense of (6b) are differentiated by the same combination of elliptical movements and nonmanual features described previously, that is, elliptical modulation accompanied by pursed lips and a slight blowing gesture for Continuative Aspect, and slower elliptical modulation accompanied by gaze aversion, lax lips with protruding tongue, and slowly circulating head movement for Habitual Aspect. **However, these modulations accompany THROUGH rather than WORK.** This is presumably because of the phonological constraint proposed previously. Thus, although the borrowed element serves as a satellite in the source language, it is treated as a sort of verb in the borrowing language. The result seems to be a serial-verb construction with an uninflected main verb, WORK, and a sort of "semi-auxiliary," THROUGH, which is inflected for aspect.

Similar examples can be found regarding the second phonological constraint, that of body contact. For example, the verb TRY is signed with the fingertips of an H-handshape touching the side of the nose—again, an articulation that doesn't allow elliptical movement. Similar to the previous example, the sequence TRY THROUGH + "aspectual modulation" is used for habitual meaning.

We use the designation "semi-auxiliary" because THROUGH does not have all of the characteristics of a verb.[8] It only occurs in combination with a full lexical verb and does not occur by itself. It does not show person agreement. It cannot be independently negated. The semantic function of THROUGH is limited to the expression of certain nuances of aspect. Syntactically, THROUGH is limited to the position immediately following the verb. This is further evidence for its assimilation into SLN syntax, because the position of *door* in Dutch, and of THROUGH in Signed Dutch, is determined by the finiteness of the main verb. In the source language and in its signed surrogate, particles such as *door* follow finite verbs, as in (4b), but are prefixed to nonfinite verbs. Compare (4b), reproduced as (7a), with its variants using a nonfinite participle (7b) and an infinitive (7c). In addition, in subordinate clauses in Dutch and in Signed Dutch a modal verb, such as *kan* 'can,' intervenes between the satellite and associated verb, as in (7d). In SLN, by contrast, a single sign order is maintained for all functions, as in (7e). This is because tense is indicated outside of the clause; subordination does not affect sign order, and finiteness of verb forms plays no role in SLN syntax. The use of a single syntactic position for all functions indicates the integration of the borrowed element into the syntax of the borrowing language.

(7) *Temporal/aspectual use of* door *in Dutch*
a. *door* as a separate verb particle
    *Hij werkte **door**.*
    'He worked through.'
b. *Door* with a nonfinite participle in Dutch
    *Hij heeft **door**gewerkt.*
    he has through-worked
    'He has worked through.'
c. *Door* with an infinitive in Dutch
    *Hij moet **door**werken.*
    he must through-work
    'He must work through.'

---

[8]For a discussion of "semi-auxiliaries" or "quasi-auxiliaries" see Heine (1993, pp. 13–16).

d. Modals (e.g., *kan*) can intervene between *door* and the verb in
    subordinate clauses in Dutch and Signed Dutch
    . . . *zodat hij door kan werken.*
    . . . so that he through can work
    . . .'so that he can work through.'
e. The equivalent of *door* in SLN occurs in a single word order
    WORK THROUGH
    'continue working' or 'work habitually'

There is additional evidence that THROUGH is becoming grammaticized in SLN. Although the citation form is two-handed, as described previously, in many instances forward waving of a single lax B-handshape is
sufficient to express the aspectual modulation. This seems to be the preferred form for younger SLN signers. Reduction of phonological form is a
well-known hallmark of advanced grammaticization (e.g., Hopper &
Traugott, 1993).

We have considered the possibility that THROUGH in SLN might be
a sort of repeated adverbial, rather than a verb-like element modulated for
aspect. There is no obvious criterion for choosing between these analyses,
except for the overall typological use of serial-verb constructions in SLN
and in other signed languages. (It should also be noted that treating
THROUGH as an adverbial would require the grammar to allow for
aspectual modulation of both verbs and nonverbs in similar fashion. The
consequences of such a move cannot yet be evaluated.) The second case
study, which presents quite a different sort of serial-verb phenomenon,
lends support to the analysis of THROUGH as a semi-auxiliary, because
both case studies are amenable to the same sort of syntactic analysis.

CASE STUDY 2: BORROWING
OF THE DUTCH PARTICLE *OP*

Bos (1994, 1996) has described an "auxiliary verb" in SLN that she
glosses as ACT-ON. Like THROUGH, this verb always occurs after a lexical verb (a "fixed verb" in the terminology of Bos), with the function of
indicating agent-patient relations. The sign is a 5-handshape that moves in
an arc in signing space from the referent locus of agent to that of patient.
For example (Bos, 1996, handout):

(8) Typical use of ACT-ON in SLN (Bos, 1996)
INDEX$_1$ BOYFRIEND INDEX$_{3a}$ LOVE $_{3a}$ACT-ON$_1$[9]
'My boyfriend loves me.'

Evidence of the origin of ACT-ON as a Dutch preposition is provided by the obligatory simultaneous nonmanual feature—a sudden bilabial closure evidently derived from the spoken word *op*. The apparent source language model is the following:

(9) Source language model (Dutch) for SLN use of op
*Hij is verliefd **op** mij.*
he is in love *op* me
'He is in love with me.'

This is a common pattern in Dutch for marking the patient of verb participles or adjectives of emotional state, such as *boos op* 'angry at,' *trots op* 'proud of', and *jaloers op* 'jealous of.' However, it is never used in Dutch to mark the patient of a finite verb as in the SLN example in (8) (**Hij lieft op mij* 'He loves *op* me'). Other examples, from our own data, are given in (10a)-(10b).

(10) Door *used to mark the patient of a finite verb in SLN*
a.   INDEX$_{3a}$ INDEX$_{3b}$ TEASE $_{3a}$ACT-ON$_{3b}$
     'He teases her.'
b.   INDEX$_{3a}$ INDEX$_{3b}$ ACCUSE $_{3a}$ACT-ON$_{3b}$
     'He accuses her.'

Again, the borrowing language has assimilated a grammatical particle to its own verbal system: *op* has been transmuted into a verb-like element, serving as a kind of fixed-position auxiliary in a serial-verb construction. And again, like THROUGH, ACT-ON is an inflected auxiliary—in this instance marking the case-roles of the nouns associated with the main verb. That is, by moving from the referential locus of the agent to that of the patient, ACT-ON indicates the semantic relation between these two loci. Again, the borrowed element is used when a phonological constraint blocks the normal SLN marking of semantic relations by means of moving the verb from one referential locus to another. For example, the verb

---

[9]"INDEX" refers to points in signing space; 1 first person, 2 second person, 3 third person, with appended lowercase letters indicating "referential loci" (Engberg-Pedersen, 1993) in signing space. Words in uppercase letters refer to lexical signs.

LOVE (8) is articulated with body contact on the chest; TEASE (10a), and ACCUSE (10b) have handshapes that cannot be freely directed to all loci (e.g., the citation form points away from the body). By contrast, a sign like CRITICIZE (11) does not require the ACT-ON auxiliary, because it is formed by a hooked index finger that can freely move from one locus to another in any direction:

(11) *An example of an SLN verb which incorporates the verb agreement loci on the verb; it does not use ACT-ON*
$_{3a}$ CRITICIZE $_{3b}$
'He criticizes her.'

The **semantic** dimensions of ACT-ON also reveal interesting patterns of borrowing. Note, first of all, that the source language model uses *op* in constructions referring to emotional **states**: in love, angry, jealous, and proud. The borrowing language applies the form to the **processes** that bring about emotional states: to love, to tease, or to accuse. This realignment allows the borrowed form to function as an auxiliary verb rather than a stative marker. In addition, the sign that functions as an auxiliary in these constructions, ACT-ON plus mouthing derived from *op,* also serves as a main verb meaning 'put a flat object on a surface.' Verbs of object manipulation are common sources of patient markers in a wide variety of spoken languages, as discussed in the literature on **grammaticalization** or **grammaticization** (see, for example, Lord, 1993). A verb like 'put on' is a conceptually available form for the marking of agent-patient relations, in that it moves from a source to a goal location while transferring an object. Such a verb can be readily construed as affecting not only the location, but also the state of the patient. Metaphorically, a state like love or anger can be 'put onto' someone else. Thus issues of metaphor (e.g., Lakoff, 1987) interact with patterns of syntax and lexicalization in accounting for the odyssey of lexical elements from a source to a borrowing language.

When spoken languages use verbs of object manipulation to express transitivity, such verbs often evolve into case markers on nouns (e.g., Li & Thompson, 1976; Lord, 1993). However, it is doubtful whether a sign such as ACT-ON could ever become a noun marker, because—in its very nature—it **moves** between two index points in space. There is also no obvious way in which it could develop into a marker on another verb, such as the case-role verbal morphemes in head-marking languages (Nichols, 1986). In such languages (e.g., Navajo, Abkhaz) verbal morphemes indicate, for example, agent–patient relations between a 3SING and a 1SING participant, or between 1SING and 2SING, and so forth. Although such elements can readily be affixed to a **spoken** verb, there is no obvious way in a signed language in which a sign such as ACT-ON can become part of another verb sign. The manual–visual modality makes it most natural to maintain serial-verb constructions, rather than to reduce semi-auxiliary verbs to either noun or verb markers. We would argue, therefore, that linguistic typology is, to some extent, dependent on the modality of the channel (manual or vocal).

CONCLUSIONS

The fate of borrowed elements provides useful clues to the underlying linguistic nature of the borrowing language. This point was made by Battison (1978) in his pioneering work, *Lexical Borrowing in American Sign Language*. In his study of fingerspelled English words in ASL he proposed that "restructuring fingerspelled words makes them 'look and act like' native ASL signs, and this therefore constitutes one promising indicator of the salient structural characteristics of the ASL native lexicon" (p. 102). Similarly, Lucas and Valli (1992) noted that although ASL borrowed English prepositions such as IN, ON, and BEHIND, they are not used in their locative meanings, but only for "extended" meanings, such as MONEY BEHIND to refer to savings. They concluded—as we have as well: "What's interesting in the ASL case is that it appears that signs were invented expressly for English prepositions with prepositional function and are either not used as such or have acquired other functions"(p. 11). To use Battison's term, our two small case studies attempt to show that restructuring Dutch grammatical morphemes makes them "look and act like" native SLN auxiliary verbs, thereby indicating the salient structural characteristics of the lexical patterns of SLN. The two case studies show SLN to be a verb-framed language of the serial-verb type, with strong tendencies to use movement modulations of signs to encode both aspect and agent–patient relations. The confrontation of the two types of language, Dutch and SLN, exists not only on the plane of linguistic typology, but also on the plane of modality. The deep-seated use of movement for the expression of both temporal and semantic relations in a signed language such as SLN makes it natural to assimilate borrowed grammatical morphemes from Dutch to patterns of verbal modulation. Thus both a verb particle such as *door* and a relational particle such as *op* are re-formed in

SLN to function as auxiliary verbs. As in all phenomena of language change, the resulting patterns are codetermined by features of syntactic and lexical patterns, in conjunction with semantic patterns—and, in this instance, features of modality as well.

Numerous spoken languages also use serial-verb constructions of the sort found in SLN and ASL (see, e.g., Givón, 1975; Lord, 1993; McWhorter, 1992). However, it is relatively rare for a semi-auxiliary in such a construction to contribute additional meaning by means of inflection, such as the aspectual information marked on THROUGH or the case-role relations marked on ACT-ON. That is, serial-verb languages tend to be analytic rather than synthetic, relying on word combination and word order rather grammatical inflection as a basic organizing principle. The manual channel, however, makes it possible to superimpose information by simultaneous combinations of handshape, movement, and nonmanual features. Therefore **inflected serial verbs** should not be unusual in signed languages.

The role of modality in our case studies is nicely highlighted in comparison with the nature of borrowing in Creole languages (John McWhorter, personal communication, January 1997). Case Study 1 is not unusual in the contact situations that lead to the development of Creoles. That is, verb particles and prepositions can be borrowed from a satellite-framed donor language and come to serve as auxiliary verbs in serial-verb constructions to express temporal notions. It is relevant to our argument, however, that such elements can also be borrowed by Creole languages to express **locative** notions. We suggest that this is because there is no way of depicting locations in space using the vocal channel; therefore the same type of linguistic construction is used for both temporal and spatial expression. In signed languages, by contrast, we suggest that such elements will be borrowed **only** for temporal expression.

Case Study 2, by contrast, is rather different. This sort of borrowing is apparently not attested in Creole languages. The use of an auxiliary verb to indicate case-role relations in a serial-verb construction may be special to sign language borrowing situations such as the one examined here. We believe that this is due to the manual–visual modality, which easily allows for the expression of case–role relations by the use of movement in space between referential loci. Creole languages use word order for agent–patient relations. In a signed language, however, pronominal referents are indicated by indexed locations rather than by lexical items. In connected discourse, most references to participants are pronominal, and therefore relations between participants are indicated by verb signs that move from one participant to another. When the relation is not encoded by a sign that moves in space (that is a sign that "inflects for agreement"), an agent-patient auxiliary such as ACT-ON provides the necessary information, in combination with a content verb. Again, the assimilation of a borrowed element is codetermined by the typology and the modality of the borrowing language—and these two factors are, themselves, interdependent.[10]

As a final note, we suggest that these two case studies have implications for bilingual language acquisition by deaf children. The contrast between the two natural languages in our study—Dutch and SLN—highlights the artificiality of the hybrid language, Signed Dutch. Although easy to use by Dutch speakers, it is dismissed as a "nonlanguage" by users of SLN. It fits neither the basic typology nor modality constraints of a signed language, though it is presented on the hands. As we have seen, elements of Signed Dutch are assimilated into SLN structure, suggesting that the hybrid language cannot be maintained for natural communication. In this regard, it should be noted that studies of the acquisition and use of various types of "manually coded English" by deaf children show that these systems, as well, are assimilated to the patterns of natural signed languages (e.g., Davidson, Newport, & Supalla, 1996; Stack, 1996; S. Supalla, 1991). Regarding our two case studies, it is striking that deaf children acquiring such artificial sign systems introduce inflections for aspect and case ("agreement") such as those discussed here.

However, even if the instruction of deaf children is limited to two natural languages, SLN and Dutch, the consequences for pedagogy are serious. The deaf child born into a country speaking a satellite-framed language—when given the opportunity to acquire a verb-framed sign

---

[10]Smith (1990) has reported evidence for several auxiliaries in Taiwan Sign Language. Although these forms are apparently grammaticizations of existing signs, rather than borrowings, they are consistent with the syntactic, serial–verb account offered here for SLN borrowings. What Smith calls AUX-1 parallels the use of ACT-ON to mark agent–patient relations in SLN. The form is a rapid and smooth concatenation of an indexed point, moving from subject to object locus. It is probably derived from pronouns, but has been grammaticized into a single transitional movement. As in SLN, this auxiliary is only used with verbs that do not, themselves, mark agreement by movement from one locus to another; that is, the auxiliary provides the agreement. The list of verbs is quite similar to those marked by ACT-ON in SLN: THINK, COMMEMORATE, SUSPECT, WANT, TOLERATE, LISTEN-TO, FEAR, DRAW, RESIST, LOVE. Smith (1990) stated: "The sole function of AUX-1 appears to be to carry subject and object agreement information. It can be used with virtually any verb, but it tends to be used more frequently with nonagreement verbs that do not inflect to convey the person agreement of their subjects and objects. The use of AUX-1 in conjunction with main verbs that are themselves marked for subject and object agreement is regarded by most signers as tiring and redundant. One signer commented that such sentences are more frequently produced by younger schoolchildren or by less sophisticated signers. These reactions suggest that when an auxiliary is present, it is ungrammatical to also mark subject or object agreement on the main verb."

language—is faced with the task of mastering two typologically distinct languages (Hoiting & Slobin, 1993). This task can be made easier if teachers and curriculum designers are aware of the differences between the two types of languages and help the learner to become bilingual. Typologically based analysis of borrowing can hopefully contribute to this end.

REFERENCES

Anderson, L. (1982). Universals of aspect and parts of speech: Parallels between signed and spoken languages. In P. J. Hopper (Ed.), *Tense aspect: Between semantics and pragmatics* (pp. 91–110). Amsterdam/Philadelphia: John Benjamins.

Battison, R. (1978). *Lexical borrowing in American Sign Language*. Silver Spring, MD: Linstok Press.

Bos, H. F. (1994). An auxiliary verb in Sign Language of the Netherlands. In I. Ahlgren, B. Bergman, & M. Brennan (Eds.), *Perspectives on sign language structure* (pp. 37–53). Durham, England: International Sign Linguistics Association.

Bos, H. (1996, September). *Serial verb constructions in Sign Language of the Netherlands (SLN)*. Paper presented at the Fifth International Conference on Theoretical Issues in Sign Language Research, Montreal.

Davidson, M., Newport, E. L., & Supalla, S. (1996, September). *The acquisition of natural and unnatural linguistic devices: Aspect and number marking in MCE children*. Paper presented at the Fifth International Conference on Theoretical Issues in Sign Language Research, Montreal.

Engberg-Pedersen, E. (1993). *Space in Danish Sign Language*. Hamburg: Signum.

Fischer, S. (1975). Influences on word order change in American Sign Language. In C. N. Li (Ed.), *Word order and word order change* (pp. 1–26). Austin/London: University of Texas Press.

Gee, J., & Kegl, J. (1983). *ASL structure: Towards the foundation of a theory of case*. Paper presented at the Boston University Annual Conference on Language Development.

Givón, T. (1975). Serial verbs and syntactic change: Niger-Congo. In C. N. Li (Ed.), *Word order and word order change* (pp. 47–111). Austin/London: University of Texas Press.

Heine, B. (1993). *Auxiliaries: Cognitive forces and grammaticalization*. New York/Oxford: Oxford University Press.

Hoiting, N. (1981). *Guyot en 'God's Uitgestotenen'. De plaats van het Koninklijk Instituut voor Doven te Groningen in de geschiedenis van het dovenonderwijs in de 19e eeuw*. Referaat sociaal-economische geschiedenis. Rijks Universiteit Groningen. [Available from Koninklijk Instituut voor Doven "H. D. Guyot", Rijksstraatweg 63, 9752 AC Haren, The Netherlands.]

Hoiting, N., Menke, R., & Kuik, E. (1990). Notities bij 200 jaar Dovenonderwijs. *Tijdschrift voor Orthopedagogiek, 29*, 608–626.

Hoiting, N., & Slobin, D. I. (1993, July). *Reference to movement in speech and sign*. Paper presented at the Sixth International Conference of the International Association for the Study of Child Language, Trieste, Italy.

Hopper, P. J., & Traugott, E. C. (1993). *Grammaticalization*. Cambridge: Cambridge University Press.

Klima, E. S., & Bellugi, U. (1979). *The signs of language*. Cambridge, MA: Harvard University Press.

Lakoff, G. (1987). *Women, fire, and dangerous things*. Chicago: University of Chicago Press.

Li, C. N., & Thompson, S. A. (1976). Development of the causative in Mandarin Chinese: Interaction of diachronic processes in syntax. In M. Shibatani (Ed.), *The grammar of causative constructions* (pp. 477–492). New York: Academic Press.

Lucas, C., & Valli, C. (1992). *Language contact in the American deaf community.* San Diego, CA: Academic Press.

Lord, C. (1993). *Historical change in serial verb constructions.* Amsterdam/Philadelphia: John Benjamins.

McWhorter, J. H. (1992). Substratal influence in Saramaccan serial verb constructions. *Journal of Pidgin and Creole Languages, 7,* 1–53.

Moravcsik, E. (1978). Language contact. In J. H. Greenberg (Ed.), *Universals of human language: Vol. 1. Method & theory* (pp. 93–122). Stanford, CA: Stanford University Press.

Nichols, J. (1986). Head-marking and dependent-marking grammar. *Language, 62,* 56–119.

Slobin, D. I., & Hoiting, N. (1994). Reference to movement in spoken and signed languages: Typological considerations. *Proceedings of the Twentieth Annual Meeting of the Berkeley Linguistics Society,* 487–505.

Smith, W. H. (1990). Evidence for auxiliaries in Taiwan Sign Language. In S. D. Fischer & P. Siple (Eds.), *Theoretical issues in sign language research: Vol. 1. Linguistics* (pp. 211–228). Chicago/London: University of Chicago Press.

Stack, K. (1996, September). *The development of a pronominal system in the absence of a target language.* Paper presented at the Fifth International Conference on Theoretical Issues in Sign Language Research, Montreal.

Supalla, S. (1991). Manually Coded English: The modality question in signed language development. In P. Siple & S. D. Fischer (Eds.), *Theoretical issues in sign language research: Vol. 2 Psychology* (pp. 85-109). Chicago: University of Chicago Press.

Supalla, T. (1990). Serial verbs of motion in ASL. In S. D. Fischer & P. Siple (Eds.), *Theoretical issues in sign language research: Vol. 1. Linguistics* (pp. 127–152). Chicago: University of Chicago Press.

Talmy, L. (1991). Path to realization: A typology of event conflation. *Proceedings of the Seventeenth Annual Meeting of the Berkeley Linguistics Society,* 480–519. [Revised version: Talmy, L. (in press). A typology of event integration. In L. Talmy, *Towards a cognitive semantics.* Cambridge, MA: MIT Press.]

Tervoort, T. M. (1953). *Structurele analyse van visueel taalgebruik binnen een groep dove kinderen* [Structural analysis of visual language use in a group of deaf children]. Amsterdam: N.V. Noord-Hollandsche Uitgevers Maatschappij.

Thomason, S. G., & Kaufman, T. (1988). *Language contact, creolization, and genetic linguistics.* Berkeley/Los Angeles/Oxford: University of California Press.

Weinreich, U. (1963). *Languages in contact: Findings and problems.* The Hague: Mouton. [Originally published as Number 1 in the series *Publications of the Linguistic Circle of New York,* 1953.]

5

The Adaptation of Loan Words in Quebec Sign Language: Multiple Sources, Multiple Processes

Christopher Miller

ABSTRACT

Quebec Sign Language (LSQ) is closely related to ASL but shows significant lexical originality due to long-term contact with French. This chapter focuses on two types of loans in
LSQ whose properties distinguish the language from ASL. Fingerspelled loans are examined in some detail, with particular attention being paid to phonological and phonetic factors involved in their adaptation into full-fledged LSQ signs. A second, little discussed loan
type is examined, namely semantic shifts in existing LSQ signs, motivated by homonymy
relations in French. The chapter finishes with a brief discussion of oral material integrated
into LSQ signs.

THE SOURCES OF BORROWINGS IN LSQ

Quebec Sign Language (henceforth LSQ, for its French designation *Langue des signes québécoise*, in accordance with usage in the LSQ sign-ing community), though closely related to ASL, differs from it in several interesting respects, at the phonological, morphological, and lexical lev-els, and perhaps also in its syntactic behavior. Some of the differences between LSQ and ASL are most likely due to the different circumstances in which the two languages developed and, as we see in this chapter, diverged; these differences are often closely related to the spoken language with which each language has been in intimate contact during its development. Much of the originality of LSQ vocabulary, when compared with that of ASL, is due to the long-term contact LSQ has had with spoken and written French.

The first section of the article provides a background to the question of borrowings via a short overview of the historical development of LSQ and the various origins of LSQ signs. The following two sections deal in greater detail with the question of lexical influence from French. In the second section, we examine the nature of fingerspelled loans in LSQ, focussing on their distinguishing characteristics, which in many cases are different from those of similar loans from English in ASL. The third section explores a category of loans that appears to have received little attention to date in the sign language literature, namely semantic shifts motivated by homonymy relations in a contact language, in this case French. The fourth section discusses the question of borrowings in somewhat more general terms and touches briefly on the question of oral material integrated into LSQ as loans. The final section summarizes the findings presented in the chapter and discusses the question of borrowings in somewhat more general terms.

A Short History of LSQ

The first references to the origins of LSQ date back to the 1830s. In 1830, a lawyer named Ronald MacDonald was sent by the legislature of the Province of Lower Canada to the United States to learn current methods in deaf education. MacDonald spent a year at the American Asylum for the Deaf in Hartford, Connecticut, where he learned sign language at the hands of Laurent Clerc. The historical record does not tell us whether the sign language MacDonald learned was the French Sign Language (LSF) that Clerc had brought with him in 1827, or the new ASL that was at the time developing from the contact between LSF and local sign languages, homesign systems, or both. In 1834, MacDonald founded the first Canadian school for the Deaf in Quebec City; due to insufficient funds, the school closed not long after.

Over the next two decades, several other schools opened and closed, first in the town of St-Hyacinthe (between Quebec City and Montreal), then in Montreal itself. There is evidence that the signs introduced in Quebec by MacDonald were transmitted through these schools: a Deaf student

FIG. 5.1.   *The Deaf friars Jean-Marie-Joseph Jung (Young) (left) and Auguste Groc (right).*

of MacDonald, Antoine Caron, played an important role in teaching at the St-Hyacinthe school, which was later relocated to Montreal; later on, a Deaf student of Caron, Benjamin Reeves, assisted in teaching in the Montreal location. According to Lafrance (no date), Reeves "had a good knowledge of the principal signs in use in institutions in the United States," which may be taken as evidence that the sign language used by Reeves, and transmitted to the students at the school, was at least similar to the ASL of the period.

In 1855, a Deaf friar, Jean-Marie-Joseph Jung (or Young), arrived from France to teach the Deaf boys at the school, now known as the *Institution catholique des Sourds-Muets* and established in a permanent home where it was to stay for the next century. It is recorded that Young used his sign language, LSF, to teach the boys and that he also taught catechism to the girls at their recently established school. In 1866, Young was joined at the boys' school by another Deaf friar from France, Auguste Groc.

During the same period, the founders of the girls' school, the Gadbois sisters, journeyed to the Peet school in New York, where they learned ASL, and to Europe, where they may have learned elements of Belgian-French Sign Language, of BSL, or of both.

According to the admittedly sketchy information in historical sources reviewed here, it seems that the sign language used in Quebec between the 1830s and the mid-1850s was probably closely related to old ASL, if not identical. This language was subsequently exposed to strong influence from LSF during the second half of the 19th century. This double influence on LSQ has influenced the language's vocabulary in interesting ways, as we see in the next section.

Multiple Origins of LSQ Vocabulary

As might be expected from the information in the historical record, important portions of the LSQ lexicon can be traced back to ASL and to LSF. In many cases, it is not clear whether a sign came from one language or the other, but in others the origin is much clearer.[1] There are, in fact, a number of interesting cases in which synonyms from ASL and LSF have come to coexist in LSQ, with varying effects on the meaning of each member of the pair. We briefly describe some of these cases in the following section. Besides the expected influences from these two languages, there is also some linguistic evidence for borrowing from BSL. In this section we survey the areas in which these different sign languages have left their mark on LSQ and we finish with a brief discussion of borrowing from French, presaging the discussion of fingerspelled borrowings and borrowings via homonymy in French in the sections titled "Borrowings Through Fingerspelling" and "Homonym Calques from French."

    ASL.   As indicated in the beginning of this section, the major source of the vocabulary of LSQ is most likely old ASL. There are several structural reasons to believe this is the case. The fingerspelling alphabet is identical, except for superficial differences, with that of ASL. Similarly, the number system of LSQ is based not on the LSF system but on the ASL system; the numbers from zero to ten are identical and the only differences appear in the separate phonological evolution of compound numerals in the two languages.[2] The major kinship terms MOTHER, FATHER, SISTER, and BROTHER are identical with the ASL signs and unrelated to the corresponding LSF terms. The sign FAMILY and the related signs GROUP, ASSOCIATION, and SOCIETY, are identical to the ASL signs and unrelated to the LSF terms; they have given rise to neologisms initialized on French words, such as *RÉUNION*/MEETING (Fig. 5.2),

---

[1]In tracing the origins of signs, it is always important to take into account the roles of iconicity and of metaphor. Similarity or identity of form in signs from different sign languages should not be taken, *a priori,* as evidence of a linguistic relationship; the similarities may be due instead to the fortuitous or culturally conditioned choice of a particular iconic model or underlying visual metaphor. In our research on the origins of LSQ signs, we have in general restricted our attention to signs that could not easily be explained by such iconic or metaphoric considerations. For a more in-depth discussion of methodological questions, see Miller and Lelièvre (in preparation).

[2]Although the standard LSQ number system is clearly directly descended from an earlier ASL number system, there are remnants of an entirely distinct system, used in the old convent school for girls, whose roots can be traced either to LSF (Boudreault, 1996) or possibly to BSL.

FIG. 5.2.   *RÉUNION*/MEETING

FIG. 5.3.   *ÉQUIPE*/TEAM

FIG. 5.4a.   HELP

FIG. 5.4b.   HELP_{ASL}

DÉPARTEMENT/DEPARTMENT, *ÉQUIPE*/TEAM (Fig. 5.3).[3] Basic color terms, including RED, YELLOW, BLUE, BLACK, and WHITE are identical or nearly so to the corresponding ASL signs. Similarly, names of countries are, except for a handful of exceptions, the same as in ASL.

Certain other signs, including basic time terms (when they are different from LSF), are from ASL: in particular, MONTH and WEEK are clearly from ASL. The basic signs of negation (#NO, NOT, and NOTHING (3 forms)), as well as YES, appear to be from ASL rather than from LSF. Additionally, certain phonological changes occurring independently in ASL and in LSF point to a likely ASL origin for LSQ signs cognate with

---

[3]In this article, glosses are generally presented in English, for two reasons. First, the fundamental purpose of a gloss is to render, in the language of a text, the sense of a lexical item in another language. Second, the use of French glosses for LSQ signs would, in our opinion, symbolically state that LSQ is in some way uniquely and specially dependent on or subordinate to the French language, when such is not the case. In accordance with this convention, glosses otherwise not identified are to be interpreted as referring to LSQ signs; signs from another sign language are identified by a subscript, for example, ASL, appended to the gloss.

The only case in which we stray from the convention of English-only glosses is in the case of loans from French, where a dependency between the borrowing and source languages does, in fact, exist. In this case, where necessary for reasons of clarity, we also present, in italics, the French word on which the loan is based. In the case of initialized signs, we underline the letter or letters whose corresponding handshape(s) is or are retained in the initialized sign. In the case of fingerspelled loans, we reproduce the English gloss (preceded by a #), followed by the French word on which the loan is based, in italics, with the letters retained in the loan underlined.

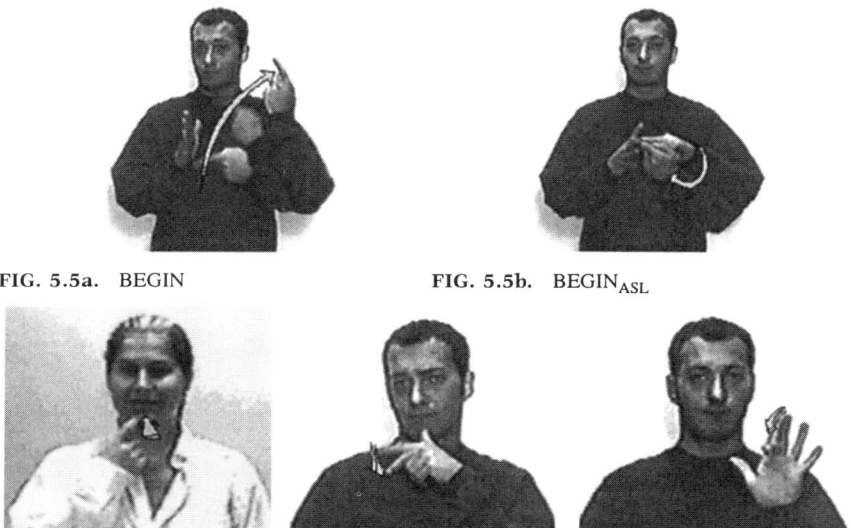

FIG. 5.5a. BEGIN   FIG. 5.5b. BEGIN_ASL

FIG. 5.6. WHO *(old form)*   FIG. 5. 7. WHO_ASL/GUY   FIG. 5.8. TWENTY-FIVE_ASL
                                                                     /TWENTY-FIVE-
                                                                     CENTS

signs in the other two languages, such as HELP and BEGIN (Figs. 5.4a, 5.4b, 5.5a, 5.5b).

In addition to the older ASL base of the vocabulary of LSQ, there exist a number of loans that appear to be of more recent vintage. Parallel to the standard sign WHO in LSQ (Fig 5.6) a phonologically changed version of an earlier ASL variant without chin contact, the modern ASL sign WHO—this time with the thumb contacting the chin—has been borrowed and, via the accompanying French mouthing *qui,* has come to be used as the name sign GUY (Fig. 5.7). Similarly, the ASL sign TWENTY-FIVE has entered LSQ with the specific sense of TWENTY-FIVE-CENTS (Fig. 5.8). Many other ASL signs are sporadically borrowed into LSQ with the same meaning as the

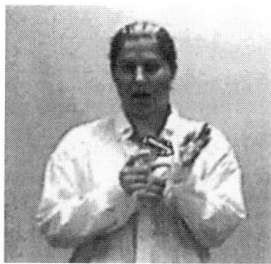

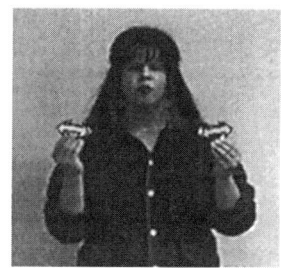

FIG. 5.9. *when*   FIG. 5.10. *where*

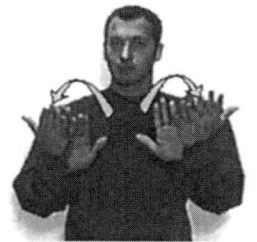

FIG. 5.11. HOW

FIG. 5.12. WORK *(verb)*

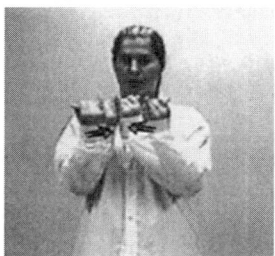

FIG. 5.13a. FIGHT <FIGHT$_{BSL}$ *(924)*

FIG. 5.13b. COLOR <COLOR$_{BSL}$ *(1172)*[4]

FIG. 5.14. WHY <WHY$_{BSL}$ *(469)*

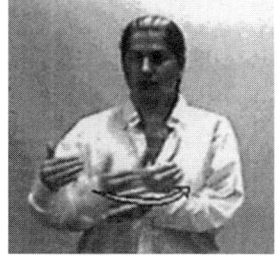

FIG. 5.15. BECAUSE <BECAUSE$_{BSL}$ *(1492)*

already existing LSQ sign: thus the fingerspelled loan #ALL or the initialized sign R̲EADY cooccur with already existing LSQ signs.

LSF. LSF, apart from LSF signs LSQ has inherited through ASL, has had an important direct influence on LSQ vocabulary. LSF provides an important number of signs, especially in the area of question words. The signs WHEN, WHERE and HOW (Figs. 5.9–5.11) are all from LSF, as may be the signs WHAT and HOW-MUCH/MANY. A number of other LSF signs coexist with originally synonymous signs from ASL. Such is the case, for example, of the LSF sign WORK (verb; Fig. 5.12a), which

---

[4]Numbers following BSL sign glosses refer to the number of the relevant sign entry in the Dictionary of British Sign Language/English (Brien, 1992).

coexists with the ASL-origin sign WORK, which is produced with the same handshape and movement, but with a different orientation.

BSL.   BSL has provided a small contribution to LSQ vocabulary, including signs such as COLOR, FIGHT (Fig. 5.13) and (possibly) WHY (Fig. 5.14) and the rarely used sign BECAUSE (Fig. 5.15). It is unclear from the historical record by what means these signs entered LSQ. Two possibilities suggest themselves: either they were borrowed through contact with the now apparently extinct, BSL-based Maritime Sign Language of the neighboring Atlantic provinces, or they may have been imported by Deaf immigrants from Britain.

BORROWINGS THROUGH FINGERSPELLING

Fingerspelling in LSQ

Whereas fingerspelling is a commonly used means of incorporating spoken language material into ASL discourse, it plays a somewhat less important role in LSQ. Fingerspelling is generally used in LSQ only to introduce names and terms unknown to interlocutors; otherwise, mouthing is the preferred strategy for introducing spoken language material into LSQ discourse. Very often, only the first letters of a word are spelled if it is clear that the interlocutor has understood the intended referent.

Changes in Form to LSQ Fingerspelled Loans

Fingerspelled loans in LSQ seem to be less numerous than in ASL and their characteristics are in general quite different from such loans in ASL. Table 5.1 presents a (non-exhaustive) list of fingerspelled loans found in LSQ.

The fingerspelled loans presented in Table 5.1 can be divided into different classes according to their surface form and characteristics. The first six signs are all derived from simple sequences of two letters, that is, either from two-letter words or from abbreviations of words. Of these, #WHERE/*OÙ* has either an oscillating, repeated closing movement or a side-to-side oscillating movement, #TV and #NO/*NON* are articulated either with a single movement or with oscillating movement, and the others have a single, unrepeated movement. Signs 7–11 are derived from words with sequences of more than two letters and are characterized by a rapid (oscillating) repetition of the first two letters or of a handshape sequence derived from the original sequence of two letters. Signs 12–17

TABLE 5.1.   *Fingerspelled Loans in LSQ*

Gr.	No.	Loan	French (or other) Source
I	1	#OK	ok (<ASL<English)
	2	#NO-GOOD/*PAS-BON*	no good (<ASL<English)
	3	#FORMER(LY)/*ANCIEN(NEMENT)*	ex (<ASL<English)
	4	#NO/*NON*	no (<ASL<English)
	5	#TV	TV
	6	#WHERE/*OÙ*	où (<LSF<French)
II	7	#COCA-COLA	coca-cola/coke
	8	#SHERBROOKE	Sherbrooke
	9	#APARTMENT/*APPARTEMENT*	appartement
	10	#WIDOW(ER)/*VEUF(VE)*	veuve/veuf
	11	#TALK-BUSINESS/*PARLER-D'AFFAIRES*	affaire(s)
		#PRIVATE/*PRIVÉ/(MES/TES)-AFFAIRES*	
III	12	#MAY/*MAI*	mai
	13	#JULY/*JUILLET*	juillet
	14	#IRD *(INSTITUT-RAYMOND-DEWAR)*	Institut Raymond Dewar
	15	#PIZZA	pizza
	16	#CLASSIFIER/*CLASSIFICATEUR*	Cl. (abbreviation)
	17	#7-UP	7-up
IV	18	#IF/*SI*	si
	19	#KING/*ROI*	roi
	20	#GREEN/VERT	vert

are derived from words or abbreviations more than two letters long but, unlike other such loans, contain sequences that do not correspond directly to the first two fingerspelled letters of the original word.[5] Signs 18–20 contain a single handshape formed by fusing features of two or more fingerspelling handshapes.

Examining the four groups of loans distinguished in the previous paragraph allows us to distinguish and examine their different phonological behaviors. In the following paragraphs, we examine each in turn to establish the reasons for the form taken by the signs in each class.

Group I Loans.   The first group of signs, #OK, #NO-GOOD, #FORMER(LY), #NO, #WHERE/*OÙ*, and #TV, all originate in two-letter words or abbreviations borrowed as such from a written language (i.e., English, except for #WHERE/*OÙ,* borrowed from the French *où*). It is a plausible hypothesis that these signs, with the obvious exception of #WHERE/*OÙ,* come to LSQ through ASL. #OK, #NO-GOOD and #NO have the same forms as the corresponding ASL signs enumerated and illustrated in Battison (1978). Battison reported only one form for this

---

[5]In the case of #CLASSIFIER, although the first two letters of the fingerspelled sequence are retained, there is an added movement that is not present in the fingerspelled sequence.

FIG. 5.16.   #TV

FIG. 5.17.   #WHERE/*OÙ (with hs change)*

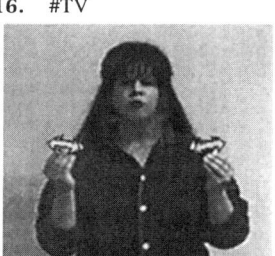

FIG. 5.18.   #WHERE/*OÙ (no hs change)*

FIG. 5.19.   #WHERE/ *OÙ (intermediate LSF form)*

sign (that he glosses #EX), in which the handshapes for -E- and -X- are both present and the forearm is in neutral rotation throughout the sign. In the LSQ version of the sign, only the -X- handshape is present and the sign moves through two orientations, pronation followed by neutral rotation. #TV is not mentioned in Battison; in all ASL sources consulted it is represented as the fingerspelled sequence T-V, executed by one hand in normal fingerspelling space. In LSQ, on the other hand, it undergoes changes in form and can be produced as a two-handed sign (Fig. 5.16).

#WHERE/*OÙ*, illustrated in two forms in (Fig. 5.17 and Fig. 5.18), is a loan from LSF, where it originated as the fingerspelled sequence O-U (French *où*). This form is attested in Lambert (1865); a partly modified form from the late 1950s, in which the orientation is changed from the forearm pronation of fingerspelling to supination (Fig. 5.19), is attested in Oléron.

Group II Loans.   The previously mentioned signs show some interesting differences with signs of the second group. As mentioned in the previous section and illustrated in Table 5.1, Group II signs are formed from the first two letters of a written word composed of several letters. In Group II signs, one or both handshapes have undergone modification. The sign #COCA-COLA (Fig. 5.20) illustrates the general characteristics of

FIG. 5.21.   #SHERBROOKE

FIG. 5.22.   #APARTMENT*(older form)*

FIG. 5.23.   #APARTMENT*(newer form)*

FIG. 5.24.   #WIDOW*(er)/veuf(ve)*

Group II signs. First, the handshape sequence is based on the first two handshapes of the fingerspelled word; second, the movement corresponding to the transition between the two handshapes is oscillated, that is, rapidly repeated.

The sign #SHERBROOKE (Fig. 5.21) shows the effect of assimilation of the selected fingers from -U-, the second handshape of the S-H sequence, onto the preceding closed S-handshape. The resulting -U§-[6] handshape probably facilitates articulation of the repeated oscillating movement.

A similar change is found in the sign #APARTMENT, which is articulated in two variants. The older of the two is the simple sequence A-P (Fig.

[6]The $\S$ in superscript position to the right of the base handshape indicates a particular thumb–finger relation in the handshape. The handshape notation system developed in the LSQ research group is an extension of variants of Stokoe notation originally developed by researchers at Berkeley in the 1970s. An innovation of the LSQ notation system is the notation of thumb–finger relations by a series of symbols in superscript position. These are as follows: " (thumb parallel to the fingers, touching the side of the first available (non-extended) finger, as in the North American manual alphabet letters -A- and -K- or the French manual alphabet -F-); ·· (thumb extended to the side); ' (thumb extended to the side); ^{c} (thumb pointing forward, no contact with fingers, as in -C-); ^{O} (thumb pointing forward, tip to tip with curved fingers, as in -O-); § (position between -O- and -S- with thumb pointing forward, covering nail of selected finger, as in twelveASL or hateASL); and ^{s} (thumb pointing forward, covering closed fingers, as in -S-).

FIG. 5.24.   #WIDOW(ER)/*VEUF*/(*VE*)

FIG. 5.25.   #TALK-BUSINESS/*PARLER-D'*
                     AFFAIRES

FIG. 5.26.   PRIVATE/*PRIVÉ*

FIG. 5.27.   NEED-*neg*

5.22). The more recent variant is a two-handed sign in which two changes have taken place (Fig. 5.23). First, the second handshape, -K-, which corresponds to the letter -P-, has changed to a -V- handshape in which both fingers are fully extended. Second, the -A- handshape of the first letter has changed to a U§-handshape, as has -S- in #SHERBROOKE.

In the sign #WIDOW(ER)/<u>*VEUF*</u>(*VE*), the selected fingers of -V- spread onto the second handshape of the sign. Instead of -E-, then, the resulting handshape is—which retains the curvature features of -E- while substituting the selected fingers of the preceding handshape /V/ (Fig. 5.24). The signs #TALK-BUSINESS/*PARLER-D'AFFAIRES* (Fig. 5.25) and #PRIVATE/*PRIVÉ/(MES/TES)-AFFAIRES* (Fig. 5.26) are particularly interesting because of the unusual handshape sequence O§-F§, which occurs only in these two signs in LSQ. Taken in the context of the general properties of handshape phonology in this and in other sign languages, this sequence is anomalous. In all other cases, a -O§- handshape opens to another handshape in which all four fingers are selected, as in NEED-neg (Fig. 5.27) or THROW. Similarly, a final F-handshape would be expected to result from the closing of an open -FC- in which the thumb and index form a -C- shape, but this is not the case in #TALK-BUSI-NESS/*PARLER-D'AFFAIRES* and #PRIVATE/*PRIVÉ*. The restrained thumb contact mode in the final handshape, in which the tip of the thumb covers the fingernail of the index finger, would normally be anomalous in final position of a handshape sequence; in this case, it can be assumed to be the result of spreading from the initial -O§- handshape. The unusual nature of the handshape sequence is a clue that the origin of this sign is in a peripheral system of LSQ grammar. Indeed, the French gloss for #TALK-BUSINESS is *#PARLER-D'AFFAIRES;* it is plausible to assume that the O§-F§ sequence is in fact derived from the initial A-F sequence of *affaires.* This hypothesis is supported by the phonological changes affecting the initial -S- and -A- handshapes in #SHERBROOKE and in #APARTMENT: the initial -U§- of these two signs would thus have the same origin as that in #TALK-BUSINESS and #PRIVATE, namely a phonological change that has the effect of easing the transition between handshapes in an oscillating movement.

The sign #PRIVATE can also be traced back to the French word *affaire.* The English expression 'my/your (etc.) business,' synonymous with the word 'private,' is mirrored by the French expression *mes/tes (etc.) affaires;* it is thus likely that this sign is borrowed indirectly from the French expression. This hypothesis is confirmed by the fact that #PRIVATE, with directional movement, can take on the meaning 'mind your own business,' or *mêle-toi de tes affaires* in French.

All of the previously mentioned signs undergo repetition (including the Group I signs #WHERE/*OÙ*, #NO/*NON,* and #TV), except for #PRIVATE. There are two possible explanations for the lack of repetition in this sign: one may be simply to distinguish it from #TALK-BUSINESS; the other may have to do with the semantics of the sign. The generalized repetition in the other signs may be related to the repetition often encountered in LSQ compound numerals and may function as a means of integrating sequences from an extraneous phonological system (i.e., fingerspelling or numeral sequences) into core LSQ phonology.

Group III Loans. Signs from the third group (#MAY/*MAI*, #JULY/*JUILLET, #INSTITUT-RAYMOND-DEWAR,* #PIZZA, #CLASSI-FIER/*CLASSIFICATEUR,* and #7-UP) show interesting differences from Group II signs. Whereas signs in the second group keep only the first two letters of the written form from which they are derived, and oscillate the transition between the two handshapes, Group III signs do not, in general, conform to these characteristics. To this extent, the properties of Group III signs resemble more closely those of ASL fingerspelling loans. These properties, different from the native LSQ loans of Group II, can be

 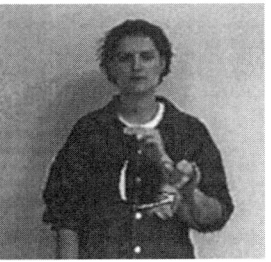 

FIG. 5.28.   #JULY/*JUILLET* FIG. 5.29.   #MAY/*MAI*   FIG. 5.30.   #PIZZA

FIG. 5.31.   #CLASSIFIER/*CLASSIFICATEUR*   FIG. 5.32.   #7-UP

explained, for the most part, by characteristics of the fingerspelled sequences on which the loans are based. The fact that the letters retained are not the first two seems to be based on necessity: for #MAY/*MAI* (Fig. 5.28) and #JULY/*JUILLET* (Fig. 5.29), the choice of -I- and -L-, respectively, as the second letter is motivated by the need to avoid confusion with other month names beginning with the same two letters (mai vs. mars (March) and juin (June) vs. juillet).

The lack of oscillation between the two handshapes retained in the sign is correlated in three of these signs with the fact that the two handshapes involved employ disjoint sets of selected fingers. In #JULY/*JUIL-LET* (Fig. 5.28) the selected pinkie finger of -I- is disjoint from the index finger of -L-, in #MAY/*MAI* (Fig. 5.29) the selected pinkie finger of -I- is disjoint from the index-middle-ring set of -M-; and in #PIZZA, the lack of oscillation is due to the inherent movement of the letter -Z- that is incorporated into the movement of the sign (Fig. 5.30).

The signs #CLASSIFIER/*CLASSIFICATEUR* (Fig. 5.31) and #7-UP (Fig. 5.32) are similar to #PIZZA in that their movement does not correspond directly to the transition between two handshapes in the source fingerspelling sequence.[7] Nor is the movement derived directly from a

---

[7]More precisely, in the case of #7-UP, the number+fingerspelling source sequence.

TABLE 5.2. *Factors Affecting the Derived Movement in* #CLASSIFIER/*CLASSIFICATEUR and* #7-UP

Articulation effect	Physiological Description
a. Wrist flexion often cooccurs with finger extension; wrist extension often cooccurs with finger flexion.	The extensor muscles of the wrist, which bend the hand backward toward the back of the forearm, act together with the flexor muscles of the fingers, which act to curl or close the fingers. Conversely, the flexor muscles of the wrist act together with the extensors of the fingers. This means that when the hand is curved back, the fingers will naturally tend to curl and vice versa; similarly, when the hand is flexed forward, toward the ventral surface, that is, the belly, of the forearm, the fingers will naturally tend to extend, and vice versa.
b. Wrist flexion often cooccurs with wrist adduction.	The muscle that extends the wrist (i.e., bends the hand backward) on the ulnar (pinkie) side, the extensor carpi ulnaris, also adducts the hand (i.e., angles it away from the thumb side).
c. Wrist adduction often cooccurs with palm supination.	The action of adduction has a greater range of motion when the forearm is in a position of supination (palm of the hand upward and visible to the signer) than when it is in a position of pronation (back of the hand upward and visible to the signer).

movement inherent to one of the fingerspelled letters, as in #PIZZA. In these two signs, the movement is a function of a 'sympathetic' change in forearm rotation triggered by the change in handshape. In each of these two signs, the first of the two handshapes retained from the source sequence (-C- and -7-, respectively) has all or most of the fingers extended at the first (i.e., metacarpo-phalangeal) joint. The second handshape in each sequence (-1'- and -K-) has only the index extended, with the middle finger neither extended nor flexed in -K-; the other two fingers (ring and pinkie) are fully flexed, that is, closed.

The source of this movement can be traced to the interaction of three articulatory factors, drawn from Kapandji (1982) (Table 5.2).

It can be argued that the movement in the derived fingerspelled loan is due to the interaction between these three factors and the characteristics of the two handshapes involved in each case. It appears that what happens is the following: In the first handshape of the two signs, the forearm is in a raised, pronated position, that is, the canonical fingerspelling posture in one-handed systems. In the -1'- and -K- handshapes, the muscles that flex the fingers—the digital flexors—are acting on the ulnar (pinkie finger) side of the hand, holding the ring and pinkie fingers in a closed position. At the same time, the extensor muscle is acting on the index finger, keeping it in a fully extended position. As a consequence, there is an automatic sympathetic extension of the wrist by the muscle actions described in Table 5.2a

FIG. 5.33.   #WHERE/*OÙ(Older LSF form; left);* #WHERE/*OÙ (Current LSQ form; right)*

FIG. 5.34.   #SHERBROOKE   FIG. 5.35.   #APARTMENT/*APPARTEMENT*

on the ulnar (pinkie) side of the hand. This ulnar wrist extension is due to the action of the extensor carpi ulnaris muscle, which also adducts the hand (Table 5.2b). By the description in Table 5.2c, it can be deduced that if adduction has a greater range or is, in other words, facilitated, when the forearm is in a supinated position, it is also facilitated, though to a lesser degree, when the forearm is in neutral rotation, between pronation and supination (i.e., thumb up, palm toward the midline of signing space). This fact, in combination with the two other factors, appears to explain why the second segment of the signs #CLASSIFIER/*CLASSIFICATEUR* and #7-UP adopts this forearm position rather than the canonical fingerspelling position. Note that in #7-UP, the handshape that triggers the change in rotation, -K-, disappears and is replaced by -7-. This fact appears to be connected with the fact that this sign has taken on a repeated, oscillating movement.

This explanation has the advantage of accounting for changes in several other fingerspelled loans. There is a similar change of forearm rotation throughout the whole sign in #WHERE/*OÙ,* #SHERBROOKE, and #APARTMENT/*APPARTEMENT.* In #WHERE/*OÙ,* the forearm is turned to a fully supinated position (palm toward the signer) in Oléron (1974; Fig. 5.33). It may well be that this position was already adopted by the middle of the 19th century, when LSF borrowings first began to enter the LSQ lexicon. The other two signs, #SHERBROOKE and #APART-

MENT/*APPARTEMENT,* have adopted, in their most recent variants, a neutral forearm rotation (Fig. 5.34) and (Fig. 5.35).

In all three of these signs, the first handshape is one in which all the fingers have the same position; the second handshape, as in the other signs mentioned, is one in which the ring and pinkie fingers are closed and the index is flexed (as is the middle finger, in two of these latter signs). It is thus plausible that the factors that account for the change in forearm rotation in #CLASSIFIER/*CLASSIFICATEUR* and #7-UP also account for similar changes in #WHERE/*OÙ,* #SHERBROOKE, and #APART-MENT/*APPARTEMENT.*

Presence Versus Lack of Oscillation.   In Group II signs, which are characterized by an oscillating transition between the first two handshapes of the source fingerspelled word, although (underlyingly) the two handshapes may have different sets of selected fingers, these are not disjoint. In each of #COCA-COLA, #APARTMENT, #SHERBROOKE, #WIDOW(ER)/ *VEUF(VE)* and #TALK-BUSINESS/*PARLER-D'AF-FAIRES,* one of the underlying (if not surface) handshapes has all four fingers selected: no matter what set of fingers is selected in the other handshape, such a set is never disjoint from the set of all fingers. Similarly, in #TV, the selected index finger of -T- is not disjoint from the index-middle set of -V-. In the derived signs, except #TALK-BUSI-NESS/*PARLER-D'AFFAIRES,* the more inclusive selected finger set always assimilates to the included finger set.

This phenomenon is related to restrictions on the possible sequences of handshapes within a syllable. Perhaps the most important of these is the Selected Fingers Constraint (SFC). This constraint states that the syllable may license only one selected finger constellation. The SFC appears to determine the surface form these fingerspelled loans take by forcing their component handshapes to adopt the same selected finger set.

Note that the SFC does not, however, account for the distinction between the movements of Group II and Group III signs. What distinguishes these two groups is a correlation between length of the movement cycle and the aspects of handshape structure that may undergo a change during the movement. Although any change of selected fingers within short oscillating movements is completely excluded, such changes appear to be possible in the longer movements of Group III signs.

This necessitates a pair of generalizations, different from the SFC as originally formulated. If we represent oscillating movements as the repetition of identical monomoraic syllables and longer, non-oscillating single or repeated movements as bimoraic syllables, shown in (1), then it becomes

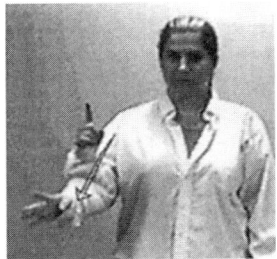      

FIG. 5.36.   SINGLE   FIG. 5.38.   HEARING   FIG. 5.38.   SEE^NEVER

possible to state two distinct generalizations, given in (2).[8] The first concerns possible handshape sequences in monomoraic syllables (i.e., each cycle of an oscillating movement). In long movements (i.e. bimoraic syllables) the condition is less restrictive. In signs with such movements, as discussed previously, it is sufficient that the two selected finger sets not be disjoint.

(1) *Contrastive monomoraic syllables in LSQ: light/short (monomoraic syllable (left)) and heavy/long (bimoraic syllable (right)).*

(2) *Revision to the Selected Fingers Constraint*

a.   Selected fingers constraint (short/monomoraic syllables SFC-σ_μ) The monomoraic syllable may license only one selected finger constellation.

b.   Selected fingers constraint (long/bimoraic syllables SFC-$\sigma_{\mu\mu}$) The bimoraic syllable may license a maximum of two selected finger constellations, which must be non-disjoint.

---

[8]This contrast is justified by a set of different types of phonological phenomena, all of which refer to a difference between long or short movements. These include positional handshape constraints sensitive to syllable length, lexical minimal pairs based on the weight distinction, derivational pairs of which one member is derived by imposition of a monosyllabic template, and metrical constraints on the presence or absence of repetitions of short movements that are crucially sensitive to both the moraic and syllabic structure of surrounding signs in a phrasal context. This conception of moraic structure in signs is different from those proposed in Brentari (1990, 1995), Brentari & Bosch (1990), and Perlmutter (1989, 1990). The models proposed in these publications make the use of the mora or mora-like weight units but do not recognize any lexical distinction between light (i.e., monomoraic) and heavy (i.e., bimoraic) syllables.

  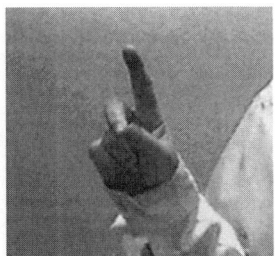

FIG. 5.39.   #KING/*ROI*   FIG. 5.40.   -D⁰-   FIG. 5.41.   -D⁰-

Under the SFC-$\sigma_{\mu\mu}$ signs such as #MAY/*MAI* M-I" sequence) and
#CL(ASSIFIER) are permitted, as is the Group I sign #OK and signs not
derived from fingerspelled sequences such as SINGLE (Fig. 5.36), one
variant of HEARING (Fig. 5.37), or the contraction SEE^NEVER (Fig.
5.38).

What never occurs within a single syllable is a sequence of handshapes whose selected fingers are completely disjoint. When the two
handshapes have disjoint selected finger sets, each must occur in a separate syllable, distinct from the other handshape.

Group IV loans.   The final group of loans, which contains signs
15–17 (#IF/*SI*, #KING/*ROI* and #GREEN/*VERT*), uses an atypical strategy for incorporating multiple fingerspelling handshapes in a sign. Instead
of sequencing the handshapes, with or without modification to adjust the
signs to phonological constraints of the language, as the case may be, features of different handshapes are combined to yield a single handshape
that corresponds directly to none of the handshapes of the corresponding
fingerspelled word.

The most striking example of this is #KING/*ROI* (Fig. 5.39),[9] in
which the selected finger sets of the -R- and -I- fingerspelling handshapes,
together with their associated finger position features, are combined
wholesale, and the curvature and thumb contact features of the O-hand-
shape are applied to the ring finger, thus forming a handshape that is found
nowhere else in the language; indeed, this handshape violates one of the
most important parameters for handshape formation, namely the possible
combinations of selected and unselected finger sets. It is a strong generalization about handshapes in LSQ that a handshape can normally contain
only one selected finger set and, at most, two unselected finger sets, each

---

[9]The usual sense of this sign is 'haughty' or 'behave arrogantly.'

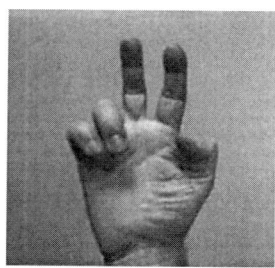

FIG. 5.42.   #IF/*SI*   FIG. 5.43.   #GREEN/*VERT* FIG. 5.44.   *Anomalous hand-*
                                                                       shape combining
                                                                       features of
                                                                       -V- and -E-

of these latter being confined to a choice between a fully open or fully closed position. Only one other handshape in LSQ violates this generalization, namely -D^{O}-[10] (Fig. 5.40), in which the unselected fingers take on the curved (i.e. neither open nor closed) position of the selected middle finger; this handshape is usually replaced by -D^{O}- (Fig. 5.41), in which the unselected pinkie and ring fingers adopt a fully closed position. The handshape of #KING/*ROI* is entirely anomalous in that it appears to contain three sets of selected fingers in one handshape, and no unselected fingers.

In the sign #IF/*SI* (Fig. 5.42), the combination of the -S- and -I- handshapes is more straightforward. The extended pinkie finger takes on the role of selected finger and the other fingers all retain a fully closed position of the -A^{S}- handshape of the fingerspelling -S-. The choice of fusion over a handshape sequence in this sign may be attributed to an avoidance of any movement for the little finger in an -I- handshape.

In the sign #GREEN/*VERT* (Fig. 5.43), the -V- and -E- handshapes are combined. In this case, however, unlike the other two described, distinct selected finger sets are not combined, each retaining its original curvature and aperture features. In this sign, the selected index and middle fingers of the fingerspelling -V- handshape take on the role of selected finger set for the derived handshape, but adopt the curvature feature of the -E- fingerspelling handshape. This curvature is the only vestige of the fingerspelling handshape -E-. It appears that this is the optimal combination of features from the two handshapes, because a handshape in which the selected fingers of -V- retain their extended position and the unselected fingers adopt the curvature of -E-, as in (Fig. 5.44), would be anomalous.

---

[10]In this handshape, the subscript "O" indicates a variant handshape in which all fingers except for the index are curled into an O-position, rather than just the selected middle finger.

Whereas in #KING/*ROI* the fusion of handshapes seems to be a case of creativity, the sign being relatively rare in LSQ usage, and in #IF/*SI* it appears to be motivated by a prohibition on handshape changes in which the pinkie finger of -I- is active, the motivation for the fused handshape in #GREEN/*VERT* seems to be of a different order.

If we ignore, for the moment, the fact that the handshape of #GREEN/*VERT* is not a handshape from the LSQ manual alphabet, we observe that this sign has, otherwise, the typical characteristics of one class of initial-ized signs in LSQ, as described in Machabée (1995). The sign has a single handshape, the forearm is raised so as to place the hand in typical "finger-spelling space," the palm faces outward as in fingerspelling, and the arm executes a small, oscillating, side-to-side movement. Given that the only characteristic that is missing in this case is the fact that the handshape is not a plain -V-, two questions seem to be relevant: why is plain -V- not used and why is a fused handshape used, rather than a handshape sequence?

As far as the first question is concerned, it seems that pressure to avoid synonymy may be an important deciding factor. There already exists a similiar initialized sign in LSQ that uses -V-, the sign FRIDAY/*VENDREDI*. This sign is part of a paradigm of initialized signs for the days of the week, all of which have the same form but for the ini-tialized handshape.[11] It would appear that although there is a likely pres-sure to avoid synonymy with other initialized signs that use -V-, the deciding factor that reserves this for FRIDAY/*VENDREDI* is the paradig-matic similarity within the set of weekday names. This explanation does not, however, clarify why a fused handshape is adopted in place of a hand-shape sequence. As far as this question is concerned, #GREEN/*VERT* seems to be in competition with #WIDOW(ER)/*VEU(F/VE)*. Again, the two signs have adopted different forms, and it is plausible to assume that a pressure to avoid synonymy plays a role in this case as well. The fact that it is the sign #WIDOW(ER)/*VEU(F/VE)* that retains a handshape sequence, leaving the rarer strategy of handshape fusion to #GREEN/*VERT*, can plausibly be attributed to the form of the base finger-spelling sequence V-E-U-V-E. This sequence, when executed rapidly, eas-ily reduces to the form of the fingerspelled loan, due to the presence of two V-E sequences separated only by a -U- handshape, which has the same selected finger set as -V-. It seems a plausible hypothesis that the

---

[11]In this paradigm, the sign THURSDAY/*JEUDI* differs additionally from the others in that it oscillates the twisting movement of the initial letter -J- and thus also orients the palm differently from the other signs.

repeated bending movement in this sign may indeed be a fortuitous reduction from the fingerspelling sequence; this would explain why
#WIDOW(ER)/*VEU(F/VE)* retains the handshape sequence and the more
peripheral process of handshape fusion is reserved for #GREEN/*VERT*.

LOAN SHIFTS VIA FRENCH

One type of borrowing of special interest is illustrated by numerous "loan
shift" signs in LSQ. Loan shifts are signs that take on a new and usually
unrelated meaning motivated by the fact that a French word synonymous
with the sign in its original sense is homonymous with another French
word with a different meaning. Although this type of borrowing is not to
our knowledge discussed elsewhere, it is nonetheless a logical outcome of
LSQ/French language contact.

Loan shifts contribute to the vocabulary of LSQ in two ways. One
type of loan shift provides a source of new common nouns in LSQ
whereas another type provides numerous proper names for persons and
places. Due to the importance of this mechanism for inventing new name
signs, these two general classes of loan shifts will be discussed in separate
sections. The next section, titled "Signs Derived via Visual Homonymy,"
is devoted to an overview of two types of homonymy responsible for loan
shifts: oral homonymy and written homonymy. The section titled "Name
signs Derived via Visual Homonymy" is devoted to a discussion of the
productive use of loan shifts for deriving new name signs in LSQ.

Signs Derived Via Visual Homonymy

Table 5.3 lists several cases in which an LSQ sign with one meaning takes
on another meaning via homonymy between the French equivalents of the
original and the derived sign. The first three signs are derived via oral
homonymy, that is, by the visual similarity of the oral French word corresponding to the original sign and its derived counterpart. The other five
signs are derived via written homonymy, that is to say, homonymy
between the written French word corresponding to the original sign and its
derived counterpart.

The first three signs in the table form homonymous pairs, the
homonymy being carried over from oral homonymy of their counterparts
in French. The first of these signs, the proper name GUY (Fig. 5.45), is
derived from the ASL sign WHO. Occasionally, WHO$_{ASL}$ is used instead
of the LSQ sign WHO (Fig. 5.46). This sign is often accompanied by the

FIG. 5.45. *GUY and* WHO_{ASL}   **FIG. 5.46.** WHO   **FIG. 5.47.** COOKIE/*BISCUIT and BUICK*

Table 5.3. *Semantic shifts via visual homonymy*

	Original sign			Derived sign
English gloss	*French gloss*	*Mouthing*	*French gloss*	*English gloss*
WHO$_{ASL}$	*QUI*	[ki]	*GUY*	GUY (PROPER NAME)
COOKIE/BISCUIT	*BISCUIT*	[biwI]	*BUICK*	BUICK
LAUGH	*RIRE*	[ri]	*RIZ*	RICE
(HEAD-)COLD	*RHUME*	—	*RHUM*	RUM
(SUBWAY)	*MÉTRO*	—	*SUPERMARCHÉ -MÉTRO*	MÉTRO -SUPERMARKET
SAVINGS	*ÉCONOMIE*	—	*ÉCONOMIE*	ECONOMICS
LAWYER	*AVOCAT*	—	*AVOCAT*	AVOCADO
NECK/THROAT	*COU/GORGE*	—	*COUSCOUS*	COUSCOUS

mouthing [ki], which corresponds to the French word *qui* 'who.' Because voicing distinctions are essentially irrelevant for the visual phonology of mouthing, [ki] serves also as the representation for the French name Guy. Via the visual homonymy between these two words, the sign WHO$_{ASL}$ has taken on a new function as the name sign GUY, which is used for certain individuals with this name, as well as for a street and a Metro (subway) station in Montreal.

The sign BUICK (Fig. 5.47) is derived from COOKIE/*BISCUIT*. The salient visual image of the French word *biscuit* is [biwi]. This sequence is similar enough to [bjuwi], the visual image of *Buick*, for the two spoken

FIG. 5.48. LAUGH *and* RICE   **FIG. 5.49.** HEAD-COLD *and* RUM

FIG. 5.50.   *MÉTRO*-SUPERMARKET   FIG. 5.51.   SUBWAY/*MÉTRO* *(new sign)*

words to be taken as visually homonymous. By association with this visual image, then, COOKIE/*BISCUIT* has taken on a new function as the sign BUICK.

The sign RICE (Fig. 5.48) is derived from the iconic sign LAUGH. When mouthing cooccurs with a verb in LSQ, it normally takes the form of the third person singular of the corresponding French verb. Thus the mouthing that corresponds to LAUGH in LSQ is *rit*, pronounced [ri]. This phonological sequence also corresponds to the French word *riz,* 'rice.' No other sign being available in LSQ, the sign thus took on an entirely distinct meaning due to the homonymy between *rit* and *riz* in French.[12]

The following examples depend on strict or partial homonymy between written words in French, one of which corresponds in meaning to an existing LSQ sign. The sign RUM (Fig. 5.49) is derived from the iconic sign HEAD-COLD by this process. 'Head cold' is *rhume* in French; 'rum' is *rhum*. The resemblance between these two written words appears to have triggered the shift to a second meaning for the original sign in LSQ.

A somewhat different case involves the sign SUBWAY (Fig. 5.50). This iconic, classifier-based sign depicts a path that makes its way underneath a surface, in this case, the surface of the earth. The French word for 'subway' is *métro,* derived from *métropolitaine,* 'metropolitan (transit system).' There exists in the Province of Quebec a large supermarket chain that bears the name Métro, and due to the homonymy between this name and the name meaning 'subway,' the original sign took on this sense. In this case, however, the original sign as almost never used in its older sense and almost always refers to the supermarket chain. The older sense of 'subway' has been reserved for another sign morphologically derived from the original by superposing the handshape of train on the dominant hand of the original sign (Fig. 5.51).

---

[12]It should be noted that the two signs are generallly accompanied by different nonmanual features. LAUGH is accompanied by a raising of the corners of the mouth in imitation of a smile, whereas RICE is accompanied by the spread lips corresponding to the mouthing *rit*.

FIG. 5.52.   SAVINGS/SAVE
-MONEY *and* ECONOMICS/
ECONOMY

FIG. 5.53.   LAWYER
and AVOCADO

FIG. 5.54. · NECK/THROAT *and*
COUSCOUS

The LSQ sign SAVINGS/*SAVE-MONEY* (Fig. 5.52) has taken on the related sense of ECONOMICS/*ECONOMY* via the French expression *faire des économies* 'save money' (cf. 'economize' in English). Because *économies* 'savings' is lexically and semantically related to *économie* 'economy' and *économique* 'economical/economics,' the shift in sense is natural to an LSQ and French bilingual in the way a shift from the related ASL sign SAVINGS$_{ASL}$ to a secondary meaning ECONOMICS$_{ASL}$ would not be to an ASL and English bilingual. Hence the preference, in ASL, for a sign ECONOMICS$_{ASL}$ initialized on MONEY$_{ASL}$.

A rather surprising case of meaning shift, for a non-Francophone, is the use of LAWYER as a base for the derived sign AVOCADO (Fig. 5.53). This, again, is due to homonymy between the French equivalents of these two terms, both being rendered by *avocat*. It seems unlikely that there would be many contexts in which the two meanings would lead to confusion.

A final example of this sort of meaning shift is provided by the sign NECK/THROAT (Fig. 5.54), which has taken on the additional meaning COUSCOUS. This is due to homonymy with the French word *cou* 'neck' with the reduplicated syllable of couscous. Unlike the other signs discussed in this section, which are known and used throughout the LSQ signing community, this is a fairly recently invented sign that is gradually spreading through the community, in competition with an initialized sign in which a fingerspelling -C-, with a typical side-to-side movement in fingerspelling space, is accompanied by the mouthing "couscous."

Two further examples of semantic shift via influence from French are relatively more complex in derivation than the examples discussed in the preceding paragraphs. These are the sign CHAMPAGNE, derived ultimately from FAN-NOSE (Fig. 5.55), and CASTLE/*CHÂTEAU,* derived ultimately from AMERINDIAN (Fig. 5.56).

FIG. 5.55.   FAN-NOSE *and* CHAMPAGNE   FIG. 5.56.   AMERINDIAN,
                                                        CASTLE/*CHÂTEAU and* WILD

The reason CHAMPAGNE is derived ultimately from fan-nose is not directly related to homonymy between the corresponding French terms, unlike the cases covered in the previous paragraphs, although homonymy does enter into the equation. According to Dubuisson and Desrosiers (1994), the name sign champagne was invented to refer to a particular individual with the surname Champagne, who was reputed to have smelly feet, hence the use of the sign FAN-NOSE. The use of the sign since that time to stand for the name Champagne eased the transition in sense from the name sign to the name of the variety of wine.

AMERINDIAN is phonologically related to the corresponding ASL sign and has the same basic meaning as in ASL. It has undergone two significant meaning shifts, unlike the ASL sign, both having to do, directly or indirectly, with contact between LSQ and French. One shift in meaning is due to a no longer used French synonym for *Amérindien* 'Amerindian,' namely *sauvage*. The basic meaning of *sauvage* is 'wild,' and because the French term was previously used both for 'wild' and 'Amerindian,'[13] the LSQ sign took on the additional meaning of 'wild.' Thus the phrase flower amerindian is equivalent to the French phrase *fleur(s) sauvage(s),* or 'wildflower(s).'

The explanation for the shift in meaning from AMERINDIAN to CASTLE/*CHÂTEAU* (Fig. 5.56) is even more indirect. The shift to is due to the partial similarity between the French word *château* 'castle' and the name of the town of Châteauguay, located across from Montreal on the South Shore of the St. Lawrence River. This does not suffice, however, to explain the connection between 'Amerindian' and 'Châteauguay.' The connection is, in fact, geographical, because the town of Châteauguay is immediately adjacent to the Mohawk/Kanienkeha:ka community of Kahnawake.[14] Once this connection was exploited, then, it was sufficient to

---

[13]In the same way as Amerindians were referred to as 'savages' in English in the past.
[14]The name of the community, formerly known by an anglicized version of its name, Caughnawaga, is a locative form in Mohawk /Kanienkeha:ka, meaning 'at the rapids.'

TABLE 5.4. *Name signs derived via visual homonymy*

Proper name	Adapted sign(s)	Motivation
SAINT-EUSTACHE (TOWN)	SAINT+MOUSTACHE	*(Eu)stache, (mou)stache*
LORANGER	ORANGE	(l)*orange*(r)
GADBOIS	WOOD	(gad)bois (=wood)
LAVERDURE	WASH+HARD	*laver* (=wash)+*dur* (=hard)
RIOUX	LAUGH+WHERE	*rit* (=laughs)+*où* (=where)
LASALLE	ROOM/PLAY	*salle* (=room)
LAVOIE	VOICE	(la)*voie* [vwa]
		(=*voice/voix* [vwa])
CONCORDIA (UNIVERSITY)	CONCORDE-AIRPLANE	Concord(e/ia)

exploit the similarity between the name of the town and the French word for castle to provide a new sign for this particular referent.

Name Signs Derived Via Visual Homonymy

Although visual homonymy is exploited to a certain extent to extend the vocabulary of LSQ, one area where this strategy is particularly productive is in the derivation of name signs. Table 5.4 gives eight examples of name signs derived from another existing sign via an existing relation of homonymy in French. Those that are institutionalized, that is, attached to places or to organizations, are universally known; the others are known to a greater or lesser extent throughout the community.

Three of the signs in Table 5.4, namely ORANGE, WOOD, and ROOM, are signs whose French equivalent is contained within both the written and the oral forms of the proper name to which they have been applied (LORANGER, GADBOIS, and LASALLE, respectively). Another sign, CONCORDE (-AIRPLANE), has a French equivalent *Concorde* that is closely equivalent to the proper name 'Concordia' to which it is applied. A slightly more tenuous relation is found in the application of *moustache* to the name Saint-Eustache. Here, the correspondence (either oral or written) is found in the second of two syllables each word (exclud-

FIG. 5.57. SAINT-EUSTACHE   **FIG. 5.58.** SAINT   **FIG. 5.59.** MOUSTACHE

FIG. 5.60.   WASH/*LAVER*

FIG. 5.61.   HARD/*DUR*

FIG. 5.62.   TO-LAST/*DURER*

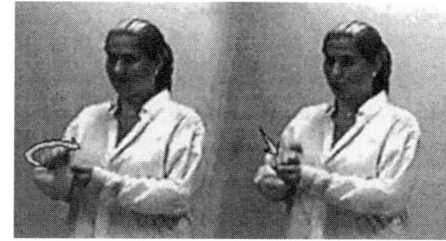

FIG. 5.63.   LAVERDURE

ing the 'Saint-' in Saint-Eustache). The form of the proper noun Saint-Eustache (Fig. 5.57) undergoes certain phonological changes, being a compound of the two signs saint (Fig. 5.58) and MOUSTACHE (Fig. 5.59). Whereas the unselected fingers of moustache are closed, in SAINT-EUSTACHE they are open: it appears that this is due to spreading of a [-closed] feature from the handshape of SAINT.

In some cases, name signs are derived by reanalyzing the French name itself and by attributing a semantically equivalent sign to the reanalyzed portion(s) of the name. This strategy is illustrated by the signs attributed to the names Lavoie, Rioux, and Laverdure. The first two names are reanalyzed in terms of oral homonymy; Laverdure is reanalyzed in terms of its written form.

The name Lavoie is derived from the phrase *la voie* 'the way.' However, the LSQ sign that is used for the name sign does not correspond in meaning to *voie;* the closest sign would be STREET/*RUE*. The sign that is used for Lavoie is actually VOICE, whose equivalent in French, VOIX, is homonymous with voie, both being pronounced [*vwa*].

A similar reanalysis has taken place with respect to the name Rioux. In this case, the name does not correspond in its written form to any other French word.[15] In its oral form [ri.u], though, the word is homonymous

---

[15]It is probably a francized version of the word *rius* 'rivers' in Occitan, the traditional language of the southern third of France (also known as Provençal, or as the "lenga d'òc" or "langue d'oc").

with the sequence *rit, où* 'laughs, where.' As a result of this play on words, it is the sequence LAUGH+WHERE that has been adopted as the name sign Rioux.

A more unexpected reanalysis has taken place with respect to the name Laverdure. The name itself derives from the French phrase *la verdure* 'verdure' or 'greenery.' Although the sense of the word is transparent, and it might have been expected that the sign #GREEN/*VERT* would have been adopted as the name sign corresponding to Laverdure, this is not what happened. In fact, the written sequence was reanalyzed as *laver+dure,* where *laver* means 'to wash' and *dure* can mean either 'to last' or 'hard' (feminine form). Of the two alternatives, it was the latter that was adopted, perhaps because it allows for a more fluid transition between the signs WASH/*LAVER* (Fig. 5.60) and HARD/*DUR* (Fig. 5.61) and does not involve a change of handshape as would be necessary were the second sign TO-LAST/*DURER* (Fig. 5.62). The resulting name sign LAVERDURE also thus contains a circle plus contact sequence that is found in a number of other LSQ signs (Fig. 5.63).

BORROWINGS VIA MOUTHING

The most direct type of borrowing from French would be the incorporation of spoken French words into the LSQ lexicon. This type of borrowing is more difficult to study than others due to the pervasiveness of the phenomenon of mouthing and the fact that it is rarely clear what the status of such mouthings is in the language.

Unlike the case of borrowings via fingerspelling, it is difficult to determine, at this stage of research, any general principles that will help establish a clear distinction between mouthings as loans and mouthings as another type of contact phenomenon, be it a type of bimodal codemixing comparable to codeswitching between two oral languages or some other cross-modal phenomenon without any parallel in situations of oral language contact. It is a fairly simple matter, at least regarding fingerspelling loans in LSQ, to establish a set of characteristics that help to distinguish them from fingerspelled sequences per se; these characteristics can be taken as criteria for evaluating the degree to which such a loan has been integrated into the core phonological system of the language. When it comes to mouthings, however, the question is not as simple. For one, it is not as simple a matter to determine whether a spoken word can be said to be phonologically "integrated" into LSQ. Although different degrees of faithfulness to the spoken model can be detected in mouthing as used by

Deaf signers, it is not obvious at first sight, except in a few isolated cases, how or whether deviations from oral language-faithful mouthings can be taken as evidence for integration into the phonological structure of LSQ.

Failing any clear general criteria for establishing when the use of mouthing is a loan rather than a case of code mixing, only a very few cases can be taken to be borrowings with any degree of certainty. The (relatively few) fairly clear cases of lexical borrowing of French words into LSQ can be divided into two main categories: those that cooccur with a particular sign and those that can occur independently of any particular sign.

In the latter category are two lexical items about which it can be said, with a fair degree of certainty, that they are in fact integrated borrowings in LSQ. One of these lexical items is *quoi* 'what.' This particular word often appears, independently of the sign WHAT/*QUOI*, either coarticulated with another sign, as in Example (3), where it is coarticulated with the sign POINT/*PTÉ* in the second line of the transcription, or on its own. In either case, it takes the place of the sign WHAT/*QUOI* in the sentence.[16]

(3) *'It was written down on the list what each person had to bring to eat.'*

gloss	WRITE	LIST	BRING	POINT	BELONG	BRING	EAT
for manual component			*APPORTE*		-TO$_{HR2,HL2}$	*APPORTE*	*MANGE*
mouthing			*apporte*	*quoi*		*apporte*	*mange*

An important argument for the the conclusion that quoi has in fact been integrated into the LSQ lexicon comes from the fact that it undergoes a morphophonological process that affects many manual signs. Many signs in phrase-final position take on, when emphasized, a repeated, oscillating form in which their lexical movement is rapidly repeated. This same process affects *quoi*. Whereas it normally has the visual phonological form [wa], in the previously mentioned context it takes on the form [wawawawawa], the number of repetitions being indeterminate, as is also the case for manual signs.[17]

---

[16]For the sake of consistency in glossing practice, as outlined in footnote 3, sign glosses are given in English; where French mouthings are identical in meaning to the sign they accompany, they are followed by an equal sign (=).

[17]I have been told by Deaf ASL signers at the 1996 LSA Linguistic Institute that the same phenomenon exists in ASL with respect to the mouthed English word 'what'. It may be the case, then, since quoi and what have a similar or identical visual phonological form, i.e. [wa(t)], that this is in fact a single loan with the same origin.

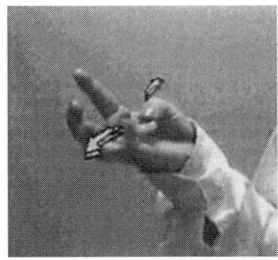  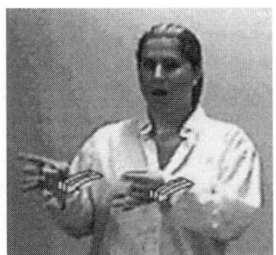

FIG. 5.64.   SMALL-OBJECT FIG. 5.65.   TIME   FIG. 5.66.   TEMPORARY

Certain other lexical items, such as the conjunction *après* ('then, afterward') and the negative adverb *pas* ('not'), share with *quoi* the syntactic characteristic of independence from any particular sign but do not undergo the same degree of phonological integration.

The second type of apparent lexical borrowing from spoken French involves what can be called 'simultaneous bimodal compounds,' where a French lexical item is twinned with a particular sign and contributes significant information that would otherwise be absent. Such is the case of certain signs without a specific meaning of their own, such as SMALL-OBJECT (Fig. 5.64), which is uninterpretable without mouthing. Only when accompanied by a mouthed French lexical item does this sign take on any specific meaning, and these oralizations derive a family of related signs including PEA/*POIS*, BEAN/*FÊVE*, STRAWBERRY/*FRAISE*, RASPBERRY/*FRAMBOISE*, SEED/*GRAINE*, and PILL/*PILULE*, among others.

Other, similar cases of simultaneous bimodal compounds involve a sort of mutual rhythmic adjustment between the manual sign and the accompanying French mouthing. An example of this is the sign TEMPO-RARY (Fig. 5.66), derived from TIME (Fig. 5.65).

Whereas TIME has a single, long (bimoraic) movement, in which the handshape transition is temporally aligned with the outward arm movement, the derived sign subdivides the outward arm movement into three short syllables, each of which is characterized by the handshape change of the underlying sign, and is aligned with one of the syllables of the accompanying French word temporaire (visually [ta.po.re]; Fig. 5.66). Beyond a very few cases along these lines, it is difficult to determine whether occurrences of mouthing with signs are in fact borrowings into LSQ, or some other type of contact phenomenon comparable to code mixing in oral language pairs.

DISCUSSION

Lexical borrowings in LSQ show a quite remarkable range of origins, attesting both to the range of languages with which LSQ has had contact and to the varied means by which borrowings can be brought into the language. Borrowings have come into LSQ from other sign languages, and from French via fingerspelled representations of written French words, via relations of homonymy between French equivalents of LSQ signs and, to some extent, in the form of mouthings.

Due to contact with ASL, LSF, and BSL at different stages during its approximate century and a half of existence as an autonomous language, LSQ has adopted a number of signs from these different languages, much in the way oral languages borrow lexical items from other oral languages with which they enter into contact.

In many cases, parallel borrowings result in synonyms with different origins. For example, LSQ has two different signs that can be glossed CAN'T, one from ASL and the other from LSF. Similarly, along with the signs SPECIAL, WINTER, and BUT, which appear to be indigenous to LSQ, ASL signs with the same meaning have been borrowed and alternate freely with the original LSQ signs. In some cases, such as the synonymous pair ACCEPT$_{ASL}$ and ACCEPT$_{LSF}$, there is a differentiation in usage: of these two signs, the sign borrowed from LSF appears to be less current than it was in the past.

To some extent, such borrowings have permitted LSQ to expand its lexicon by specializing the semantic range of one or both of two originally synonymous signs with distinct origins. This is the case, for example, of the doublet WORK$_{LSF}$ and WORK$_{ASL}$: the first of these two signs has retained its full range of senses whereas the second has specialized and can only be used as a noun in the sense of 'work to be done.' Similarly, LSQ has two signs from different languages, with the same original meaning: ENGLAND$_{ASL}$ and ENGLAND$_{LSF}$. The first of the signs has specialized to an essentially adjectival meaning 'English (nationality/language)' whereas the second has specialized in another direction and can only be used to refer to the country ('England' or 'Great Britain').

A fairly important route taken by borrowings from French (or, occasionally, from English) is through fingerspelled representations of words from these languages. It seems to be the case that fingerspelled loans from English are in fact borrowed through ASL. Whereas fingerspelled loans in ASL appear, in the unmarked case, to restructure the fingerspelling sequence from the edges in, LSQ adopts a different default strategy,

retaining only the first two letters and restructuring them into an oscillating short movement with an identical finger set in both handshapes. The
only cases where such a strategy is not adopted are those where extraneous factors of two types come into play. In a couple of cases, semantic factors enforce the adoption of a peripheral strategy of handshape fusion. In
the majority of cases, though, the typical restructuring strategy is blocked
for phonological reasons, either because of a movement inherent to one of
the letters (-J- or -Z-) or, most commonly, because the two handshapes
involved have disjoint selected finger sets that cannot be assimilated into a
single set, thus rendering impossible the typical oscillating movement
shape of LSQ fingerspelled loans.

In several cases, the original sequence of two letters with the typical
palm-outward orientation of fingerspelling (i.e., forearm in pronated position) is restructured such that either the second handshape or both handshapes adopt a neutral forearm rotation in which the palm faces sideways,
or even a supinated position, with the palm toward the signer. This type of
restructuring can be traced to the interaction of a number of anatomical
factors that favor a neutral or supinated rotation for handshapes in which
the index is extended and the other fingers are closed. This explanation
can be extended to certain signs with the same characteristics—including
an oscillating handshape sequence—mentioned in Battison (1978): #DO
and #WHAT.

It is interesting to speculate on the possible reasons for the seemingly
unique LSQ strategy of restructuring the first two handshapes of a fingerspelling sequence into an oscillating handshape change.[18] In the section
titled "Borrowings Through Fingerspelling," it was noted that this type of
oscillating handshape change appears to derive almost automatically, in
the loan #WIDOW(ER)/*VEU(F/VE),* from the underlying fingerspelled
sequence V-E-U-V-E. It is tempting to speculate that this loan may have
been the original model for the LSQ strategy, perhaps reinforced by the
common oscillating repetition found in the sign #NO/NON, whose handshape change corresponds in LSQ, unlike in ASL, to the transition
between the first two of three letters. This explanation has a certain plausi-
bility about it; however, it must remain a hypothesis unless and until further evidence can be found pointing to these two signs as the oldest
fingerspelled loans in LSQ to have such an oscillating handshape change.

---

[18]Battison (1978) notes that this would be a logical alternative for ASL fingerspelling loans which,
instead, typically conserve the initial and final handshapes and simplify or delete the intermediate
handshapes of the source fingerspelling sequence

Apart from fingerspelling, LSQ also uses the indirect strategy of loan shifts to derive new signs. Loan shifts exploit the fact that a French word equivalent to an LSQ sign is homonymous with another French word to superimpose the meaning of the second word on the original sign, thus deriving a new LSQ sign that forms a homonymous pair with the original, mirroring the homonym pair in French. This type of loan shift could also be termed "homonym calquing." A particularly productive use of this strategy is in the derivation of new name signs from existing signs.

The most direct way by which spoken language material is integrated into LSQ discourse is via mouthing of French (and sometimes English) words. Unlike the case of borrowings that enter LSQ via the oral channel, it is difficult, at the current stage of research, to determine for the majority of cases whether mouthings are in fact instances of borrowing or of simultaneous code mixing.

What is clear, though, with respect to borrowing in LSQ, is the fact that as a sign language, LSQ has a large variety of channels through which new words can be integrated into the language, both from other sign languages and from oral languages, whether directly or indirectly through secondary representations such as fingerspelling or homonym calquing. In this chapter, we have only been able to present an overview of the borrowing phenomena found in LSQ, together with some of their accompanying characteristics. Much work remains to be done in further clarifying the extent of loan vocabulary in LSQ and the nature of the constraints and processes that determine how the various borrowing types are integrated into the language. This is especially true in the area of integration of oral French material into sign language discourse, and it is to be hoped that this area will receive greater attention in the future.

REFERENCES

Battison, R. (1978). *Lexical borrowing in American Sign Language*. Silver Spring, Maryland: Linstok.

Boudreault, P. (1996). L'usage des chiffres standards en LSQ avant et après la réforme scolaire du Québec. Unpublished manuscript, Université du Québec à Montréal.

Brentari, D. (1990a). *Theoretical foundations of American Sign Language phonology.* University of Chicago dissertation. University of Chicago Occasional Papers in Linguistics.

Brentari, D. (1995). Prosodic constraints in American Sign Language: Evidence from fingerspelling and reduplication. In H. Bos & T. Schermer (Eds.), *Sign language research* (pp. 39–52). Hamburg:Signum.

Brentari, D.,& Bosch, A. (1990). The mora: Autosegment or syllable constituent. In M. Ziolkowski, M. Noske, & K. Deaton (Eds.), *CLS 26. Papers from the 26th Regional Meeting of the Chicago Linguistic Society* (pp. 1–15). Chicago: Chicago Linguistic Society .

Brien, D. (Ed.). (1992). *Dictionary of British Sign Language/English.* London: Faber and Faber.

Desouvrey, L-H., Dubuisson, C., & Vercaingne-Ménard, A. (1992). L'épellation en langue des signes québécoise. In C. Dyck, J. Ghomeshi, & T. Wilson (Eds.), *Proceedings of the Annual Conference of the Canadian Linguistic Assocation/Actes du Congrès annuel de l'Association canadienne linguistique* (pp. 63–78). Toronto: Linguistic Graduate Course Union, University of Toronto.

Dubuisson, C., & Desrosiers, J. (1994). Names in Quebec Sign Language and what they tell us about Quebec Deaf culture. In I. Ahlgren, B. Bergman, & M. Brennan (Eds.), *Perspectives on sign language usage* (pp. 249–260). Durham, England: International Sign Linguistics Association.

Dubuisson, C., Vercaingne-Ménard, A., Pinsonneault, D., & Desouvrey, L-H. (1992). L'oralisation en langue des signes québécoise. *Revue de l'ACLA/Journal of the CAAL, 14*(2), 95–106.

Kapandji, I./A. (1982). *The physiology of the joints. Annotated diagrams of the mechanics of the human joints.* London: Churchill Livingstone.

Lafrance (Abbé, no date). *Renseignements antérieurs aux Ordos de l'Institution sur les professeurs, élèves, éphémérides etc. du 26 novembre 1848 à 1895.* Montreal: Institution Catholique des Sourds-Muets pour la province de Québec.

Lambert (Abbé, 1865). *Le langage de la physionomie et du geste mis à la portée de tous.* Paris: Lacques Lecoffre.

Machabée, D. (1994). *L'initialisation en langue des signes québécoise.* Unpublished masters thesis, Université du Québec à Montréal.

Machabée, D. (1995). Description and status of initialized signs in Quebec Sign Language. In C. Lucas (Ed.), *Sociolinguistics in Deaf Communities* (pp. 29–61). Washington, DC: Gallaudet University Press.

Machabée, D., & Dubuisson, C. (1995). Initialized signs in (or outside of ?) Quebec Sign Language. In H. Bos & T. Schermer (Eds.), *Sign Language Research 1994* (pp. 69–83). Hamburg: Signum.

Miller, C. (1997a). *Metrical structure of movement in Quebec Sign Language.* Unpublished manuscript, Université du Québec à Montréal.

Miller, C. (1997b). *Phonologie de la langue des signes québécoise. Structure simultanée et axe temporel.* Unpublished doctoral thesis, Université du Québec à Montréal.

Miller, C., & Lelièvre, L. (in press). *Les origines de la LSQ.*

Oléron, P. (1974). *Éléments de répertoire du langage gestuel des Sourds-Muets.* Paris: CNRS.

Perlmutter, D. (1989). A moraic theory of American Sign Language syllable structure. Unpublished manuscript, University of California, San Diego.

Perlmutter, D. M. (1990). Handshape sequences as evidence for syllable structure in American Sign Language. Unpublished manuscript, University of California, San Diego.

Author Index

175

Subject Index